Building New Labour

D1806124

Building New Labour
The Politics of Party Organisation

Meg Russell
Senior Research Fellow,
The Constitution Unit, University College London

First published 2005 by
PALGRAVE MACMILLAN
Houndmills, Basingstoke, Hampshire RG21 6XS and
175 Fifth Avenue, New York, N. Y. 10010
Companies and representatives throughout the world

PALGRAVE MACMILLAN is the global academic imprint of the Palgrave Macmillan division of St. Martin's Press, LLC and of Palgrave Macmillan Ltd. Macmillan® is a registered trademark in the United States, United Kingdom and other countries. Palgrave is a registered trademark in the European Union and other countries.

ISBN-13: 978-1-4039-3993-7 hardback
ISBN-10: 1-4039-3993-4   hardback
ISBN-13: 978-1-4039-3994-4 paperback
ISBN-10: 1-4039-3994-2   paperback

This book is printed on paper suitable for recycling and made from fully managed and sustained forest sources.

A catalogue record for this book is available from the British Library.

A catalogue record for this book is available from the Library of Congress.

10   9   8   7   6   5   4   3   2   1
14   13   12   11   10   09   08   07   06   05

Printed and bound in Great Britain by
Antony Rowe Ltd, Chippenham and Eastbourne

To Iris Elizabeth Russell

Contents

List of Tables and Figures

Tables

Figure

List of Abbreviations

ACTT   Association of Cinematograph, Television and Allied Technicians.

AEEU   Amalgamated Electrical and Engineering Union, formed in 1992 as a result of a merger between the AEU and EETPU.

AEU   Amalgamated Engineering Union. Later became part of the AEEU.

AM   Assembly Member (in Wales).

APEX   Association of Professional, Executive, Clerical and Computer Staff. Became a section of GMB in 1989.

ASLEF   Associated Society of Locomotive Engineers and Firemen.

AUEW   Amalgamated Union of Engineering Workers. Later became AEU.

CAC   Conference Arrangements Committee.

CLP   Constituency Labour Party.

CLPD   Campaign for Labour Party Democracy.

CLV   Campaign for Labour Victory.

COHSE   Confederation of Health Service Employees. Later became part of UNISON.

CWU   Communication Workers Union, formed in 1995 as a result of a merger between the NCU and UCW.

EC   Executive Committee (of the CLP).

EETPU   Electrical, Electronic, Telecommunications and Plumbing Union. Later became part of the AEEU.

EPLP   European Parliamentary Labour Party.

FBU   Fire Brigades Union.

GC   General Committee (of the CLP), also known as General Management Committee (GMC).

GLA   Greater London Authority.

GLC   Greater London Council (abolished in 1986).

GMC   See GC.

GMB	General Municipal and Boilermakers' union.
GMWU	General and Municipal Workers' Union. Following a merger with the Boilermakers became known as GMB in 1987.
GPMU	Graphical, Paper and Media Union.
ISTC	Iron and Steel Trades Confederation.
JPC	Joint Policy Committee (NEC/government).
LCC	Labour Co-ordinating Committee.
MEP	Member of the European Parliament.
MP	Member of Parliament.
MSF	Manufacturing Science and Finance union.
MSP	Member of the Scottish Parliament.
NCU	National Communications Union. Later became part of CWU.
NEC	National Executive Committee.
NGA	National Graphical Association.
NPF	National Policy Forum.
NUM	National Union of Mineworkers.
NUPE	National Union of Public Employees. Later became part of UNISON.
NUR	National Union of Railwaymen. Later became part of RMT.
OMOV	One Member One Vote.
POEU	Post Office Engineering Union. Later became NCU.
PLP	Parliamentary Labour Party.
RMT	Rail, Maritime and Transport Union.
SDP	Social Democratic Party.
SERA	Socialist Environment and Resources Association (Labour Environment Campaign).
SPD	German Social Democratic Party.
TGWU	Transport and General Workers' Union.
TSSA	Transport Salaried Staffs Association.
UCATT	Union of Construction, Allied Trades and Technicians.
UCW	Union of Communication Workers. Later became part of CWU.
UNISON	Public services union formed in 1993 as a result of a merger between COHSE, NUPE, and NALGO (National and Local Government Officers Association – previously non affiliated).
USDAW	Union of Shop, Distributive and Allied Workers.
WAC	Women's Action Committee (originally part of CLPD).

Acknowledgements

There are many people and organisations without whom this work would not have been possible.

Financial support for the project came primarily through a Research Fellowship from the Leverhulme Trust. I am very grateful to the Trust, and also to Jean Cater for administering the grant so efficiently. An additional smaller grant came from the Mactaggart Trust. Both of these were essential in helping me make time available for research and writing. I am grateful to Alison Howson, Guy Edwards and John Smith at Palgrave Macmillan for their advice on the planning of the book, and for helping me bring it to completion. The comments of their anonymous readers, and those of the readers for the Leverhulme Trust, were also extremely useful. And the book would not, of course, be what it is without its cover. I am therefore very grateful to Steve Bell for making available the cartoon.

Of central importance were the many people who gave up time to be interviewed, some on more than one occasion, for the project. These include Graham Allen MP, Ann Black, Anne Campbell MP, Peter Coleman, Robin Cook MP, Jon Cruddas MP, Angela Eagle MP, John (Lord) Evans, Bob Fryer, David Gardner, Anne (Baroness) Gibson, Joyce (Baroness) Gould, Dianne Hayter, Diana Holland, Diana Jeuda, Maggie Jones, Neal Lawson, Ben Lucas, Frances Morrell, Maureen O'Mara, Mike Penn, Ann Pettifor, Vicky Phillips, David Pitt-Watson, Margaret (Baroness) Prosser, Tony Robinson, Tom (Lord) Sawyer, Paul Simpson, Clare Short MP, Nick Smith, Nigel Stanley, Pam Tatlow, Matthew Taylor, Larry (Lord) Whitty, Pete Willsman, Phil Wilson and Daniel Zeichner. Others kindly helped with specific queries, and these include Tony (Lord) Clarke, Renee Finan, Nicky Gavron, Joe Irvin, Andrew Pakes, Mike Power, Richard (Lord) Rosser, Andrew Sharpe and Tony (Lord) Young. I hope that I have not misinterpreted the many valuable things that they told me.

Various people and places were also essential in making documents available for the project. Central to these was the Labour History Archive and Study Centre managed by the John Rylands University Library of Manchester. Stephen Bird, Jennette Martin, Roy Lumb and Darren Treadwell were very welcoming and efficient during my visits. Giles Wright at the Fabian Society was, as ever, also extremely helpful. I am particularly grateful, however, to those individuals who searched through their own papers, or gave me access to them, to find less accessible material. These include Vladimir and Vera Derer, Peter Hain MP, Roy (Lord) Hattersley, Dianne Hayter, Ben Lucas, Frances Morrell, Nick Smith, Nigel Stanley, Pam Tatlow, Paul Thompson and Pete Willsman.

A number of people took the time to read and comment on earlier drafts of the chapters. These include Sarah Childs, Philip Cowley, Diana Jeuda, Joni Lovenduski, Tony Robinson, Ben Seyd, Paul Simpson, Alan Ware, Paul Webb and Daniel Zeichner. Their comments were very valuable, and I only hope I have done them justice. Eric Shaw heroically read a draft of the whole manuscript, and I am immensely grateful for his many useful comments on detail, and for his general encouragement. Alan Ware and Patrick Seyd were also very supportive of the project at its earlier stages.

This work has been, like most of its kind, very sapping of personal resources and far more time consuming than I had hoped. I would thus like to thank my friends, and my colleagues at the Constitution Unit and School of Public Policy at UCL, for tolerating my absences and occasional bad tempers throughout the project. I am particularly grateful to Philip for his constant support, and his advice and help in the final stages of editing. Lastly, a list of tributes would not be complete without a mention of my dear cat, whose company was so much appreciated during the writing of the book. She sat approvingly on many of its pages in draft, but sadly died, aged 19, just before it went to press.

1

Introduction

The renewal of Labour is not a distraction from winning power. Indeed the modernisation of the Labour Party is the first step to the modernisation of Britain. That is why the task of regenerating Labour must lie at the heart of a political strategy for winning and sustaining power.
Gordon Brown, in *Making Mass Membership Work*, 1993

In this last year we have transformed our party – our constitution rewritten, our relations with the trade unions changed and better defined for today's world, our party organisation improved ... I did not come into politics to change the Labour Party. I came into politics to change my country, and I honestly believe that if we had not changed ... we could not change the country.
Tony Blair, speech to Labour Party conference 1995

I have always believed that the politics of organisation is as important as the politics of ideas.
John Prescott, speech to Labour Party conference 2000

There is no shortage of books about 'new' Labour. The repackaging of the British Labour Party in the 1980s and 1990s has been the subject of much academic study and even more journalistic speculation. Numerous volumes and articles have sought to dissect the personalities involved, the policy directions pursued and the extent to which the party's underlying values have or have not changed.[1]

During this same period the Labour Party also underwent far reaching reform to its internal organisation, which generally appears in the background of these various studies. Yet, as demonstrated by the quotations above, Labour's leaders did not regard organisational reform as a secondary matter. Instead they saw it as central to the drive to 'modernise' the party. The vigour of campaigns such as that over 'one member one vote' for the selection of Labour candidates, or the press hostility that Labour was prepared to face over 'all-women shortlists', illustrate how serious many in

1

the party were about reform. More recent examples, such as the controversy in 2000 over the way Labour's candidate for Mayor of London was selected, illustrate how internal democracy has resonance beyond the party itself, and can affect both its public image and its electoral prospects. As far back as 1981, party organisational matters helped spark the breakaway of many Labour members, including 28 MPs, to form a new party (the SDP). In 1993 other similar matters nearly forced the resignation of John Smith as party leader. Since then issues concerning Labour's internal democracy have caused several major embarrassments to Tony Blair.

Political parties have many functions in modern democratic politics. They aggregate interests and draw up policy programmes for government. They select candidates for public office, who are then responsible for implementing policy decisions. They bring together like-minded individuals to campaign for these candidates, and to participate in discussions about future policy directions. In all of these ways they create important links between politicians and the public, and opportunities for dialogue and persuasion. How these internal party functions are carried out, and particularly who has influence within them, is thus crucial to shaping the broader political system. The raft of reforms implemented by Labour in the 1980s and 1990s touched all of these central functions. Significant changes were made to the composition and role of the party conference, to the powers of local parties, and to the ways in which Labour's candidates and leaders were selected. Such changes have potentially far reaching consequences in terms of the party's policy positions, the kinds of candidates it puts into office, and how it communicates with the electorate. Given that Labour is one of the two main parties that seek to govern Britain, they also have important wider implications for British politics.

This book is designed as a resource for those who engage with Labour Party politics at many levels: as active participants, interested observers and commentators, or students of political parties. It is intended to be accessible to all of these audiences and, it is hoped, will provide each of them with something new. The purpose of the book is to chart the internal changes undergone by the Labour Party since 1979 – and particularly during the late 1980s and the 1990s, when much of this change actually took place. As well as providing a record of how each major reform was devised and put into effect, the book also seeks to analyse the collective importance and overall impact of approximately 25 years of internal party change.

The reforms during this period represented the first major alteration to the Labour Party's democracy since the agreement of its 1918 constitution. The changes challenged some of the original principles of the party's internal organisation, and in many ways really did create a 'new' party in organisational terms. From its roots as a 'federal' organisation where affiliated trade unions at least formally had overwhelming power, Labour's structures have gradually been transformed to give greater representation to other groups. From being an extremely male dominated organisation, the party developed mechanisms that now see men and women equally represented at almost every level. And from having a strong tradition of internal representative democracy, Labour increasingly moved towards empowering members individually, through systems of 'one member one vote'.

Many common assumptions about Labour's organisational reform are challenged by the material in the book. First, it is often assumed that change was made largely as a result of the leadership of Tony Blair. As this study shows, many important reforms did take place in the 1990s, particularly after the shock of Labour's fourth successive general election defeat in 1992. This in part accounts for their association with the birth of 'new' Labour, which was proclaimed after Blair was elected party leader in 1994.[2] Yet most of the reforms, like so much else about 'new' Labour, had enjoyed a long gestation. Some had been discussed ever since the first decades of the party's existence, and most were on its agenda since at least the 1970s. Many important changes were made during the period of Neil Kinnock's leadership, from 1983-92, and significant further agreements were reached during John Smith's brief period as leader from 1992 to 1994. These changes between them established most of the principles, and many of the procedures, that became more familiar under Tony Blair.

Second, there is a common perception that reform in the party was driven by Labour leaders, often in the face of opposition from the party. In fact, as the material in the book demonstrates, the opposite was often the case. Most of the reforms that came to be implemented were first proposed by party activists, and some of them by the leader's opponents. Reform was generally a process of negotiation, which often took place over many years. During this process leaders conceded to the demands of activists and trade unions, just as these groups could eventually be persuaded to com-promise to accommodate leaders' views. The result was reform that drew on competing visions of internal party democracy, rather than implementing the pure model favoured by any single individual or group. Consequently, as the book concludes, it is not straight-forward to deduce who has benefited from the reforms. There are no simple winners and losers. The third common assumption – that Labour's internal reform has resulted in a shift of power towards its leaders and away from its members – is thus found to be questionable at best. Two major changes in particular – the reduction of the trade unions' formal powers in the party, and the enfranchisement of inactive members through one member one vote – have shown themselves to have effects which are ambiguous in terms of leadership power.

Labour's internal debates opened up some of the most fund-amental questions about 'intra' party democracy, which have vexed politicians and political scientists alike from the early days of mass politics. Ever since Ostrogorski (1902) questioned the influence of Liberal activists over the party's elected representatives, contro-versies have existed about the potential conflict between parliamentary democracy and the internal democracy of parties outside parliament. In 1915 Robert Michels suggested that, despite some parties' stated intentions to empower their members to take decisions, power would inevitably become concentrated in the hands of party leaders – a tendency described as his 'iron law of oligarchy' (Michels, 1962). In a detailed study in the 1950s Robert McKenzie (1963) concluded that this was largely the case in the British Conservative and Labour parties. This was despite their ostensibly different principles of organisation, and the statement in Labour's constitution that the annual party conference was formally responsible for decision making, rather than the leadership in parliament.

In a backlash against the very situation described by McKenzie, Labour Party activists through the 1960s and 1970s increasingly came to assert the rights of the conference and of local parties, as described in Chapter 2. After Labour lost power in 1979, the demands of these groups led to some of the first major organ-isational reforms since 1918. After this, organisational reform was a constant theme in internal Labour debates, particularly during the 1980s and early 1990s. Amongst the leadership, and its supporters on the party's moderate and right wings, there was a perceived need to move Labour's organisation back to its old equilibrium. But the change that had already taken place, and the leadership's new interest in organisational matters, also opened up opportunities for further reform which would challenge other aspects of Labour's traditions.

The intense period of internal debate and reform since 1979 leads to many interesting questions, which this book seeks to answer. The main body of the text explores the origins of each individual reform, and charts the involvement of various protagonists in the negotiations which brought about organisational change, particularly from the mid 1980s onwards. In doing this the book seeks to explore what drove each of these reforms, and what their individual effects have been. But by looking at a wide range of reforms together, and over a period of more than two decades, the material also allows us to see emerging patterns, and to evaluate the overall impact on the party. In particular an assessment is made of the success that various proponents had in achieving change (or indeed blocking the proposals of others), and the extent to which their objectives were realised as a result.

The book also considers what factors helped to ensure that certain reforms proposed by the party leadership were implemented, despite opposition, whilst leaders themselves came to accept others that they had originally opposed. As suggested above, assumptions that leadership power will tend to be enhanced over time (as proposed by Michels in his 'iron law') are questioned. In fact it is suggested that there are significant constraints on leaders, including those created by the media and public opinion, as well as by actors inside the party itself.

Finally the book asks how Labour's original principles of democracy have changed as a result of reform, and to what extent they have been replaced with a model that is either internally coherent or likely to prove stable over time. These bigger questions are each addressed in the 'evaluation' sections at the end of the main chapters, and then more substantially at the end of the book.

Whilst there are many benefits in presenting a general study of Labour's organisational reform, the attempt to cover such a broad subject over a relatively long period (in what is necessarily a short book) also brings limitations. It has been necessary to condense the material covered, and also to take hard decisions about the omission of certain issues. The topics chosen are those that were most central, most high profile, and potentially had the most profound effects on both how the party operates and how it is perceived. For example whilst covering the transformation of women's representation within the party, the book does not discuss parallel issues of youth and ethnic minority representation, whose progress in comparison was relatively limited. Whilst looking at the selection of candidates for parliament and devolved government, the analysis does not extend as far as local government. The book also includes no general coverage of changes resulting from devolution in Scotland and Wales.[3] And its focus is firmly on the extra-parliamentary party, rather than attempting to explain the organisation of the party in parliament or in government.

THE STRUCTURE OF THE BOOK

The remainder of the book is in ten chapters. Seven of these tell the stories of particular aspects of reform. Before turning to the specifics, however, Chapter 2 considers the context in which reform took place. Here the history of Labour's organisation is briefly reviewed, culminating in the organisational and political crisis that engulfed the party after 1979. The chapter then identifies the main protagonists in reform debates, and what they were seeking to achieve. It also briefly reviews some of the main 'packages' of reforms that are referred to in greater detail in subsequent chapters.

Chapters 3 and 4 look at the selection of Labour candidates for public office, and particularly at the party's attitude to one member one vote (OMOV). The adoption of OMOV challenged some of the most central principles of Labour's traditional democracy, and consequently debates over its introduction were heated and took place over many years. Chapter 3 considers the growing support, particularly after 1979, for applying the OMOV principle in selecting local candidates and the party leader. This ended with dramatic decisions at the 1993 conference over both of these matters, which largely cemented the principles governing internal party elections today. Chapter 4 then considers the later period, when Tony Blair was party leader. Here OMOV was called into question, and its frequent absence from selection contests caused various controversies. Following pressure from within the party, but also from the media and public opinion, it was later re-established and seems to have achieved a stable place as one of the central organising principles of 'new' Labour.

Chapter 5 considers the wide range of changes that affected women's representation in the party. These included moves to achieve gender balance amongst candidates for public office, starting with the dramatic decision in 1993 to adopt all-women shortlists. However this breakthrough was crucially predated by changes to women's representation throughout the party's structures, which themselves followed years of friction between leaders and women activists. After 1997 Labour achieved impressive levels of women's representation in the new devolved institutions, and the issue of gender balance in the party became increasingly mainstream.

The next three chapters examine the party's central decision-making organs, and particularly their influence on policy. Chapter 6 considers the new structures established to develop policy in the period between annual conferences, which centred on the 'National Policy Forum'. The chapter addresses not only how and why these reforms happened, but also how they operated in practice after Labour's election to government in 1997. It suggests that whilst there are many weaknesses in these arrangements, they have also created important new sites of dialogue between leaders and members. In effect they took over roles previously performed by the National Executive Committee (NEC) and its subcommittees behind closed doors, with little input from the wider party. Chapter 7 examines changes to the NEC, which was traditionally responsible for overseeing the party between annual conferences. This body was reformed first in terms of its structure and method of election, and then with respect to its powers and functions. Both of these sets of changes have tended to marginalise its role. Chapter 8 goes on to consider how Labour's traditionally sovereign body, the annual conference, was itself also reformed in terms of composition and powers. It traces the constitutional position of the trade unions at conference – challenged from the early 1980s onwards and changed in the 1990s – which marked a major shift at the heart of the party's democracy.[4] This reform had knock-on effects for the leadership's relationship with the conference, and was accompanied by further reforms to the policy-making process outside, which increasingly compromised its traditionally central role.

Chapter 9 completes the review of specific areas of reform by looking at the impact of change on local parties and members. It notes that the vision of some reformers to create a 'mass membership' party has largely failed, both due to the difficulty of recruiting members and because of leaders' lack of clarity about what to do with them. Meanwhile the various visions for reform of local parties have not been realised, and no single programme of local party reform came to be agreed. Nonetheless the impact of other changes has been significant at the grassroots level.

The book concludes with two chapters that reflect on these wide ranging reforms, and tackle some of the big questions mentioned above. Chapter 10 first examines the process of reform – seeking to explain why certain changes happened when they did, and which bodies and individuals proved influential. In particular it concludes that outcomes were necessarily negotiated, and that leaders' motivations in pursuing reform were more complex than is often assumed. However, the tendency by leaders to 'spin' reform as benefiting themselves had an important impact on how it came to be perceived, contributing to how 'new' Labour has been myth-ologised. Chapter 11 then looks at the overall outcome of reform, considering what it means for power relations in the party. It concludes that Labour's internal democracy has become a complex hybrid as a result of reform, and new dynamics are developing inside both the parliamentary and extra-parliamentary parties. It is difficult to conclude that the party leadership has more freedom than it did in 'old' Labour, when the role of the unions in the party meant that leaders could often negotiate policy and organisational matters to their own satisfaction. Instead leaders in the modern party face new constraints, which are more diffuse and also more unpredictable.

Tracing Labour's reform since 1979 is complex, as there are many inter-related factors, both in terms of external factors driving reform and between the different changes themselves. In the Appendix is a timeline, which provides a snapshot of the reforms discussed in the main chapters, on a year-by-year basis. This provides both a summary and a visual indication of the connections between the different aspects of reform.

By 2005 the internal democracy of the Labour Party was fundam-entally different from that which had endured for most of the twentieth century. Whilst the imprint of the original party is still visible, many new principles of democracy, and new organisational conventions, have been established since 1979. The impact of Labour's internal reforms for the party, and for British politics more widely, has yet to be fully felt or fully understood. Meanwhile over this same period many of the organisational changes undergone by Labour were mirrored in other parties (Dalton and Wattenburg, 2000a; Katz and Mair, 1994; Webb, Farrell and Holliday, 2002). It is hoped that this detailed study of Labour and its reforms can therefore help us better understand not only the events as they happened, and their impact on Labour's democracy, but also the implications for British politics and political parties in the wider world.

Notes

1. See, for example, Anderson and Mann (1997), Brivati and Bale (1997), Coates and Lawler (2000), Driver and Martell (1998), Fielding (2003), Finlayson (2003), Giddens (2002), Gould (1998), Hay (1999), Jones (1996), Ludlam and Smith (2000, 2004), Macintyre (2000), Mandelson and Liddle (1996), Panitch and Leys (1997), Rentoul (2001), Routledge (1998), Sopel (1995).
2. The slogan 'new Labour, new Britain' was unveiled on the set of the Labour Party annual conference in autumn 1994.
3. The impact of devolution on the party's organisation is the subject of a study by Martin Laffin, Eric Shaw and Gerald Taylor (2004, 2005).
4. Note that within the party the annual conference is often simply referred to as 'conference', without the definite article. Often in the book this form is used.

2

The Context for Reform

The following seven chapters describe the key organisational reforms that took place within the Labour Party between the early 1980s and the early 21st century. Each seeks to explain a particular aspect of change to the party's democracy. But first, this chapter provides some necessary historical and political context.

The reforms that took place over this period represented a significant break with the past. Many of Labour's traditional principles of organisation were questioned, and new models of party democracy were proposed. To appreciate the significance of these changes therefore requires some knowledge of Labour's original party structure, which had remained little changed throughout most of the twentieth century. A brief summary is provided here, followed by a description of the breakdown in consensus on both policy and organisational matters which occurred in the party from the 1960s onwards.

The second form of context needed to understand the nature of Labour's internal reform is an insight into the conflicting currents of opinion within the party. The protagonists in these debates, who were broadly aligned with the party's 'left' and 'right', appear regularly throughout the book. In particular, proposals from various activist groups within the party, themselves largely reflecting this ideological divide, provided many of the proposals that were discussed and went on to be implemented. To understand this process it is also important to identify the motivations of these competing groups in the party – and, in particular, what drove the so called 'modernisers' – in proposing reform. Finally, there were a number of reform 'packages' which were presented by the party leadership from the late 1980s, each of which spans several of the chapters that follow. The chapter closes with a brief review of these packages.

Later chapters will then examine the numerous specific reform proposals that were debated and came to be agreed. After this we will be able to consider which, if any, of the protagonists came to see their vision realised, and what the overall impact of the party's organisational reforms has been.

PARTY ORGANISATION BEFORE 'NEW' LABOUR

According to the party theorist Angelo Panebianco, the way in which 'the cards are dealt out and the outcomes of the different rounds played out in the formative phases of an organization, continue in many ways to condition the life of the organization even decades afterwards' (1988, p. xiii). This must rarely have been more true than with respect to the British Labour Party.

Unlike the Conservative and Liberal parties, the Labour Party was formed as an extra-parliamentary body. Created by the coming together of trade unions and socialist societies in 1900, the party's original purpose was to achieve representation for working people in parliament. The central organising logic of the party was, from the start, its federal structure. This reflected the partnership between autonomous founding organisations, with each group guaranteed seats at an annual conference and on an executive committee. Initially the party had no individual members – leading it to be classified by Maurice Duverger (1954) as having an 'indirect' rather than a 'direct' structure. Instead individuals could gain representation only via one of its affiliated organisations, such as a trade union, the Independent Labour Party (ILP) or the Fabian Society. The second founding principle of the party's organisation was thus one of representative democracy. The various affiliates reached their own internal decisions and then expressed opinions inside the party with a collective voice. This mirrored the traditions of Labour's main founding organisations. As Henry Drucker has observed, at the birth of the party 'many of its organizational principles were taken unreflectively from the characteristic properties of the trade unions' (1980, p. 266). A classic study by Drucker (1979) was influential in demonstrating how the party's organisational 'ethos' was equally important to its identity as was its 'doctrine'.

Labour's 1918 constitution, which for the first time formally adopted socialist objectives (in Clause IV), also allowed individuals to join the party for the first time. At this point local Labour parties gained formal representation. They were organised both at constituency level (i.e. corresponding to seats in parliament) and through smaller geographic branches. Both of these had their own elected officers and programme of regular meetings. Locally, the principles of federalism and representative democracy were replicated, with trade unions and socialist societies affiliated to constituency parties, thereby gaining representation on the bodies that controlled local decisions. The core unit of decision making was the constituency-wide 'general committee' (GC), which brought together elected representatives from branches and local women's sections with delegates from affiliated organisations.[1] One of the most important duties of the GCs was selection of the local parliamentary candidate, within a framework of rules set down by the National Executive Committee (NEC). Each local constituency party also gained representation at the party's sovereign decision making body, the annual conference – to which the GC would elect a delegate or delegates (depending on the size of the local membership). The local parties collectively were also given a small number of seats on the NEC, which was elected at the conference.

From the outset the MPs that made up the Parliamentary Labour Party (PLP) were responsible for electing their own leader, who quickly became recognised as the leader of the party as a whole. However, on policy matters the PLP was to be guided by the annual conference. In theory control was thus firmly with the extra-parliamentary party. Each constituency party, and each national affiliated organisation, was able to submit one motion per year for the conference to consider. When the delegates gathered, these motions were boiled down, in strictly organised pre-meetings, to a manageable number of 'composite' resolutions. Any resolution that went on to be supported by at least a two-thirds majority at the conference officially became part of the party's policy 'programme'. The conference also voted on statements from the NEC, which in practice determined much of its policy direction, and on any changes to the party's rules.

Despite the formal subordination of the PLP, and the elaborate local structures, Labour's organisation did little to empower ordinary members. The party's organisational 'affiliates' continued to hold most of the formal power, with the trade unions providing the vast majority of both party funds and voting strength. The unions held up to 90 per cent of votes at the annual conference, controlled most of the seats on the NEC and could also potentially dominate local party GCs. The effect of empowering trade unions within the party traditionally tended to benefit the parliamentary leadership. The general understanding between trade union and parliamentary leaderships was that the former would set the terms on industrial policy, giving the latter significant freedom on other matters (Harrison, 1960; Minkin, 1980; 1992; Reid, 2000). The lack of influence held by grassroots members was, according to some, essential to the party's stability. Richard Crossman wrote of activists that 'since [they] tended to be "extremists", a constitution was needed which maintained their enthusiasm by apparently creating a full party democracy whilst excluding them from effective power' (1963, p. 41-2). Hence the conclusion of Robert McKenzie's careful study of democracy inside the Conservatives and Labour was that 'whatever the role granted in theory to the extra-parliamentary wings of the parties, in practice final authority rests in both parties with the parliamentary party and its leadership. In this fundamental respect the distribution of power within the two major parties is the same' (1963, p. 635).

THE BREAKDOWN OF CONSENSUS

This state of affairs caused understandable frustration amongst activists on the Labour left, whose strength in the constituencies was rarely reflected in the decisions of the party's ruling bodies. Tensions over the internal balance of power were apparent from at least the 1930s, and were prominent in disputes between the 'Bevanite' left and more 'moderate' or right-wing elements in the 1950s, and then between the 'revisionists' and more traditional elements into the 1960s. But though there were occasional reviews of party organisation, none touched on these central issues. Thus in 1955 a committee chaired by Harold Wilson reported on possible organisational changes in the wake of the party's general election defeat, but confined itself largely to issues concerning the organisation of local campaigns (Labour Party, 1955). In 1966 the NEC established a 'Committee of Enquiry', which only proposed some changes to the party's women's and youth organisations, and a restructuring of the NEC which was never brought into effect (Labour Party, 1968). By the 1970s, the organisational structures set down in the party's 1918 constitution remained in most major respects untouched.

Frustrations amongst party activists grew during Harold Wilson's governments in the 1960s. Having had high hopes of Wilson, who was seen as coming from the party's left, many were disappointed by the timidity of the Labour administrations of 1964 and 1966. In particular, changes in the mood of some trade unions meant that the conference inflicted increasing numbers of defeats on the party leadership.[2] The fact that Wilson frequently chose to ignore these led to greater tensions. In 1970 the party conference passed a resolution stating that it 'deplore[d] the Parliamentary Labour Party's refusal to act on conference decisions'.[3] From this point on, disputes about party organisation became increasingly bitter. During Labour's years of opposition from 1970-74 the complaints were largely contained. However, disappointments with the 1974-79 governments made activists on the left increasingly determined to achieve reforms that would make the parliamentary party more accountable. Meanwhile Labour's relationship with the unions had reached a new low. In the early 1970s the NEC had – for the first time – come under the control of the party's left. It therefore became more sympathetic to the calls for organisational reform. After the party lost power in 1979 arguments over internal party democracy became central to 'Labour's multiple crises' (Shaw, 1994, p. 1).

The pressure for organisational change in the 1970s, realised in 1979-81, therefore resulted from activists' desire that the extra-parliamentary party should achieve the *de facto* authority over the parliamentary party that it in principle already held. Ministers and MPs, it was felt, were too prey to influence by establishment voices and insufficiently bold in implementing socialist values. To achieve cultural change left-wing activists, co-ordinated by the new Campaign for Labour Party Democracy (CLPD – see below), made three key organisational demands. The first of these was 'mandatory reselection' of MPs, meaning that each constituency should hold an open contest to select its parliamentary candidate once in every parliament. This, it was argued, would make individual Labour MPs more accountable to their local parties. Second, activists demanded that the party leader should be elected by and accountable to the party as a whole, rather than just to Labour MPs. This was again seen as an important means of boosting accountability to the extra-parliamentary party. Third, it was proposed that the responsibility for agreeing the party's election manifesto should rest with the extra-parliamentary party alone, in the shape of the NEC, rather than also involving members of Labour's cabinet or shadow cabinet.

After defeat at the 1979 election the party leader Jim Callaghan, and others from the party's right wing, sought to hold back the growing pressures from the left for reform. At the suggestion of

loyalist trade union leaders it was agreed to set up a new Commission of Enquiry, with a broad remit to investigate party organisational matters (Panitch and Leys, 1997). This was in part a delaying
tactic and in part an attempt to encourage a more rounded look at
potential reform. However, although the Commission gathered
over 2,000 pieces of evidence on a wide range of organisational
matters, it did not succeed in blocking the CLPD's demands. As
summarised in Chapter 3, the first two of these were realised
between 1979 and 1981. The third was agreed in principle in 1979
but failed, by an extremely narrow margin, to be voted into the
party's rules at the annual conference in 1980.[4]

These debates, and the reforms that were agreed, placed a new
focus on the party's internal democracy. As the CLPD's campaign
gathered pace, the annual conference agenda was increasingly
dominated by organisational matters, culminating in a special
conference in 1981 with the sole purpose of deciding a method for
electing the party leader. After this reform was agreed, and with
mandatory reselection now in place, the pressure from the left for
change became less intense, but by no means abated. The left
sought to protect the gains they had made, and to deploy their
successful tactics in order to achieve further change. At the same
time moderates and right wingers in the party sought to tackle the
crises that had grown since the 1960s and 1970s with their own
reform proposals, and to rebalance the gains of the left.

One way or another this period brought to the fore many
questions about Labour's traditional internal democracy. Much of
what followed can be seen as a reaction to the organisational,
ideological and cultural changes that occurred in this tempestuous
period. However, the next major internal reforms in the party did
not occur until the late 1980s and 1990s, as documented in the
chapters that follow.

THE PROTAGONISTS

In considering the structure of opinion within the Labour Party it is
traditional to talk of the 'left' and the 'right'. This is a necessarily
simplistic distinction, too crude to capture both the breadth and
multi-dimensionality of views that at any time exist. However,
these terms are freely used as shorthand within the party by those
wishing to categorise both their own positions and those of others.
They will thus appear regularly throughout the text. But such terms

must be used with care. A more precise and meaningful way of considering the protagonists in debates on party organisational reform is to look at the views of formally organised pressure groups inside the party. Although these had always existed, the events of the 1960s and 1970s had spawned new groups, with organisational reform high on their agendas. Whilst not being formal factions, such groups were broadly aligned with the 'left' and the 'right'. They had no direct power to bring about reform, but played a key role as intermediate organisations in articulating claims and building coalitions for change. Formal power was held by the traditional stakeholders, such as the unions or constituencies. But these unofficial groups of like-minded party members were influential in setting the terms of most reform debates. They formulated demands, lobbied for change, mobilised supporters in the unions and constituencies, and sought to gain majority support at the party conference and on the NEC for their positions.

Groups on the left

The earliest and most important of these groups, which has already been mentioned, was the Campaign for Labour Party Democracy (CLPD). This organisation, formed in 1973, was, unlike virtually all other groups, created principally to achieve organisational reform in the party. The specific trigger for its formation was Harold Wilson's immediate dismissal of proposals in an NEC policy statement, and his announcement that he would not even endorse them if they were approved by the annual conference.[5] The publication of this programme, which proposed the nationalisation of 25 major companies, demonstrated the hold that the left of the party had gained on its NEC. Once this had been achieved the CLPD sought to assert the NEC's power, and that of the extra-parliamentary party in general, over Labour's parliamentary leaders.

The CLPD was an emphatically grassroots organisation, in contrast to the left-wing Tribune Group, which organised amongst MPs. Its founding secretary and powerhouse was Vladimir Derer, who organised the group out of his north London home. Other key members included Victor Schonfield, Francis Prideaux and Pete Willsman. Despite its extra-parliamentary focus the CLPD was launched with the support of ten MPs. These included Neil Kinnock, who increasingly disagreed with the organisation's objectives from 1979 onwards, and ended his membership in 1982.

In the 1980s the group became associated with Tony Benn, although he had not joined until after the 1979 election defeat. However by this time his Special Adviser, Frances Morrell, was already a member of the organisation's executive.

The CLPD was associated with the 'new left' of social movements which had flourished in the 1960s, and its members supported a more radical policy agenda than the cautious parliamentary leadership wanted to embrace.[6] However, rather than being explicitly ideological its central principle was that 'policy decisions reached by annual conference should be binding on the Parliamentary Labour Party'.[7] Given the current political balance in the party, the group expected this to benefit the left. Its primary campaign method was to mobilise constituency parties, by circulating 'model resolutions' which the group's leaders proposed should be submitted to annual conference. This tactic, increasingly successful during the 1970s, was also used by other organisations. In addition the CLPD worked hard to mobilise support amongst left-wing trade union activists for its positions, seeking to win backing from trade union conferences and union delegations at the Labour Party conference.[8] Given the balance of votes in the party this was essential to success. The public service union NUPE affiliated to the CLPD at a national level in 1976 and its Research Director, Bernard Dix, became the organisation's vice president.

Following the adoption of mandatory reselection of MPs and the new 'electoral college' for choosing the party leader (discussed in Chapter 3), the CLPD developed and campaigned on further organisational demands. Its vision was of an 'activist democracy', where decisions were determined by those who populated the structures of the extra-parliamentary party. In 1980, as discussed in Chapter 5, the organisation formed a Women's Action Committee (WAC) which campaigned on issues of women's representation within the party. Although the high point of the CLPD's success was in 1979-81, it continued campaigning throughout the 1980s and 1990s, and its organisers continue to include Derer, Prideaux and Willsman.

The Labour Co-ordinating Committee (LCC) was founded in 1978.[9] The group was originally set up by Michael Meacher (then a junior minister), and Frances Morrell. In its early years it had a significantly overlapping membership to the CLPD and was also seen as associated with Tony Benn. Its core objective was not to focus on organisational matters, but instead to encourage policy discussion in the party and stronger policy links with outside interest groups. However, given the dominance of debates about party democracy at the time of its formation, it was quickly drawn into these issues. The CLPD's three core demands commanded broad consensus on the left, and the LCC joined forces to support these as part of the 'Rank and File Mobilising Committee'.[10] But this alliance soon began to crumble. The first differences emerged when Tony Benn decided to test the new electoral college arrangements in 1981 by challenging Denis Healey for the party deputy leadership. The LCC was divided over whether to support Benn, whilst the key members of the CLPD became central in his campaign. The organisations were also in disagreement over whether the loss of many leading right wingers to the breakaway Social Democratic Party (SDP) in 1981 was a cause for celebration or mourning. By the time of the 1983 general election defeat the two groups were largely opposed. The LCC's response was not to see the defeat as a vindication of the left, but rather to argue that the party should embrace more moderate positions. Leading LCC members were increasingly intolerant of the 'ultra' left and became convinced of the need to expel the Trotskyist Militant Tendency from the party (an objective achieved in 1983[11]). As a result the group attracted new members sympathetic to this cause. It was also supportive of Neil Kinnock's election as leader in 1983, whilst the CLPD was not. This split between the 'hard' and 'soft' left in the extra-parliamentary party mirrored parallel developments inside the PLP. Here the broad left Tribune Group had split over many of the same issues, leading to the formation of the Campaign Group in 1981, which took a more 'hard left' position.

Current and future parliamentarians were more visible amongst LCC members than they were in the CLPD. Peter Hain was a member of the executive from 1981, and vice chair from 1982. Harriet Harman took over the chair from Michael Meacher in 1983, and John Denham became chair in 1984. By the mid 1980s executive members included Joan Ruddock and Ken Livingstone, as well as Maggie Jones of NUPE (who later served on the NEC) and Cherie Booth. Much of the organisation's work was however managed by grassroots members, and it employed a paid organiser from 1979. Using similar tactics to the CLPD, the LCC mobilised support for a 'soft left' agenda. Central to this was the vision of a mass membership party based on 'participatory democracy', with a culture of political education, policy discussion amongst members, and stronger links to other groups in the community.

Over time a series of factors led the LCC to move further and further away from its former allies the CLPD. One was the desire to broadly support Kinnock once he had become leader. Another was the absorption of increasing numbers of activists who opposed the hard left, and who gradually gained ground on the LCC's executive. These factors were coupled with shifts in the attitude of existing members in response to consecutive election defeats. Whilst the CLPD's organisational demands were primarily concerned with making the party responsive to its activists, the LCC became ever more concerned with changing the party's image to make it more appealing to the electorate. As one former LCC activist put it, many came to believe that 'any price was worth paying to get Labour into government'. LCC members thus increasingly found common cause with those on the right of the party who were interested in embracing change. It was this grouping in the late 1980s and early 1990s that came to be known as the 'modernisers' – opposed to the 'traditionalists' to both their left and their right.

Despite its original intention to focus on policy, the LCC continued, until it was wound up in 1998, to expend considerable energy on party organisational matters. In particular it convened two commissions on party democracy, in response to major consultations by the national party in 1989 and 1996. Although the recommendations from the first of these proved too controversial to win support from the LCC as a whole, the ideas in both reports were influential (LCC, 1989; 1996). In both cases members of the commissions went on to hold high office in the party and thus were centrally involved in implementing change.[12] After the CLPD's first flush of success the LCC became at least as successful at achieving support for its proposals on party organisational reform. This in part resulted from its greater sympathy with the leadership's perspective. For example its conversion in 1987 to the cause of one member one vote (OMOV), which had been long supported by groups on the right, was a sign that the centre of gravity in party opinion had shifted.

Groups on the right

Groups on the party's right wing (or as many of its members prefer to be called, the 'moderate' wing) tended to organise less publicly than those on the left. Whilst the aspirational left needed to work hard to mobilise members in local parties, the right had a natural constituency amongst non-ideological trade union leaders and those faced with the politics of compromise in the PLP. As alliances between these groups had generally been enough to swing the support of Labour Party conference, organisation on the ground was largely unnecessary.[13] Whilst the left was largely defined by its policy objectives – such as public ownership or unilateral nuclear disarmament – the traditional 'trade union' right was as much a cultural as an ideological phenomenon. Having always held control in the NEC and parliamentary party, the ethos of this group was synonymous with respect for and loyalty to leaders. This implied a pragmatic approach to policy often defined more by what it was against (i.e. the left) than explicitly by what it was for. However there was also a more intellectual right, including the 'revisionist' thinkers in the PLP from the late 1950s. These two strands of the right generally made common cause, though on some matters (notably including the role of the unions in the party) they could find themselves in conflict.

Prior to 1981 there were two main right-wing pressure groups in the party. From 1974 the Manifesto Group operated in the PLP, in opposition to the left-wing Tribune Group. The momentum of the CLPD then resulted in the establishment of the Campaign for Labour Victory (CLV) in 1977, to oppose it in the constituencies. However, the CLV's grassroots organisation was relatively less successful and its leadership rested with parliamentarians. Like its opponent, the CLV embraced organisational objectives in order to secure political advantage. In this case tactics included seeking enhanced powers for 'ordinary' less active members, at the expense of activists and trade unions. The organisation was thus always supportive of the principle of OMOV.

When a group of senior right wingers split from Labour in 1981 to form the SDP, both the Manifesto Group and the CLV lost many of their key supporters. At this point the need for the remaining members of the party's right to organise became more urgent, and a new group was formed. The Labour Solidarity Campaign (generally referred to as 'Solidarity') was jointly chaired by MPs Peter Shore and Roy Hattersley (Hayter, 2005). It set out to be more broadly based than its predecessor, and to attract members from both the Tribune and Manifesto Groups in parliament. Other MPs involved included Giles Radice, John Golding, George Robertson, John Smith and Donald Dewar. Although Solidarity's steering committee was comprised entirely of parliamentarians it also set out to organise in the constituencies, with an objective of fighting back against the advance of the left. This was seen as key to its other main objective – that of persuading remaining right wingers not to defect to the SDP. The group was firmly committed to OMOV, as a means of disempowering left-wing activists, and campaigned for this until its demise in 1988. Outside parliament early Solidarity members included Peter Mandelson, then a councillor in Lambeth, and Tony Blair, then a barrister living in Hackney (Macintyre, 2000; Rentoul, 2001). Members like Blair, who was also a member of the LCC from 1982, exemplified the fusion between the soft left and elements of the more intellectual right that occurred from the early 1980s.

A key priority for the right was regaining support in the trade unions, which had drifted leftwards from the 1960s. In 1981 the 'St Ermin's Group' of senior trade unionists was formed, and organised more covertly to this end (Golding, 2003; Hayter, 2005). Through their joint efforts these groups on the right had significant success. Like the CLPD the right also sought to organise amongst grassroots union activists, and within trade union delegations at Labour Party conference, to win support for their favoured positions. In this way they managed to reverse the majority that the left had achieved on the NEC in the 1970s. The 'moderates' gained five seats in 1981 and won a narrow majority on the body in 1982. Their other objectives included various party organisational reforms – many of which had previously been championed by the CLV – which sought to reverse or neutralise the gains of the left.

Other key protagonists

In addition to pressure groups on the left and the right, there were important organisational and individual actors holding key posit-ions within the party, whose consent was generally needed in order to achieve reform.

First, the National Executive Committee was central to all disc-ussions about organisational change. This body was responsible for proposing most of the rule changes considered by the annual conference, but also for indicating to the party which proposals from others it was willing to accept. The view expressed by the NEC was generally (but by no means always) influential with conference delegates. The composition of the NEC is described in Chapter 7. As already noted, the left gained control of this body in the 1970s, but a majority more loyal to the leader was established from 1982 onwards.

The key block, both on the NEC and at the conference, was the trade unions. They held an effective veto over reform, thanks to their majority of votes on both of these bodies. Any coalition for change therefore needed significant trade union support. However, it is important to remember that the unions are a diverse and complex set of organisations, often with different perspectives from one another. And, in any case, each union is itself a democratic organisation, with policy determined by its own executive committee and conference. Trade union leaders are influential in these forums, but do not have absolute power. In deciding how to vote at the party conference or on the NEC, trade union representatives must thus take account of the views expressed within their own organisations. Appreciation of this dynamic is essential to understanding how some of the changes within the Labour Party were, or were not, ultimately agreed.

Finally there were, of course, many key individuals who centrally influenced the direction of reform. The most obvious of these – Kinnock, Smith and Blair – were the ones who went on to lead the party. Others were influential not because of their position in elected office but due to their role on the Labour Party staff. The most important amongst them were those who reached the highest office of party General Secretary. Larry Whitty took up this post in 1985, having joined the party from the General and Municipal Workers Union (GMWU), and was generally sympathetic to the soft left. Tom Sawyer replaced him in 1994, having previously been Deputy General Secretary of NUPE and a long serving member of the NEC. He, like many around the LCC, had by then made the journey from the relatively 'hard' left to become a fervent 'moderniser'. Along with others key politicians, NEC members and trade union representatives, such individuals played an important role in defining the trajectory of reform.

THE MOTIVATIONS FOR REFORM

Given the range of individuals and groups involved, there were clearly various and conflicting motivations for party organisational change. All sides argued that they were seeking to pursue greater democracy within the party, although their visions of how that democracy should work were very different. The CLPD's objective, as we have seen, was to wrest control of party policy from over-cautious leaders by making them more responsive to the demands of ideologically-driven activists in both the constituencies and trade unions. In contrast, the LCC sought a mass membership party with a stronger culture of member participation, extending beyond the current activists. For moderates and right wingers the primary objective was to stabilise the party and, in particular, to make it more responsive to the views of the electorate.

At the 1983 general election Labour hit its electoral low point, winning just 28 per cent of the vote and narrowly avoiding coming in third place, behind the new SDP-Liberal Alliance. Splits over policy, which led to the SDP breakaway and culminated in the infamous 1983 manifesto, had done the party huge electoral damage. Internal rows over party organisation had also been highly visible, and their results threatened to make it harder to shift the party's policy positions towards the centre ground. When Kinnock was elected leader he thus took over a party that was 'demoralised, deeply polarised and virtually ungovernable' (Shaw, 1994, p. 202).

From this point on the absolute priority for the leadership, the right, and growing numbers on the soft left, was to build the party's electoral popularity. In practical terms this meant regaining the old balance between the parliamentary and extra-parliamentary parties – initially through rebuilding coalitions of support for the leadership at the party conference and on the NEC. But organisational reform was also seen as central to cementing this objective. Changes to internal democracy therefore came to be prioritised not only by internal pressure groups but, for first time, in a concerted way by the party leadership itself.

This focus continued, indeed intensified, following the party's further general electoral defeats in 1987 and 1992. For those concerned with electoral strategy organisational reform had taken on both a substantive and a symbolic importance. In *substantive* terms it promised a shift in power inside the party, away from those who resisted the policy changes needed to bring Labour back to the centre ground. In *symbolic* terms internal party reform was also a means, alongside these new policy directions, of communicating to the public that the party had changed. Philip Gould, for example, who acted as a senior adviser on Labour's communications strategy from 1985, continually emphasised the centrality of symbolic organisational reform, and proposed after each electoral defeat that the party had not changed far and fast enough (Gould, 1998). For both substantive and symbolic reasons internal democratic reform had become central to debates about the party's 'modernisation'. And as far as the 'modernisers' were concerned there were two primary targets of reform: the activists and the trade unions.

Curbing the powers of the activists

The desire to enhance activist power had been central to the campaigns of the CLPD, and by 1981 these had achieved significant success. However, Labour activists, who showed their commitment to the party primarily through attendance at local meetings, were generally perceived as being out of step with the views of the wider electorate. Not only this, but they were seen by the party leadership as being unrepresentative of Labour's membership as a whole. There was a general belief (to which the CLPD also quite openly subscribed) that party activists were more left-wing in their views than 'ordinary' inactive members. In particular in the 1970s and 1980s the perceived influx of new left-wing party members, and the problems of ultra-left 'entryism', which culminated in the proscription of the Militant Tendency, enhanced suspicion of the activist base (Seyd, 1987). The experiences of figures such as Tony Blair, Peter Mandelson and Charles Clarke (who worked for Kinnock from 1981) in the bitterly factional London Labour Party in this period convinced them that party activists were unrepresentative of wider opinion both inside and outside the party.

This was a pattern familiar to those who studied political parties. Ostrogorski (1902) had expressed concern about this phenomenon in his early study of the Liberal Party's Birmingham caucus. Later it had been described by John May in his 'law of curvilinear disparity' (1973). This suggested that party 'sub leaders', amongst whom would be counted activists, were strongly motivated to protect ideological positions, whilst party leaders were more responsive to the views of the electorate, and thus would adopt more moderate positions. The instinctive understanding of May's law in the party at this time held that those who were most active were likely to be the most left-wing, whilst less active members would hold views closer to the electorate, and to party leaders. Evidence from a survey of Labour members in 1989 appeared to show this to be the case. This found that 59 per cent of those classified as 'very active' considered themselves to be on the party's left, whilst only 20 per cent of inactive members said the same (Seyd and Whiteley, 1992). The power that activists held in the party thus mattered to leaders substantively, in terms of the impact it would have on decisions taken. It also mattered symbolically as, even after 1987, focus groups showed that target voters continued to believe Labour to be 'extreme' (Gould, 1998). There were thus multiple motivations for seeking to limit activist power in party decision making.

There were also various means by which this might be achieved. One would be to reduce the powers of activists by directly increasing the power of party leaders. However, such a blatant move would be unlikely to achieve support in the party. Another tactic would be to displace activists by recruiting new members to the party from amongst its more moderate supporters outside. A third would be to dilute activists' impact on internal party decisions by giving new rights to less active party members. According to Seyd and Whiteley's survey, 43 per cent of party members were barely active at all, and 58 per cent attended party meetings no more than occasionally. As the first LCC commission complained, the activist model of party democracy as pursued by the CLPD 'cast [these] members in the role of spectator' (1989, p. 2). Extending decision making power to less active members in the party might strengthen their commitment by offering them greater influence. But crucially it also seemed likely to result in more moderate and representative decisions. For leaders, therefore, proposals from the right for OMOV, and from the soft left for a mass member party, both had major attractions.

Renegotiating the relationship with the trade unions

The second specific target for party modernisers was the trade unions. In the traditional party structure the unions had offered stability to leaders, generally insulating them from the demands of the left. As Lewis Minkin put it, the trade unions considered that they had a 'parental obligation to the Party to play a stabilising role' (1992, p. 38). They operated as what Ralph Miliband called 'a knightly order for the defence of the political leadership' (1961, p. 320), and what other writers referred to as the leadership's 'Praetorian guard' (McKenzie, 1963; Minkin, 1992). This gave leaders considerable policy flexibility, and the ability largely to control the annual conference and the NEC.

However, from the height of the unions' loyalty in the 1950s, these conventions began to disintegrate. Frank Cousins replaced arch loyalist Arthur Deakin as General Secretary of the mighty TGWU in 1956, and was more sympathetic to the claims of the left.

With TGWU support the leadership was defeated at the 1960 party conference on the issue of nuclear disarmament. In the same period widespread opposition in the unions prevented the party's then leader, Hugh Gaitskell, from achieving his desired objective of revising Clause IV (Brivati, 1997; Jones, 1996). At that time 'revisionists' in the party began to see injustice in the 'block vote' of the trade unions, which had long stifled minority left-wing voices, but was now being used to block their own policy proposals.[14] They also saw escaping from the party's traditional 'cloth cap' image as an important ingredient in regaining electoral popularity.

In the 1970s, the unions helped establish a left-wing majority on the NEC, and fed the growing conflicts between the parliamentary and extra-parliamentary parties. Outside the party, the unions had been unhappy with the policies of the Wilson governments in the 1960s, leading up to the crisis over the white paper *In Place of Strife*.[15] However, tensions between Labour leaders and the unions reached their height during the governments of 1974-79, culminating in the widespread strikes of the 'winter of discontent'. This action by the unions severely damaged perceptions of Labour's ability to govern, ultimately contributing to its fall from power. But it inflicted even greater damage on the image of the unions themselves. Whilst 70 per cent of the public in 1964 believed the trade unions were 'generally a good thing' and only 12 per cent saw them as a bad thing, by 1979 public opinion on this question was split at 44 per cent each way. The proposition that the unions had become 'too powerful' was supported by 84 per cent of the public (Taylor, 1993).

After the 1979 defeat backing from key unions facilitated, through their votes on the NEC and at the annual conference, the agreement of the two successful CLPD reforms. Not only did the unions help secure the mandatory reselection of MPs, but they had voted themselves additional power through the establishment of the electoral college in 1981. This culmination of events was an absolute reversal of the party's traditions, whereby the unions' behaviour was guided by restraint (Minkin, 1992). Both their actions and the new powers that they had gained were openly criticised by Labour's political opponents, including many of those who defected to form the SDP. The new party was created without union affiliations, and was free of such controversial features as the block vote. This helped it establish an image as a centre-left competitor that was more modern and internally democratic than Labour. Meanwhile an assault on the trade unions' powers in the economy was a central policy of the Thatcher governments, and had popular support amongst the electorate. Amidst high unemployment and manufacturing decline, trade union membership fell by two thirds between 1979 and 1993 (Wrigley, 1997).

By the early 1980s changes to the party's relationship with the unions had thus, like the role of activists, taken on both substantive and symbolic importance. Within the party itself the moderates soon regained control of the trade union block, but by then the seeds of change had already been sown. Whilst proposals to reduce trade union power had long come from the party's left they were now supported by many moderate and right-wing members. The substantive reasons for seeking change might have declined, but symbolic motivations came to be increasingly important. There was a strong desire to change the party's image in a way that distanced it from those elements that had become associated in the public mind with Labour's internal battles and failures in government. The controversy over the electoral college had simply reinforced the view that some diminution of the unions' role was a necessity. As three moderates writing for the Fabian Society suggested in 1987, Labour's organisation gave the trade unions 'more power than they want[ed]' and the constituency parties 'far too little power for their own good' (Sawyer, Linton and Mitchell, 1987, p. 6).[16]

Visible reform to the trade union relationship was thus seen by 'modernisers' as essential to showing that the party had changed, and to regaining the electorate's trust. The connection with the unions was used against the party relentlessly by its opponents over many years. Focus group research from the mid 1980s showed that Labour's relationship with the unions deterred electors from giving the party their support. Even after the 1992 election these views continued to be expressed to the party's pollster, Philip Gould. His focus groups suggested that 'Labour lost because it was still the party of the winter of discontent; union influence; strikes and inflation; disarmament; Benn and Scargill' (1998, p. 158). Although major changes to the party–union relationship had by this point already been made, the 1992 defeat led some in the party to argue that this was still not enough. Debate increasingly moved on to the possibility of 'divorce'.[17] By 1992 Ken Livingstone was able to suggest that 'the term modernisation has ... become a code word for ending the union link' (quoted in Alderman and Carter, 1994, p. 322). At this point change took on a symbolic importance to the trade unions as well and, although further reform of their role in the party was achieved, this was at times bitterly resisted.

There were paradoxes in these positions. The attack on both activists and the unions was motivated in large part by the hold that the party's left had gained over these groupings. The immediate response in both cases was for the moderates and right-wingers to seek to regain control of the NEC and the party conference. Yet despite their successes, the pursuit of structural reform continued, long after a majority supportive of the leader had been secured in both of these forums. In fact, the right found itself pressing through reforms to the union relationship of a kind that had previously been championed by the party's left. Meanwhile left-wingers ultimately became the defenders of union power.

If both the unions and the party's activists were to be weakened, this required a third group to be strengthened. Neither side would readily consent to handing control directly to the leadership, so the 'ordinary member' became the target of empowerment. Whilst argued on the basis of widening internal party democracy, many anticipated that this shift would in practice strengthen the leadership's hand (the extent to which this proved to be the case is discussed in Chapter 11). However, the new vision of a party democracy that enfranchised individual members on a mass basis was a major challenge to Labour's organisational traditions. The federal nature of the party, embodied by trade union involvement (and numerical dominance) in all forums of decision making, was potentially threatened. So too was the representative tradition, which existed both within the structure of local parties and within its founding affiliated organisations.

THE REFORM PACKAGES

As the above introduction indicates, the proposals for Labour's organisational reform came from numerous sources. Some ideas had been long under discussion, and many were put on the table by internal pressure groups in the party. It would thus be inaccurate to suggest that the changes that took place all came in neatly defined packages. However, there were also several attempts by the party leadership to promote 'joined up' reforms, partly in response to these various pressures. The remaining chapters of the book take a thematic rather than a strictly chronological approach to describing the different reforms that were debated. Thus references to cross-cutting packages of reform appear in several different places. Before turning to these discussions it is therefore appropriate to briefly summarise four particularly important reform packages that were presented to the party by the NEC in the 1990s. As well as providing a link between the material in different chapters, this gives some indication of the development in the thinking of the Executive, and of the party leadership itself.

The first example is the programme of quotas for women that was brought forward by the NEC from 1990. To call this a 'package' is strictly a misnomer, as proposals on women's representation were in fact presented to annual conference in three consecutive years, and before this had been driven by mounting activist demands. The most dramatic decision taken was that to adopt 'all-women shortlists', at the conference in 1993. However, before this a raft of quotas had been agreed applying to virtually all of the party structures discussed in the chapters that follow, including the new policy forums, the NEC, local parties and the conference itself. The broad context of these reforms, and the way in which they were developed, are described in Chapter 5.

Another discernible 'package' had its origins at a similar time, and was the particular brainchild of party General Secretary Larry Whitty. Its purpose was to cement a new relationship between the PLP and extra-parliamentary party that would prove stable when Labour entered government – a transition anticipated in 1991 or 1992. The document *Democracy and Policy Making for the 1990s* was published after a consultation with affiliates and local parties, and included responses to a wide range of complaints about party organisational issues raised during the 1980s.

Claiming that the Labour Party was 'on the brink of power' this document suggested that it was 'essential that we now gear ourselves to be the party of government for the rest of the 1990s and beyond' (Labour Party, 1990a, p. 1). It proposed a reform of the party's traditional method of policy making, as discussed in Chapter 6. Alongside this were plans to resolve the long-running debate about the balance of votes between trade unions and constituencies at annual conference, as discussed in Chapter 8. The review also considered submissions on restructuring the NEC (for which see Chapter 7) and on possible changes to the constitution of local parties (covered in Chapter 9). Coinciding as it did with the first major NEC document on quotas for women in the party, this represented the most ambitious programme for internal party reform ever presented by the party leadership.

In assembling the proposals Whitty sought explicitly to learn from the practice in socialist and social democratic parties overseas. The recommendations were first tested out on NEC members from the soft left, as 'squaring' this group would mean there was a good chance of winning the NEC's support, and then the approval of the party conference.[18] The proposals therefore largely coincided with Whitty's own soft-left perspective, and that of groups such as the LCC. But they also represented a compromise, between the leadership and the claims of groups such as the CLPD. In some ways the package can now be seen as cautious, as it included – for example – no structural change to the NEC and no major restriction on local parties' rights to submit items to the annual conference. But in other ways it was extremely radical, promising to formalise joint working between the NEC and PLP, and to create a culture of greater consultation and deliberation over policy – with a new 'National Policy Forum' at the heart of the system. In the event the 1992 general election defeat prevented these proposals from being fully implemented. However, they provided a skeleton which was later built upon, with modified proposals implemented under the 1997 Partnership in Power package, discussed below.

After the 1992 defeat attention focussed increasingly on the party's relationships with the trade unions. Consequently the NEC decided to set up a Trade Union Review Group, which reported in 1993. This was a time of high tension, and the party's relationship with the unions was under intense scrutiny. Some 'modernisers' saw the Review Group as an opportunity to break or severely weaken the party–union link. However, others treated it as an opportunity to reaffirm and redefine the party–union relationship for modern times. In the event the proposals from the Review Group – the majority of whose members represented the unions – were relatively cautious (Labour Party, 1993). The most important concerned the selection of candidates and leaders, and are discussed in detail in Chapter 3. The Review Group's proposals also had a significant impact on the organisation of annual conference, as discussed in Chapter 8, and were connected to the reform of party membership, covered in Chapter 9. That even these relatively cautious proposals proved so difficult to agree demonstrated the constraints upon change created by the party's existing structures. But it also reflected a growing defensiveness by the unions in the face of aggressive language and press 'briefing' by some of the modernisers.

The final major package of reform was that of 1997, under the title *Partnership in Power*. The genesis and objectives of this project, initially named 'Partners into Power' in 1995, were remarkably similar to that of *Democracy and Policy Making for the 1990s*. It too represented a wide-ranging series of changes, designed to cement a constructive partnership between the leadership and the party outside parliament, with more joint forums to underpin Labour in government. Although Larry Whitty had now departed, the core group included many of the same individuals.[19] This was the only major reform package to be implemented after Tony Blair became leader and he influenced the project heavily. His own constituency of Sedgefield moved the resolution at the 1996 party conference which asked the NEC to bring forward proposals for reform.

The work of the project was organised in four taskforces, formally under the auspices of the NEC, but acting relatively independently. Each taskforce was chaired by an NEC member. These covered 'relationships in power' (chaired by Mo Mowlam), the democracy of policy making (Margaret Wall), the NEC (Maggie Jones) and local parties (Diana Jeuda). In practice a core group, comprising the taskforce leaders, external advisers, senior party staff and representatives from Blair's office, did most of the work. By this time the soft left, and activist groups in general, were relatively weak, and the key to achieving approval was to gain the support of key individuals in the trade unions.

The consultative document issued to the party shortly before the 1997 general election suggested that 'The Labour Party has been changing and needs to continue to change to prepare it for effective and continuous periods of national office. A Labour Party in power will need to rely on a united, co-operative approach in which the Party constitutes a decisive link between the Labour Government and the people' (Labour Party 1997, p. 5).[20] In order to achieve this, ambitious changes to the policy-making process were proposed, which would reduce the role of annual conference and encourage a more consensual approach, centred on a strengthened National Policy Forum. These proposals are discussed in Chapter 6. They were accompanied by major reforms to the structure and role of the NEC (detailed in Chapter 7), and to the annual conference agenda (Chapter 8). Some had hoped that they would also include changes to local parties (Chapter 9), but the unions were resistant to these proposals, and indeed to several others. Although the reforms were agreed by the 1997 party conference, riding on the celebratory mood after Labour's general election win, they did not go as far as some of their proponents would have wished.

After all of these changes, Labour's structure in 2005 still retains key features of the 1918 constitution – although in many other ways the party has been transformed. Many of the central tensions in Labour's internal democracy, such as how much control the parliamentary leadership should have over policy, and how the relationship with the trade unions should function, were left unresolved even after Partnership in Power. These issues are returned to in Chapter 11. But the chapters in the main body of the book begin with a discussion of the wide-ranging changes to the procedures for selecting Labour candidates and leaders. This is where the CLPD's first gains were made in 1979-81, and these set off a long process of debate, leading to the well publicised and highly symbolic adoption of the OMOV principle in 1993.

Notes

1. Before the 1980s these structures were generally known as General Management Committees (GMCs), and still are in some areas.
2. Between 1948 and 1959 there was only one conference vote won against the 'platform'. Between 1964 and 1970 there were 13 defeats over policy. Between 1970 and 1973 there were nine platform defeats, and between 1979 and 1986 there were 52. (Minkin, 1980; 1992).
3. Composite 16.
4. For a fuller discussion of this period and the negotiation of these reforms see Cocks (1989), Golding (2003), Kogan and Kogan (1982), Minkin (1992), Mitchell (1983), Panitch and Leys (1997), Shaw (1988; 1994; 1996), Seyd (1987).
5. The document in question was *Labour's Programme, 1973*. For a detailed discussion of the formation and early years of CLPD see Kogan and Kogan (1982).
6. For an account of the broader politics of the 'new left', within both the CLPD and early LCC fitted, see Davis (2003), Panitch and Leys (1997), Wickham-Jones (2004).
7. CLPD newsletter, 1975.
8. The extent of the organisation's success in the unions is in part demonstrated by the number of trade union branches affiliated. This rose from eight in 1975 to 47 in 1978, and 112 in 1980 (Kogan and Kogan, 1982).

9. For a brief (and not wholly objective) history of the LCC see Thompson and Lucas (1998).
10. This also included the Socialist Campaign for Labour Victory, Institute of Workers' Control, National Organisation of Labour Students, the Militant Tendency and other groups. From May 1980 it sought to defend the CLPD demands, and later supported Tony Benn's deputy leadership challenge. The LCC withdrew from the coalition late in 1981. See Kogan and Kogan (1982), Seyd (1987).
11. For details see Seyd (1987), Shaw (1988).
12. Maggie Jones sat on the 1989 commission and went on to be elected to the NEC in 1991, later chairing the Partnership in Power taskforce on the future of the NEC, which later implemented many of the proposals in this commission's report. Matt Carter, later the party's head of policy, and General Secretary from 2003, sat on the 1996 commission.
13. The obvious exception was the Campaign for Democratic Socialism, set up by supporters of party leader Hugh Gaitskell in 1960. This group campaigned to reverse the 1960 conference decision on nuclear disarmament and had significant success in the constituencies (Brivati, 1997).
14. The term 'block vote' indicated the way in which a trade union would cast all of its votes at the conference for one side of the argument or the other, rather than splitting them in proportion to its members' views. See Chapter 8.
15. See, for example, Pelling (1992), Perkins (2003), Shaw (1996), Taylor (1993).
16. If the unions had more power than they wanted they were certainly sometimes very reluctant to give it up, as later chapters demonstrate.
17. See, for example, Sassoon (1993), Walsh and Tindale (1992).
18. For this purpose an unofficial meeting was held at Northern College, facilitated by its Principal, Bob Fryer, who had worked with NEC member Tom Sawyer on organisational change in NUPE. The meeting involved Larry Whitty, Charles Clarke (by now Kinnock's Chief of Staff), NEC members Tom Sawyer, Diana Jeuda of USDAW, Margaret Beckett and Clare Short, and party historian Lewis Minkin – who had published a respected work on the history and dynamics of party conference (Minkin, 1980). Minkin also sat on the trade union review group and was centrally involved in Partnership in Power.
19. Tom Sawyer, having replaced Larry Whitty as party General Secretary in 1994, was central to its organisation. Advisers included Bob Fryer and Lewis Minkin.
20. Despite the rather awkward timing of the consultation, given the focus on campaigning, 842 responses were received, including 380 from constituency parties (Labour Party, 1997a).

3

Selecting Candidates and Leaders: The Battle for One Member One Vote

No question has been more central to debates about the internal democracy of the modern Labour Party than that of how candidates and leaders should be selected. Choosing candidates for public office is one of the most important functions of any political party, and how Labour went about this task became a core battleground in the 1970s and 1980s. The initiatives of the CLPD, which pressed for the relationship between Labour's elected representatives and the wider party to change, started in the 1970s with successful moves to reform the selection process. Later the dramatic decision to adopt the 'one member one vote' (OMOV) system in 1993 was a symbolic step on the path to creating new Labour. The OMOV package was presented as a fundamental shift in the party's democracy. However it was also the long overdue conclusion of a 15 year debate about reform, which is charted in this chapter. And the debate did not end in 1993 – as further discussed in Chapter 4.

Throughout these discussions there were two issues at stake. The first was the selection of individual parliamentary candidates, which traditionally in Labour (as in the other British parties) was the responsibility of local constituency parties. Until 1987 the final choice of candidate lay with the local General Committee (GC), comprising representatives of branches and affiliated trade unions and socialist societies. Each of these organisations could nominate one aspirant candidate, and the GC made its choice from among the nominees. However, the concern of the left was that this process took place infrequently, with many Labour MPs enjoying long careers in parliament without effective recall to their constituency parties.

The second issue was the election of the party leader. In stark contrast to their involvement in selecting local candidates, party members and affiliates had no role at all in this decision until the CLPD achieved change in 1981. Prior to this, responsibility for electing the leader rested with the Parliamentary Labour Party (PLP) alone.[1]

The initial CLPD reforms, which are summarised in the first section of this chapter, were driven by a desire to gain greater power for activists over both of these important processes. After this had been achieved, however, moderates and right wingers in the party saw further reform as essential. Their immediate priority was to wrest control from activists, who were seen as being dominated by the left. But the moderates' preferred outcome – OMOV – would necessarily also restrict the collective powers of the unions, by taking power away from delegates on local GCs. The unions valued their role in local selection contests, which had always been a key sphere of influence. They had also, alongside activists, won involvement in the leadership electoral college in 1981, and were reluctant to see this compromised. With both left-wing activists and trade unions, for different reasons, unhappy about further reform, it proved extremely difficult to achieve.

THE LEGACY OF 1979–83

The issues of both leadership election and local parliamentary selection became the focus of increasing attention during the 1970s, primarily due to the demands of the left. In 1972 the pamphlet *Party or Puppet?*, written by three left-wing MPs for the Tribune Group, raised questions about both of these processes. It claimed that MPs were 'freelance' – not sufficiently accountable to their local parties (Allaun, Mikardo and Sillars, 1972). Activists were concerned that under current selection rules, Labour MPs were automatically deemed to be reselected unless their local GC passed a resolution asking them to retire. This in itself set a high hurdle, but even where such resolutions were passed the NEC had the power to reverse the local party's decision.[2] One of the earliest claims of the CLPD, founded in 1973, was therefore to ensure greater accountability of MPs to activists, by increasing local parties' control over this process. Their demand, supported also by the LCC and other groups on the left, was that all MPs should face a mandatory reselection contest once in each parliament, where they were considered alongside other candidates. The proposal made in the Tribune Group pamphlet with respect to party leadership elections was also taken up by CLPD. This claimed that the leader should cease to be chosen by the PLP alone, but instead should be elected by, and accountable to, the party as a whole.

During this period there was also growing interest in extending the involvement in parliamentary selections beyond the GC, to include all members of the local party. The OMOV cause was particularly taken up by those on the party's right, and was seen as a way of neutralising a potential move to mandatory reselection. The CLV made this one of its founding claims from 1977, and campaigned for OMOV to be adopted. The proposal continued to feature in various pamphlets, including one in 1978 co-authored by the young Peter Mandelson.[3] It was made in many submissions to the Commission of Enquiry that was established after the 1979 defeat, including that coming from the right-controlled union the EETPU. However, support for such ideas was not entirely confined to those on the right. For example Frances Morrell, a leading figure in both the LCC and CLPD, proposed in a *Guardian* article in 1979 that mandatory reselection of MPs should be balanced by local OMOV.[4] At this stage there was limited incentive for the NEC to support this reform, however, and it was rejected in the mid-1970s (Kavanagh, 1982). However views soon changed after the CLPD's constitutional changes had been driven through, and the 'moderates' regained power on the Executive.

The achievement of the left's first constitutional demands has been well documented elsewhere, so only a brief summary is provided here.[5] With respect to mandatory reselection of MPs, the efforts of the CLPD and other groups resulted in the issue being raised at annual conference each year from 1974, with the number of resolutions on the subject ever growing. There was one such suggestion in 1974, rising to 12 in 1975, and by 1977, 79 such proposals reached the agenda (Kogan and Kogan, 1982). Despite the opposition of the PLP and the party's right wing, the leftward drift on the NEC made it increasingly sympathetic to the demand. Having initially opposed mandatory reselection the NEC finally recommended acceptance of the principle at the post-election conference of 1979, and this was approved. It passed formally into the party's rules at the 1980 conference. From this point on there were constant concerns that the new mechanism would be used by far left activists to deselect moderate and right-wing Labour MPs.

The debate over leadership elections was more controversial and difficult, and had wider repercussions.[6] The matter first reached the conference agenda in 1972 and was the subject of regular conference resolutions from then onwards. The left's frustrations with the status quo were heightened by the PLP's election of right-winger Jim Callaghan after Harold Wilson stepped down as leader in 1976. A working group was established that year and, following consultation, proposed three possible options for the election of leader: no change, giving the power to the annual conference, or establishing an 'electoral college' composed of three sections, representing the PLP, affiliates and constituencies. These options then became the basis of future conference debates, with changes to the status quo rejected in both 1978 and 1979. This did not close the matter, however, due to the persistence of the reformers and the support by the NEC for change. A more general proposal to 'extend the franchise for the election of the Leader' narrowly passed the 1980 conference, though specific mechanisms to put this into effect were all rejected.

This issue split the PLP and the shadow cabinet. Support on the left was crystallising around an electoral college and some, including Callaghan, came to see this as the inevitable outcome and concentrated on maximising the share of votes within it that the PLP would hold. Others on the right, meanwhile, argued that 'widening the franchise' should not be synonymous with either of the two options for change put forward and instead that all party members should be involved. The Manifesto Group and CLV thus proposed that OMOV, which for some years had now been their favoured means for selecting parliamentary candidates, should be adopted for the election of the leader. Indeed OMOV had been proposed by more constituencies during the consultation than either of the other two reform options, but had been rejected by the working group.[7] The left's opponents believed that OMOV would be beneficial because 'ordinary' members were more moderate than the constituency activists and trade union leaders who would be empowered by an electoral college. Many on the right would really have preferred to leave the responsibility for electing the leader with the PLP, but saw this as untenable within the current environment. To them, broadening the franchise to the whole membership was a second-best solution. To others amongst this group it represented a genuine improvement.

Amongst the proponents of OMOV were many of those who went on to leave Labour and form the SDP. For them the process for electing the leader became a deciding issue. Already frustrated by the left's hold over policy, the constitutional reforms pushed them to the brink.[8] Had the electoral college been agreed at the 1980 conference some had already decided to quit the party (Bradley, 1981). The outcome being unclear they instead decided to stay and fight for OMOV. The issue was finally resolved at a special conference convened at Wembley in January 1981. Here the various options for widening the franchise were debated. Bob Maclennan, MP for Caithness and Sutherland and later an SDP defector, proposed that 'the only way in which this Party can widen the choice and extend the franchise ... is through one member one vote' (Labour Party, 1981, p. 127). David Owen spoke strongly against trade union involvement in leadership elections, suggesting that the electoral college 'will be shown to be totally illegitimate' and 'totally undemocratic', and that '[t]o allow the block vote to choose the future Prime Minister of this country is an outrage. It is a disgrace' (Labour Party, 1981, p. 128). These were, however, minority views. At the conference – where trade unions controlled nine-tenths of the vote – 6,283,000 votes were cast in favour of the principle of an electoral college, whilst OMOV was supported by a mere 431,000 votes. The conference then decided that the share of votes in the electoral college should be 30 per cent for the PLP, 30 per cent for the constituencies and 40 per cent for the trade unions.

The link to the SDP split was made clear by the publication of the 'Limehouse Declaration' the very next day, and formal creation of the new party two months later (Bradley, 1981; Crewe and King 1995a).[9] Not only was this a huge blow to Labour, but the decision to adopt the electoral college was itself portrayed very negatively in the press, with allegations that the party was now dominated by militant unions.[10] A poll showed that two thirds of those who had heard about the decision said it would make them less likely to vote Labour at the next general election (Stark, 1996). Michael Foot, who had been elected party leader in 1980, quickly stated his intention to reverse the decision. The image of a party at war was however then amplified when Tony Benn chose to cement the electoral college arrangements by challenging Denis Healey for the deputy leadership.

The establishment of the electoral college and mandatory reselection gave added impetus to many who had been campaigning within the party for OMOV. The new centre-right organisation Solidarity, formed after the SDP split, made it a central campaign priority. Even MPs on the left were uneasy about the greater power that local GCs had been given as a result of the mandatory reselection rule. Whilst there had previously been concerns that OMOV would weaken trade union rights, Solidarity hoped that moderates would now see it as a means of neutralising the power of local activists. Similarly for leadership elections, many MPs who had previously wanted to protect their monopoly of power became more sympathetic to a further broadening of the franchise, as a means of taking power out of the hands of trade unions and activists. The unions themselves, however, were reluctant to give up their powers, including those that they had just gained through the electoral college. Following the SDP split OMOV had also lost of some of its most vocal supporters, and their defection from the party reinforced the impression amongst many on the left that it was a fundamentally suspect proposal.

KINNOCK AND OMOV, 1983–92

After Labour lost the general election of 1983 Neil Kinnock became the party's first leader to be chosen using the new electoral college. The procedure had already of course been used for a deputy leadership contest in 1981, as a result of Tony Benn's unsuccessful bid against Denis Healey.[11] At this time questions had been raised about the way constituencies and affiliates had decided to cast their votes. Each CLP cast a single block vote and Benn had won 83 per cent of this part of the college. However, in some constituencies the GC had taken the decision alone and in others there had been membership ballots or wider consultation. Likewise in the unions, some had run internal ballots and others had not. Believing that rank and file trade union members would be more moderate than leaders or activists, Healey had publicly called for balloting. This strategy showed some success. Notably, when the left-wing union NUPE balloted its members, they decided that the union's block vote should go to Healey.[12] Despite Benn's success in the constituencies, Healey won the contest narrowly, thanks to the votes of trade unions and MPs.

Following this experience there was added pressure for OMOV in both sections of the leadership electoral college. Thus when the leadership and deputy leadership fell vacant in 1983 the right wing contender, Roy Hattersley, pressed for ballots in both the unions and constituencies. Over 200 constituencies did ballot and all of them supported Neil Kinnock for leader, over Hattersley and the other candidates (Eric Heffer and Peter Shore). All of them also supported Hattersley as deputy over Michael Meacher. In the affiliates' section too, every single trade union that balloted came up with the same result. The fact that ballots had unanimously backed the ticket supported by the PLP served strongly to reinforce the belief amongst moderates that OMOV was to their advantage.

Kinnock himself had been a founder member of the CLPD and spoke in favour of the electoral college at the 1978 conference. He had, however, parted ways with the organisation over the Benn deputy leadership challenge in 1981. He believed, along with many others on the soft left, that now the CLPD's two main objectives had been achieved it was time to re-establish stability. As leader his central mission was to pursue reforms that would end the internal battles and improve the party's image with the electorate. This soon resulted in support for the OMOV principle. As Eric Shaw suggests, 'Kinnock regarded constituency activists as the main power-base of the hard left and this he sought to dismantle by devolving rights and responsibilities traditionally a prerogative of constituency General Committees to the individual membership as a whole' (1994, p. 204).

A new leader having just been elected, and likely to stay in place for some time, the organisational priority was to change the local selection procedure for MPs. Although there had actually been just eight successful deselections prior to the 1983 general election, amongst moderates there remained a concern that the PLP could be destabilised through loyalists being deselected by the left.[13] In any case, the reselection process was sapping of MPs' time and energy. However, to achieve any change to the party's selection rules required substantial support amongst the trade unions, which still controlled 90 per cent of annual conference votes. And getting the unions to support OMOV was going to be far from an easy matter. Ending the role of GCs in local selection decisions would not only disempower activists, but would also end the involvement of the unions in the final choice of the parliamentary candidate. Given that the party's founding purpose had been to gain seats for trade unionists in parliament, this was an important symbolic change. Even in recent years the unions' role in parliamentary selections remained significant, especially in safe Labour seats. Some of these seats were considered the 'fiefdoms' of particular trade unions which, through financial sponsorship and places on the GC, could secure support for their own favoured candidates.[14] Thus even trade unionists who were sympathetic to Kinnock's political concerns could find reasons to resist moves to OMOV. Meanwhile some unions on the left (notably NUPE and the TGWU) had enthusiastically supported the mandatory reselection proposal and were reluctant to see it weakened. Even on the right some were resentful of the idea that trade unions, having just helped the leadership reestablish a loyal majority on the NEC and at conference, should now be required to sacrifice some of their rights.

The broader political context heightened these sensitivities. The trade unions were under attack from the Thatcher governments and sought solidarity from colleagues in the party. Indeed there were important parallel developments going on with respect to internal trade union democracy, whose impact on the thinking of those involved in party debates cannot be discounted. The Conservative manifesto of 1979 had stated that 'too often the trade unions are dominated by a handful of extremists who do not reflect the common-sense of most union members' (quoted in Taylor, 1993, p. 283). Forcing internal ballots on the unions was one of the government's tactics to try – just as Kinnock wished to do in the party – to moderate the outcome of decisions. The 1984 Trade Union Act introduced the right to internal ballots on strike action and for the election of executive committees, and the 1988 Employment Act extended this to the election of trade union leaders. These developments helped feed hostility amongst trade unionists towards replacing internal representative democracy with compulsory balloting. As it turned out, the reforms imposed by the Conservatives had unexpected consequences for the unions, being widely seen as strengthening their legitimacy. A similar pattern was later to be seen in the party.

The issue of broadening the franchise for internal party elections appeared on the conference agenda in autumn 1983, at the same time that Kinnock was elected. The proposals made related largely to leadership elections. Solidarity had circulated model resolutions calling for OMOV in the constituency section of the electoral college in future, as well as for parliamentary selections, and a composite resolution to this effect was moved by Old Bexley CLP.[15] Although this was defeated, another resolution, moved by Gillingham CLP, simply supported a ballot in the CLP section of the leadership college. Eric Heffer, speaking for the NEC, urged the movers to 'remit' this resolution to the Executive for consideration, promising that there would be investigations into 'an even further extension of democracy ... worked out in an intelligent way' (Labour Party, 1983,

p. 272).[16] This was agreed, and allowed the NEC to investigate internal selection issues and bring proposals to a future conference.

In 1984 OMOV returned to the agenda, this time with respect to parliamentary selections. John Evans MP, an NEC member and Kinnock ally, had narrowly managed to win the Executive's support for a motion on this matter.[17] His proposal sought to modify the process for the reselection of MPs, to allow constituencies if they wished to extend voting rights beyond the GC, to include all local members. This was an extremely modest suggestion, not only because the change was voluntary, but also because the existing rules would have continued to apply to all other selection contests. This left trade union rights untouched in the contests they really cared about – where seats fell vacant and new parliamentary candidates were to be chosen. However even this package had only shaky support. Kinnock's allies in the TGWU, the party's largest affiliate by far, had advised him that they could get their union delegation to support it, despite their own executive committee having already voted against OMOV (Westlake, 2001). The NEC itself remained split on the proposal, and almost decided on the eve of the conference not to push the matter to a vote. But Kinnock persuaded his colleagues to press ahead.

Moving the proposal at conference on behalf of the NEC, John Evans insisted that it was consistent with the commitment to mandatory reselection but constituted a further 'small but important step in the campaign for increased democracy in the Labour Party' (Labour Party, 1984, p. 58). But the proposal was widely seen as an attempt by the right to neutralise mandatory reselection. It thus met resistance from the CLPD and LCC. The CLPD, in particular, sought to protect the model of activist democracy, arguing that OMOV would weaken the accountability of MPs, as the local GC was the forum to which they were required to regularly report. If the reforms were passed, the members that MPs reported to would not necessarily have the power to remove them. Concerns were also expressed that trade union delegates would be excluded, whilst OMOV would instead involve less well informed members, who might be overly influenced by what they heard in the media. Ironically the attempt to limit OMOV only to certain contests, which had been necessary in order to make it more palatable to the unions, also made it appear inconsistent and thus easier to attack. The party's largest union affiliates were split on the proposal, with NUPE and the AUEW opposing it, whilst the

GMWU was in support. Despite the earlier assurances given to Neil Kinnock the TGWU's delegation met at the conference and voted by 28 to 16 to oppose. This meant that all 1,250,000 of the union's votes were cast against the proposal. Kinnock thus suffered a major blow when the conference rejected it by 3,041,000 votes to 3,992,000.[18]

The existing procedures thus remained in place in the run-up to the 1987 election. This meant that right-wing MPs had no option but to contest their reselections as best they could under the current arrangements. This often involved a contest with the hard left to 'pack' GCs with sympathetic delegates. Right-winger John Golding MP, who advised colleagues on these tactics, boasted that 'they pack, we pack, but we pack better than they do'.[19] These time-consuming games provided another argument for reform.

The OMOV issue however did not go away, reaching the conference agenda again the following year, in 1985. On this occasion the CLPD's model resolution, which sought to shut the question down until after the next general election, was lost on a show of hands. A competing resolution, again moved by the EETPU, called on the NEC to bring forward further proposals for OMOV. Moving the resolution, the union's political officer John Spellar – a central organiser on the right – presciently suggested that '[i]f this composite is not carried today, this issue will come back year after year, because the opponents of members' democracy are swimming against the tide of history' (Labour Party, 1985, p. 192). Speaking in support, fellow Solidarity member George Robertson MP made clear the extent to which the left and right had competing visions of party democracy, proposing that 'if the arguments over all these years in which we have considered reselection are valid, they were done in the name of democracy and accountability. And if that is the real motive ... then why are we not interested in extending the franchise to all party members?' (Labour Party, 1985, p. 193). On the NEC's recommendation the resolution was remitted. As a result a new working group on widening the selection franchise was set up, which was to carry out a full consultation and report back to the 1987 conference.

The consultation document issued by this group took as a starting point that trade unions would continue to be involved in local selections, through rights to make nominations and through shortlisting by the GC (Labour Party, 1987). But the consultation focused on how the crucial final choice of candidate would be made. In total a complex array 11 different options were put, in an attempt to build support – particularly in the unions. These ranged from the status quo to mandatory full OMOV. Alternatives included restricting OMOV only to reselections (as had been proposed in 1984), or introducing a local electoral college to mirror the one now used nationally for leadership elections. Solidarity circulated material urging support for OMOV, whilst the CLPD campaigned against it.

The results of the consultation were reported to the 1987 conference, which followed the party's third successive general election defeat.[20] These showed a clear polarisation of opinion amongst constituencies, with 107 favouring mandatory OMOV and 100 preferring the status quo. Only 23 constituencies supported a local electoral college, and 18 favoured other options. Given that responses were prepared by activists, rather than by the less active members that OMOV would have enfranchised, and given the vigour of the CLPD's campaign, the result seemed to demonstrate a real change of mood in the party. It arguably offered the leader the mandate he needed to press for full OMOV.

However the unions continued to hold the key, and amongst them opinion remained rather different. Three of the five biggest unions, the TGWU, GMB and USDAW, favoured the local electoral college whilst another, NUPE, wanted no change at all. Although five unions were prepared to back OMOV, these all held far fewer votes.[21] Furthermore now the unions had had more time to debate the idea, several had policy explicitly against OMOV.[22] This left Kinnock with a potentially dangerous dilemma. The leader could not afford another conference defeat on OMOV, but it had by now become, in the words of Robin Cook, a 'respectable consensus issue'.[23] The LCC had switched its position to one of support, and OMOV was winning increasing backing from others on the soft left as well as amongst traditional supporters on the right.[24] However, the proposal was still unlikely to be passed by the party conference. In these circumstances a compromise was reached between the leader and the unions to support a local electoral college – despite the unpopularity of this idea in the constituencies. This would actually strengthen the unions' role in local selections, by giving them up to 40 per cent of the vote, with local members holding the remainder. The procedures for deciding affiliates' votes would be left to them to decide. But the members' share would be cast by OMOV.

At the 1987 conference both OMOV and the local electoral college were considered. The working group's report suggested that OMOV was 'a logical extension of democracy' but also conceded that there were arguments against enfranchising 'armchair members' (Labour Party, 1987c, p. 4). Again opening debate on behalf of the NEC, John Evans pointed out that in selections for the 1987 election there had been 205 constituencies where fewer than 30 people took part in the final decision on the parliamentary candidate, and in some cases there had been fewer than 10 participants.[25] He suggested that this illustrated a real need to broaden the franchise, and that OMOV would 'greatly enhance the perception of the party's democratic image', as well as being simple to understand and administer (Labour Party, 1987a, p. 16). In contrast he conceded that the electoral college would be far more complex and in some ways 'not particularly satisfactory' (Labour Party, 1987a, p. 17). The proposal was described as 'virtually unworkable' by the LCC, and was widely seen as a fudge.[26]

The CLPD remained opposed to both change options, claiming they were designed simply to enhance MPs' job security and weaken their accountability to the proper structures of local parties. It was claimed that they would do little to improve the party's image, but were supported by its 'enemies in Fleet Street' who sought to attack trade union rights.[27] However, a CLPD-backed resolution defending the status quo was heavily defeated, as was a competing resolution supporting full OMOV.[28] The only thing agreed was the NEC's document, which included a commitment to widening the franchise. This meant that the compromise of the electoral college was adopted by default. Although this was a proposal with few real supporters it gave both sets of power players some of what they wanted. The leader had extended participation in parliamentary selections to all local party members, ending the grip of activists on the process. Meanwhile the trade unions had retained – and indeed strengthened – their own role. As TGWU General Secretary Ron Todd suggested 'the one person, one vote principle is an idea whose time has come' (Labour Party, 1987a, p. 20). But the unions were still not prepared to support it.

The uneasy compromise of the local electoral college was not to last for long. There had been rumours when the decision was taken that right-wing unions would manipulate the system in order to deselect left-wing MPs.[29] Although this did not actually happen, the new arrangements introduced other problems, familiar from the

national leadership college. Previously trade unions had particip-
ated in parliamentary selections through their delegates on GCs,
who at least were required to be party members. Now there was no
control over how their local votes were cast, meaning that a single
regional official, or a group of trade unionists who were not party
members, could potentially decide the fate of an MP. The new
system also made it more evident when the views of trade unions
and local members were in conflict. Particular problems arose when
two MPs (Ron Brown and George Galloway) held their seats thanks
to union votes, having been rejected by local members, and another
(Frank Field) lost his despite winning a majority of individual
members' votes (Minkin, 1992).[30]

All of these difficulties focused attention on the role of unions
(rather than activists) in the selection process. After the Frank Field
case Neil Kinnock gave 'virtually a public promise' to implement
OMOV (Minkin, 1992, p. 381). The NEC agreed to yet another
consultation on parliamentary selection procedures, which took
place in 1990. This time a simple choice was offered, between
retaining the local electoral college or moving to full OMOV. Of the
265 constituencies that responded, 200 wanted to end the college
arrangements and 218 now supported OMOV. The leadership could
argue that having given local parties a taste of OMOV their
commitment to it had grown (although, crucially, this time no
return to the previous status quo had been offered). The NEC thus
proposed to the 1990 conference that the local electoral college
should be scrapped and 'in all constituencies where there is a
selection contest, the final selection vote should be on the basis of
one member one vote of all individual members' (Labour Party,
1990, p. 1). Yet the problem with the trade unions remained. In
order to gain their support for the document on the NEC, a
concession had been added stating that 'further consideration'
would be given to how members of affiliated trade unions could be
involved in the final selection decision. This enabled those unions
opposed to pure OMOV to support the document, and the 1990
conference agreed it. But the difficult task of putting these
competing principles into practice was deferred to another
occasion.[31]

Over this period most attention was devoted to the question of
local parliamentary selection, given the urgency of responding to
the environment created by mandatory reselection. However there
was also some movement on the conduct of leadership elections. In

1988 Tony Benn challenged Neil Kinnock for the leadership (with Eric Heffer and John Prescott challenging Roy Hattersley as deputy). For these elections the NEC once more encouraged constituencies to ballot their members before deciding how to vote. Kinnock and Hattersley won easily, and analysis of the results again showed that their support was stronger amongst the roughly 60 per cent of constituencies that had balloted (Punnett, 1990). Throughout the 1980s Solidarity had continued to campaign for balloting in the CLP section of the college to be compulsory. At the 1988 conference the NEC finally backed a resolution asking for this to be put into effect, and this was passed in the face of opposition from the CLPD.[32] The following year a rule change to implement the proposal was agreed. Having no impact on the trade union side of the college these changes passed the conference easily.

Thus by 1988 the perceived difficulties of activist control of the selection process had been dealt with. The principle of OMOV ballots amongst members had been established for both leadership elections and local selections. This began a weakening of the representative tradition in local parties and a greater emphasis on the individual Labour member. The remaining concerns stemmed from the party's federal tradition – manifested through the trade unions' role in local and national contests, which was seen as damaging to Labour's image. It was by now clear that the unions were very resistant to any interference in these powers. This left the scene set for further confrontations in future years.

1992: DEFEAT AND A NEW LEADER

The blow of the general election defeat on 9 April 1992 was profound. Despite all of Neil Kinnock's work to present the party as more moderate and responsive to the views of the electorate it faced a further 4-5 years in the wilderness of opposition. The defeat was immediately followed by Kinnock's announcement that he intended to step down as leader. Labour thus faced a painful post mortem on why defeat had occurred alongside a contest to choose his successor.[33] The two issues became intertwined, particularly with respect to the role of the trade unions – the association with whom, polls suggested, had cost Labour crucial votes.

Already by Sunday 12 April the role of trade union leaders in deciding the outcome of the impending leadership contest had been thrust into the spotlight. The *Observer* newspaper reported that supporters of John Smith were confident of the support of the GMB and AEEU for their candidate, and that the outcome of the contest thus effectively rested with TGWU General Secretary Bill Morris. At this time Smith had not officially announced his intention to stand as leader, but was widely seen as the inevitable replacement for Kinnock. Responding to the controversy when appearing on television that same day, Smith's challenger Bryan Gould indicated his desire to change the system for selecting the party's leader and 'move as quickly as possible to a party of one person one vote'.[34]

From this point on the involvement of the trade unions in the contest, and the need for reform of their role within the party more generally, became a matter of widespread debate in a way that had not occurred when Kinnock was elected in 1983. Although Gould did not expect to win the leadership contest, he used his campaign to highlight the issue of the trade union link, and the press were happy to oblige. On 19 April the *Sunday Times* reported 'the return of the red barons' with specific references to the role of Bill Morris, and John Edmonds of the GMB, in deciding the future party leader. An earlier paper had similarly referred to Edmonds as a 'king maker'.[35] This was a controversy that had not existed under the old system, when the PLP chose the party leader behind closed doors. An unnamed Labour frontbencher was quoted as saying that the unions' involvement made the contest 'a stitch up that could cost us the general election'.[36]

The role of the unions was particularly controversial given that there was still no requirement on them to ballot their members (unlike the rule that now applied to the CLPs). How unions would come to their decisions thus also became a matter of public debate. The rules of the AEEU (formed by a merger of the pro-OMOV AEU and EETPU) required a members' ballot, but the union's General Secretary Bill Jordan said that this would be 'a waste of time and money' given that Smith was the certain winner.[37] When the NEC met on 14 April they agreed to an extended timetable for the election, explicitly to allow more time for member consultation. The candidates themselves urged the unions to ballot, with likely winners John Smith and Margaret Beckett believing this would boost their legitimacy as leader and deputy leader, and contenders Bryan Gould and John Prescott believing it would maximise their support.[38] Under pressure, the AEEU in the end balloted a random sample of its members before deciding how to vote. Other unions used different methods – UCATT decided at its annual conference,

MSF consulted branches, and the GMB, NUPE and USDAW ran full ballots (Alderman and Carter, 1993; McSmith 1994). However, even where ballots had been conducted, the rules required affiliates (and CLPs) to cast their vote as a block, rather than breaking it down to reflect the balance of their members' views.

Throughout the contest candidates gave assurances, under pressure from the media and party members, that the system in future would be different. Bryan Gould's concentration on the issue, in particular, helped push other candidates towards making firmer commitments. John Smith was a long-standing member of Solidarity – which had campaigned hard for OMOV in parliamentary selections, although it had taken a softer line with respect to trade union involvement in leadership contests. In a situation where union votes could be decisive, and with a view to future negotiations as party leader, his approach had initially seemed cautious. But in his personal manifesto *New Paths to Victory* Smith proposed the use of OMOV for local parliamentary selections, and a 50:50 electoral college for leadership elections, comprising only the PLP and individual members (McSmith, 1994). At a hustings meeting hosted by the Fabian Society he stated that 'my own view is that the trade unions should not be involved in electing the leader' (Fabian Society, 1992, p. 8).

As predicted, the outcome of the election was an overwhelming victory for Smith, who gained 90.9 per cent of the total electoral college to Bryan Gould's 9.1 per cent. This result was exaggerated, however, by the nature of the block vote. In the ballot of GMB members, for example, Smith had won 110,177 votes to Gould's 30,267, yet the GMB's support went entirely to Smith (McSmith, 1994). A similar pattern applied in the constituencies. Here Smith won 597 CLP votes to Gould's 12. Although the result was not in doubt, Gould's humiliation was worsened by the block vote in both sections. Once the contest was underway and the controversial elements of the electoral college were out in the open, one poll of party members found that 81 per cent supported replacing the system with OMOV.[39]

THE 1993 PACKAGE OF REFORM

The resolution of selection rules at the annual conference in 1993 can therefore correctly be described as John Smith 'transacting an unfinished item of business' (Shaw 1994, p. 221). However, despite all that had gone before, this was by no means an easy matter.

The obvious forum in which to resolve the unfinished business was the annual conference of 1992. Neil Kinnock initially favoured this approach. However despite his wishes, and its instruction in 1990 to implement OMOV, the NEC chose to delay the decision until 1993. As a result of the events in the electoral college, the unions' role in leadership elections, as well as local selections, was now under the spotlight. But instead of treating selection as an isolated issue the NEC responded to the post-election atmosphere of controversy by establishing a new review group to 'examine the principles of the relationship between the party and the unions' in the round (Labour Party, 1993, p. 3). This included the nature of the union link at local, regional and national level, the rights of individual trade union levy-payers in the party, and the appropriate balance of votes held by the unions at annual conference.

A majority of the 15 members of the review group represented the trade unions, which led some to allege that it would comprise a 'stitch up' (Alderman and Carter, 1994). Most members were drawn from the NEC, though the group also included some trade union outsiders. Originally Bill Morris and John Edmonds (not members of the NEC due to their status as General Secretaries and members of the TUC General Council) were included, but they chose to delegate their positions to other representatives of their unions. Lewis Minkin, author of a detailed study on the history of the party–union relationship (Minkin, 1992), was also included as a member. John Smith himself did not take a seat on the group.

In its early stages the group concentrated on how to reduce the problems caused by the block vote, whilst maintaining trade union involvement. Attention focused in particular on options for franchising individual trade unionists. There were almost four million members of affiliated unions paying the 'political levy', yet the party had only around 260,000 individual members. Since the late 1980s, and particularly since the in-principle decision on OMOV in 1990, there had been proposals that recruiting these trade unionists into party membership should be made a priority (see Chapter 9). Achieving this goal would potentially enhance the party's democratic image in two ways: both by diminishing the block vote and by boosting the membership figures. Various options were discussed in the review group. An 'associate membership' scheme, whereby trade union levy payers gained the right to vote in internal elections as individuals, found particular support.

By the 1992 conference, at which OMOV was again a major topic of debate, the group was still deliberating on the proposals that it would put to the party.[40] At this stage the NEC elections resulted in a change in its composition. Bryan Gould had stepped down from the NEC, creating a vacancy on the review group. In replacing him attention turned to the three new members who had been elected to the NEC constituency section. At its first meeting the new Executive decided that Tony Blair, who had until July been Shadow Employment Secretary, and thus had experience of dealing with the unions, should be the one to take Gould's place.

Within weeks of joining the NEC Blair was therefore thrust into its most important area of current work. He had not had easy relationships with the unions during his frontbench role, and was known to support a radical reform of the party–union relationship. When he joined the review group he was 'horrified to discover' that the associate membership scheme, rather than a restriction of rights to full party members through OMOV, was its favoured option (Rentoul, 2001, p. 210). He responded aggressively, insisting on a change of course, and this was undoubtedly influential. What is less clear, however, is the extent to which he was acting with John Smith's blessing. His intervention upset many on the group and the new leader was said to be 'constantly telling Blair to slow down' (Gould, 1998, p. 190). Whilst Smith was comfortable with the tradition of the union link, Blair was seen as one of the most senior proponents of breaking it. The decision to put him on the review group was therefore in part an attempt to get these arguments aired in their proper setting. But by pushing for radical reform Blair also kept up the pressure on Smith to pursue specific reforms. Although the latter's caution since becoming leader had unsettled many modernisers, he had a long record of supporting OMOV.

Tony Blair was backed in his campaign by his allies Gordon Brown and Peter Mandelson but, as a member of the review group, he was the most visible 'outrider' for reform of the union relationship. Appearing on *On the Record* in early 1993 he maintained that 'We have block votes determining everything. That's all got to go' (quoted in Rentoul, 2001, p. 207). Whilst this more confrontational approach may have changed the course of the review group's work, it also greatly aggravated the unions. Unattributed press briefings suggested that the desired outcome was to break the link with the unions altogether. Clare Short, another member of the review group, spoke of 'a clear attempt to bounce our leader into "taking on" the unions'.[41]

In February 1993 the review group agreed its interim report, for consultation in the party (Labour Party, 1993b). This proposed options for change in three main areas: selection of parliamentary candidates, election of the party leader, and balance of votes at annual conference.[42] On parliamentary selections it proposed five options. Three of these effectively revived the local electoral college in different forms, and depended on separate ballots of local members and trade union levy payers. The other two represented 'full' OMOV. This would either be restricted to party members, or allow trade unionists to sign up for equivalent rights under a 'levy plus' system that involved payment of a reduced party membership fee.

For leadership elections the group offered three options, none of which maintained trade union involvement at its current level, but none of which were pure OMOV. Two of them provided for an electoral college of thirds, comprising the PLP, an OMOV ballot of members, and a ballot of trade unionists. The last of these might either extend to all levy payers or only to those who were also members of the party. The third option was for the 50:50 college that John Smith had proposed the previous year. Smith let it be known that he remained committed to this model, and that he supported OMOV at a local level for parliamentary selections, possibly including registered trade union supporters.[43] There were others who wanted to go even further – frontbencher Jack Straw MP notably had proposed that leadership elections should exclude both the trade unions and grassroots members, and revert to the PLP alone (Straw, 1992).

The consultation in the party showed mixed support for Smith's proposals. Amongst the 288 CLPs responding there was backing for OMOV in parliamentary selections: 100 favoured this option, with an additional 43 supporting 'levy plus' and only 51 a reformed electoral college. However just one of the larger unions, the AEEU, favoured OMOV, with NUPE, COHSE and the RMT prepared to compromise on some kind of registered supporters' scheme or 'levy plus'. The two largest affiliates, the TGWU and GMB, were opposed to any of these schemes. On leadership elections, none of the unions supported the 50:50 college. This was also favoured by only 35 CLPs, against the 140 that supported continued involvement by the unions (Labour Party, 1993). Smith's preferred reform of leadership elections therefore appeared to be dead, and his attempt to complete the Kinnock reform of local selection methods was also in serious trouble.

Throughout this period, campaigning within the party had been vigorous. The LCC now openly backed OMOV and had sent materials and speakers urging support to local constituencies. The Solidarity successor organisation 'Labour First', co-ordinated by John Spellar, also campaigned for change. The CLPD remained opposed, and had been joined by a new purpose-built group, the 'Keep the Link' campaign, organised by the unions themselves. By claiming that the reforms were only the first step in a campaign by 'modernisers' to eject the unions from the party, this campaign won significant support amongst CLPs. A vocal member of the campaign was Smith's supposed 'king-maker', John Edmonds, who had earlier told the 1989 Labour Party conference that 'whenever possible we should make our decisions by one member one vote' (Labour Party, 1989, p. 139). But now that this reform had taken on such symbolic importance, and with rumours flying about impending divorce, he and other union leaders sought to draw a line in the sand.

Seeing the difficulties, John Smith tried to offer the unions a deal: that he would accept their continuing membership of the leadership electoral college in return for their support for OMOV in constituency selections.[44] But Bill Morris publicly responded that 'I don't think we are in the business of trading off one part of our members' democratic rights for another'.[45] One by one the unions adopted policy at their own conferences to oppose OMOV. The first to do so was USDAW, in April 1993, followed in May by the CWU, FBU and MSF, in June by the GMB and NUPE and in July by the TGWU (Stuart, 2005). Between them these accounted for two thirds of the union votes at Labour Party conference, and more than half of conference votes overall.

The debate over OMOV had become far more than a dry discussion of the mechanics of how candidates were selected – for many it had come to symbolise the future of the unions' relationship with the party. On the left there were concerns that the response to the 1992 defeat must not just be ever greater abandonment of traditional principles. The final report of the review group had been frank about the extent to which reform was linked to changing the appearance of the party, citing 'the mass media image of the link, and the effect this has on public perceptions and voting' which, encouraged by opposition parties, presented the unions as 'sectional, male, industrially irrelevant, conservative and old-fashioned ... dominating the party and acting as rigid obstacles to modernisation' (Labour Party, 1993, p. 4). However the response of many, particularly in the unions themselves, was that these stereotypes should be countered rather than perpetuated, through the party mounting a strong defence of the union link. Their opponents considered it essential to Labour's survival that the response to such pressures was concrete reform.

Smith's campaign to win trade union support took him to the TUC conference early in September. Here he emphasised the importance of the union link and made policy promises – including full employment as a central goal of a future Labour government, and concession of rights for workers from day one of their employment. These commitments were a reversal of the cautious approach that had been taken by Tony Blair when he held the employment brief. Blair was said to be 'furious' (Sopel, 1995, p. 162). Yet when Labour gathered in Brighton for its own conference later in the month, the unions had still not been won over to reform.

The proposals put before the conference were the most moderate amongst those that had been previously discussed. The 50:50 electoral college for leader had been dropped, and the change now proposed would implement a college of thirds – with a national ballot of Labour members and compulsory ballots on the trade union side. This change was so minor that it aroused relatively little opposition. The remaining difficulties surrounded the proposals for parliamentary selection, where OMOV would be restricted to full party members, but the 'levy plus' scheme would allow trade union members to join for the reduced rate of £3.[46] The organised voice of trade unions would thus be taken out of the final selection decision, though unions would maintain nomination rights and involvement in shortlisting candidates.

This relatively modest proposal became a crucial leadership test. Smith had let it be known to colleagues that he was prepared to resign as leader if the reforms were not agreed, and behind the scenes arrangements were made for the potentially grim conseq-uences of defeat.[47] On the eve of the conference *The Independent on Sunday* ran a story on its front page which indicated to delegates that the leader might be about to resign. Smith himself opened the conference debate, presenting the reform as a sensible, gradualist step and claiming that '[i]t is not a choice between one member one vote and a role for the trade unions. It is the chance for more trade unionists than ever before to take part in all the decisions and the campaigns of the Labour Party' (Labour Party, 1993a, p. 133). Emphasising the link between internal party reform and credibility as a governing party, he suggested that 'the changes I propose today are vital – absolutely central – to our strategy for winning power' (Labour Party, 1993a, p. 134). Whilst this may have been true, it had more to do with the leader's ability to show he could impose his will on the unions than about the detail of parliamentary selections – which were little understood and largely hidden from public view.

At the conference the LCC held a star-studded fringe meeting to demonstrate the breadth of support for change, with speakers including Neil Kinnock, Tony Blair, David Blunkett, Mo Mowlam, Hilary Armstrong, Gordon Brown, Robin Cook, Clare Short and Jack Straw. Such displays were seen as crucial to winning the support of constituency delegates, who mattered as never before. Following reform to reduce the share of conference votes held by the trade unions (see Chapter 8) this was the first year that constituency votes amounted to 30 per cent, rather than 10 per cent, of the total. Nonetheless, the views of the traditional trade union block, holding most of the remaining 70 per cent of conference votes, continued to be decisive. Supporting OMOV, the AEEU's General Secretary Bill Jordan proposed to his colleagues that 'A chain is as strong as its weakest link. The block vote is now this Party's weakest link' (Labour Party, 1993a, p. 134).[48] In a passionate speech closing the debate John Prescott, a shadow cabinet member long seen as a strong ally of the unions, sought to assure delegates that this was not the first step to divorce. Emphasising the importance of perception, he argued that 'there is a moment in time in the history of every movement, when the issue does not look to be important, but what is important is the issue as it is seen from outside' (Labour Party 1993a, p. 164). Change had become symbolic of the party's readiness to modernise, and of the authority of its leader.

The vote itself was exceptionally close. The crucial rule change passed by just 45.7 per cent to 44.4 per cent. The mechanism used to achieve this was vital, and provides an obvious link between this and the developments explored in Chapter 5. In an attempt to maximise support amongst unions for the reform, party officials had drafted a single rule amendment to implement all changes to parliamentary selections. This included both OMOV and the introduction of all-women shortlists in half of Labour's winnable seats. The coupling of these issues consciously exploited the dilemma that would be faced by unions that had policy supporting one and opposing the other. It allowed sympathetic trade union officers to argue to their delegations that their mandate on OMOV should be broken. This most famously happened within the MSF delegation, which decided by 19 votes to 17 to abstain. However other unions behaved similarly – the switch of the shopworkers' union USDAW to break its conference mandate and vote in favour of the rule change was also enough to be decisive.[49] Many major trade union affiliates continued to oppose change, however, including the TGWU and GMB, though NUPE – which had opposed Kinnock on OMOV – now switched sides to support Smith.[50]

The shift in the balance of conference votes towards the constituencies also seems to have made the difference between the leadership winning and losing: constituencies voted 60:40 in favour of change. And another recent reform, to apply a quota for women amongst both constituency and trade union delegates (see Chapters 5 and 8) may well have played a part. This potentially increased support for the rule change in both delegate groups.

The knife-edge vote had turned the debate into a dramatic showdown, and the newspapers afterwards wrote of Smith's high-risk victory against the traditionalists in his party. The symbolic impact was large. Yet the final package fell well short of what many had wanted, particularly in that the trade unions remained part of the leadership electoral college. Although the process had almost cost the leader his job some modernisers expressed disappointment with the result. Tony Blair himself is said to have concluded that 'the settlement was too timid' (Gould, 1998, p. 190). Yet it is difficult to see how any more radical reform could have been achieved. Meanwhile the earlier briefings from the modernisers themselves had played their part in turning a relatively modest reform into a major showdown with the unions.

THE LEADERSHIP ELECTION OF 1994

The new mechanism for electing a leader came into practice unexpectedly soon, following John Smith's sudden death in May 1994. In the circumstances there was an official moratorium on campaigning until June, and Smith's deputy Margaret Beckett took over the position of leader on a temporary basis.[51]

The rules still gave the PLP the sole right to nominate leadership candidates, with the support of 12.5 per cent of members (34 MPs in 1994) required to win a place on the ballot paper. Three candidates, Tony Blair, Margaret Beckett and John Prescott, secured the required number of nominations to stand.[52] In addition, Beckett announced that she was officially resigning as deputy leader in order that there could be a simultaneous contest for this position. There were two successful nominees: herself and John Prescott.

The new balloting requirements meant that a longer timetable was set for this than for previous contests, with nominations to close on 16 June, ballot papers to be posted on 30 June and the result on 21 July. Although there was no longer a need for a conference where votes would be cast, it was agreed to hold a 'gathering' where the result would be announced. Ballots of levy payers would be administered separately by each union. The new rules required such members to tick a box indicating that they were a Labour supporter in order for their vote to be valid.

Although some unions chose not to ballot and thus excluded themselves from the contest (the NUM and UCATT claimed that a ballot was too expensive), the new arrangements brought hundreds of thousands of trade unionists into the process who had never been involved in the party before. The need to reach around four million of these individuals, as well as all the party's members, gave the media an unprecedented role in the process. Many union members were not familiar with Labour politics and formed their impressions of the candidates through the press. Thus ironically, given their criticisms of the previous contest, 'the media took the place filled by the union barons in 1992 in immediately identifying a frontrunner' (Alderman and Carter, 1995, p. 452). Within days of John Smith's death Tony Blair was tipped as the leading candidate.

The result was as predicted, with Blair elected on the first round of voting, winning 57 per cent of the total. In the deputy leadership contest Prescott won 56.5 per cent to Beckett's 43.5 per cent. In both cases the winner had secured support in all three sections of the ballot.[53] Although the process ran smoothly some concerns were raised which were later echoed in other OMOV contests. Whilst turnout amongst party members was relatively high at 69.1 per cent, only 19.5 per cent of trade union levy payers used their vote. There was also controversy about the costs of the contest, not only

Building New Labour

to the party and its affiliates, but also to the candidates themselves. Figures published in the *Independent on Sunday* suggested that Blair had raised £88,000 and spent £79,000 on his campaign, Beckett had spent £17,000 and Prescott had spent £13,000 (quoted in Alderman and Carter, 1995). Without major campaign finance, coupled with a sympathetic media, it was difficult to see how a leadership contest with such a large and diffuse electorate could be won.

EVALUATION

The story of Labour's adoption of the OMOV principle is a long and eventful one. First rising to prominence in the early 1970s, the campaign for OMOV received its most significant boost as part of a counter-reaction to the CLPD reforms of 1979-81. After these changes had disturbed the balance of Labour's traditional democracy, the involvement of 'ordinary' members in party decisions became the primary means by which leaders attempted to re-establish equilibrium. The initial reforms had been driven by the left, in protest against the control enjoyed by a relatively disconnected PLP. Through the introduction of mandatory reselection and the leadership electoral college, the CLPD sought to make this group and its leader more accountable to the wider party, and particularly to the CLPs. This handed significantly greater control to constituency activists, then seen as being dominated by the left. It thus gave impetus to the long-standing demands of the right to involve all members in local selection decisions. The potential threat to moderate and right-wing MPs posed by regular reselection contests gave these demands a new urgency as far as the leadership was concerned. The fact that few MPs ever were deselected (and for many on the left reselection had been more about creating accountability than about facilitating vendettas against particular individuals) did not prevent the right's drive continuing, once it had been begun. In summary, looking back, it was therefore the mutually reinforcing reforms proposed by those on both the party's left and its right that together shaped the new equilibrium eventually achieved in the package agreed under John Smith in 1993.

The motivations for OMOV were complex, and the new principle cut across the two fundamental principles of Labour's traditional democracy. The first was the representative nature of local parties, where decisions had always been taken by activists elected to the GC. For leaders it was the likely substantive impact of activists gaining control of mandatory reselections, and a share in the leadership electoral college, that triggered support for OMOV. In order to weaken activists' influence, an extension of voting rights to all local members became attractive. This was agreed as part of the fragile compromise of the local electoral college in 1987, and subsequently within the leadership electoral college in 1988. The trade unions were content to use their votes at the party conference to cement these reforms, and – despite the best efforts of the CLPD – the proposals also won considerable support in the CLPs themselves. As a result, constituency GCs lost important powers, weakening the tradition of collective decision making at the local level (as further discussed in Chapter 9).

OMOV also brought into question the party's federal traditions, however, in the shape of its relationship with the trade unions. Here change was much harder to achieve. Whilst the unions were prepared to support the leadership in moves to disempower activists, the response was very different when it came to the powers they held themselves. Yet it proved impossible to find a workable system that would extend the franchise locally beyond members of the GC, whilst retaining trade union involvement at its current level.

Although the unions had largely reassumed their position of leadership loyalty after Neil Kinnock became leader, the problem of their role in internal selections and elections took on increasing symbolic importance. It was not that union participation would result in outcomes that were unsatisfactory for leaders; rather that the image generated by their involvement was seen as increasingly problematic. Meanwhile, in the unions, there were growing suspicions that the attempt to reduce their role was part of a plan to edge them out of the party altogether. However, for them the argument was more than simply symbolic; its substance also mattered. The party had originally been founded in order to gain representation in parliament for the trade unions, and this role was still considered important. In the 1960s Ian Aitken had suggested of the unions' involvement in local parliamentary selections that 'it is this citadel, rather than the crumbling fortress of the trade union block votes at conference, which has often proved to be the real stronghold of power in the structure of the Labour Party' (1966, p. 18).

The unions were thus strongly opposed to their delegates on local GCs being disenfranchised, which explains why the agreement of

OMOV for parliamentary selections took more than 10 years of painful negotiation. Throughout this period the more intransigent the trade unions' grew, the more symbolic the issue became for party 'modernisers'. In turn, growing pressure from this group, and from the media, simply led the unions to defend their position more staunchly. This created a very dangerous situation for John Smith, who was forced to face the unions' anger over rumours of 'divorce' when he himself, though being a supporter of OMOV, was solidly committed to the union link.

In some ways this story supports the commonly perceived belief that Labour leaders got what they wanted out of party organisational reform. After all, OMOV was backed by the leader and went on to be agreed. Yet any suggestion that this demonstrates Labour leaders' power must be strongly qualified. First, reform took a very long time. It was initially proposed by Kinnock in 1984, but blocked then and in 1987, and only eventually accepted in 1993. Indeed it was finally agreed only after the leader had made clear that failure to achieve change would force him to resign his position. This was an extremely high-risk strategy, and obviously not one that could be readily repeated. Second, even when reform was agreed it fell far short of what leaders had originally wanted. John Smith was drawn from the party's traditional right wing that had never supported the leadership electoral college in the first place, but was forced to accept it in 1981. However, a return to election of the leader by the PLP was seen as politically impossible. Even Smith's attempt to modify the college by removing the trade union section resulted in total failure. In the end the compromise reached on leadership elections in 1993 did relatively little to erode union power. Even when this reform was agreed, 22 years after the CLPD's victory on the electoral college, the PLP held only a third of the votes for leader, compared to the monopoly that it had held before. The only real victory in 1993 was therefore over parliamentary selections. And although providing a symbolic win for the leader, and an equally symbolic break with the past, this simply removed the unions from the least visible element of the party's internal selection processes.

Initially, moves to introduce the new principle of OMOV were underpinned by a belief that the 'ordinary' members empowered by this change would have more moderate views than the activists. This logic was used with respect to ballots both in the trade unions and amongst the party's own membership. John May's law of curvilinear disparity (see Chapter 2) was thus instinctively understood by campaigners on both the left and the right of the party. Similar beliefs had also informed the trade union reform laws brought in by Conservative governments, which ran concurrently with these reforms. However, the application of the principle in both settings did not always have the anticipated effect. In the party, examples such as the NUPE ballot for the deputy leadership contest in 1981 were held up as proof that less active members were more moderate than activists. However, the full evidence was actually rather less decisive. The ballot in the NUM in this same election resulted in support for Tony Benn. More importantly, in the 1983 leadership contest, although it was Roy Hattersley who called for balloting, every single constituency and trade union ballot supported Neil Kinnock – the centre left candidate. These results suggested that the ballot effect might not be so simple as originally thought – a suggestion that went on to be borne out by future results, as discussed in Chapters 4 and 7.

The story in this chapter raises some interesting 'what ifs'. For example, it is difficult to guess whether Smith would have had more or less success in securing the reform he hoped for if negotiations had been conducted in an environment free of 'spin' about impending divorce. Similarly, we can also only wonder what would have happened if the package of reform had been defeated and he had been forced out as party leader. With the unreformed electoral college remaining in place it is very unlikely that Tony Blair – the very man who had been pushing Smith to go further – would have been his successor. After 24 years of the electoral college we might also ask how the stability of Labour leaders would have been different if the old system of annual election by the PLP had been retained. Whilst the intention of the college was to increase accountability, in its final form it also creates significant obstacles to sparking a leadership contest.[54] Particularly with Labour in government the potential damage done by a leadership challenge, with speculation lasting weeks whilst balloting is conducted, appears prohibitive.[55] Although no Labour leader has ever been forcibly removed by the party, the electoral college has made their position less precarious. The speed with which the Conservative parliamentary party was able to remove Margaret Thatcher in 1990 (or, indeed, Iain Duncan-Smith in 2003) offers a stark contrast.

The media have a major role throughout the story of OMOV. From 1981 onwards, and particularly after 1992, they kept up pressure for the trade union role in the electoral college to be reformed. The media's focus on the unions, and the damage that this was seen to be doing to the party, was a major factor in bringing about reform. The potential role the media would have with OMOV in place, however, had frequently been cited by its opponents as a reason for its rejection. The CLPD repeatedly claimed that 'armchair members' might be overly influenced in internal elections by the views of the right-wing tabloids. This was certainly pessimistic – Seyd and Whiteley (1992) found that only 1.3 per cent of Labour members read *The Sun* and 1.4 per cent read *The Daily Mail*. However the number of trade unionists in the electoral college that did so was undoubtedly much higher. One way or another, reform did give the media a far more central role in setting the agenda of internal party elections. In national leadership elections (though to a far smaller extent in local selections), sympathetic treatment by the press and broadcast media has become essential to candidates in their communication with the widened party electorate. This may be an appropriate test for one who will need to communicate through the media once elected as party leader. But its impact on Labour's internal democracy has been profound.

In summary, therefore, the CLPD reforms, followed by the moves towards the OMOV principle during the 1980s and early 1990s, had fundamental effects on both the federal and representative traditions of the party. They changed the relationship between the party and the unions, between individual members and local parties, between the party inside and outside parliament, and between Labour and the media. Some of the implications of these changes are discussed further in Chapters 10 and 11. But controversies over candidate selection did not end, as some had expected, in 1993. This latter part of the story is therefore told in Chapter 4.

Notes

1. In fact historically the leader of the parliamentary party was formally not leader of the party as a whole. Only after 1922 was the Chairman of the PLP (then Ramsay MacDonald) effectively recognised as party leader. In 1981, with the widening of the franchise, the office of 'party leader' was formally created for the first time (Stark, 1996).

2. This power was regularly used before the 1970s, and although the NEC's attitude had latterly become less interventionist, activists were angered by the pressure put on members of Lincoln CLP in 1972 over the deselection of Dick Taverne (who later stood for election against the party) and Newham North East CLP in 1975 over the deselection of Reg Prentice (who later joined the Conservatives and went on to become a minister in the first Thatcher government). See Wainwright (1987), Shaw (1988).

3. Mandelson's 'manifesto' was written with fellow Lambeth councillor Paul Ormerod (Routledge, 1999). Other examples are Bing (1971), Hayter (1977).

4. Brian Sedgemore and Frances Morrell, 'Setting Labour on the Long Road to Democracy', *Guardian*, 26 November 1979.

5. For more detail see for example Kogan and Kogan (1982), Panitch and Leys (1997), Seyd (1987), Shaw (1988), Stark (1996), Wainwright (1987).

6. See Stark (1996) for a detailed discussion of how party leaders have been selected since Labour's foundation.

7. OMOV was backed by 18 CLPs and one trade union, whilst 11 CLPs supported the electoral college and 36 CLPs and nine unions favoured the status quo (Stark, 1996).

8. For some SDP defectors the decision on mandatory reselection was also influential, as those with left-dominated local parties were now in a less secure position (Crewe and King, 1995).

9. Ironically when the new party was formed there was a lengthy wrangle over the method of selecting the leader, with David Owen and Shirley Williams favouring OMOV and Bill Rodgers and Roy Jenkins supporting election by MPs. Ultimately OMOV was narrowly chosen, and this method of choosing the leader later became a condition of the party's merger with the Liberals in 1988 (Stark, 1996).

10. For example, the front page of *The Sunday Times* on the day after the special conference was headed 'Shock Labour vote: unions to dominate choice of Labour leader'. This was noted as a 'stunning setback' for Michael Foot. Such responses were fed by the SDP defectors, with Shirley Williams quoted as saying that 'Four trade union barons in a smoke-filled room is no way to elect a Prime Minister'.

11. Note that whilst some on the right had feared that the electoral college would deliver the party leadership to Tony Benn, he was ineligible to stand in 1983, having lost his parliamentary seat at the general election.

12. The other unions to ballot included COHSE, the POEU, FBU and NUM. The NUM ballot supported Benn, whilst all the others supported Healey.

13. This was only two more than had occurred prior to the election of 1950 (Ranney, 1965). However, the number deselected might well have been higher if many right-wingers had not defected to the SDP in 1981 – see Crewe and King (1995).

14. On occasion one single union could have a majority or near majority on the GC. For example Rush (1969, p. 175) tells us that for the selection in 1963 in Ilkeston the Derbyshire Miners' Association had 84 delegates on a 199-strong GC, whilst the TGWU had 23.

15. A resolution from the right-wing EETPU union went further, and proposed the replacement of the electoral college for leader by an all-member ballot. This was also defeated.

16. The option to 'remit' was frequently used by the party conference as a way of leaving a proposal on the table for consideration on a future occasion. If the movers chose to push such a proposal to the vote they would usually be defeated as the NEC would ask the conference to oppose it. Remittance to the NEC formally required them to give the issue attention, and where this was agreed they would often promise to bring proposals back in a subsequent year.

17. The Evans proposal had been agreed at the July NEC by eleven votes to seven.

18. There is some dispute about the winning figure, which was recorded in the party's record of decisions as 3,592,000 (the figure reported in *The Times*) whilst the conference report suggests the figure was 3,992,000. Minkin (1992) picks the latter figure and I have followed his example.

19. Quoted in Wainwright (1987, p. 308).

20. In the run up to this election the number of deselections – six – was again modest.

21. These were UCW, EETPU, TSSA, APEX and ACTT. In addition COHSE backed the electoral college. NUR, NUM, National League of Blind and Disabled supported no change. Three unions – AEU, NCU and NGA – backed other options.

22. In addition to the defeat of 1984, the unions had shown their unease at the 1986 conference by supporting a resolution urging the NEC to desist, which was carried against the wishes of the platform.

23. Interview, 2 December 2003.

24. The LCC voted to support the policy in March 1987. Its executive had been split, so it had conducted its own internal ballot of members to decide its position (*Guardian*, 12 March 1987).

25. Many of these were undoubtedly safe Conservative seats where there was little real contest to be the candidate. Interest within Labour-held seats would generally have been far higher.

26. LCC *Labour Activist*, 28 September 1987, p. 1.

27. Dorothy Macedo, Hendon South CLP (Labour Party, 1987a, p. 19).

28. Composite 46 calling for no change was lost by 1,851,000 votes to 4,548,000, with the NEC calling for opposition. Composite 44 supporting OMOV was lost by 1,762,000 votes to 4,425,000, with the NEC taking a neutral position.

29. Those seen as likely to be targeted included Terry Fields, Dave Nellist and Chris Mullin (*Times*, 3 October 1987).

30. Frank Field won 165 members' votes to his opponent's 113. Field later appealed to the NEC and the selection was rerun, with him winning the second time.
31. The stated intention was to bring a rule change to the 1991 conference. This did not happen, however. Instead this conference took a further in-principle decision to move to a 'weighted franchise' whereby individual trade union levy payers living in the constituency would have a vote worth one third of that of ordinary members. This was never actually put into effect.
32. Resolution 71, moved by Leeds North East CLP.
33. For a full account of the leadership contest see Alderman and Carter (1993).
34. Appearing on BBC's *On the Record* and quoted in *The Guardian*, 13 April.
35. *The Guardian*, 13 April.
36. *The Sunday Times*, 19 April. It seems quite likely that this comment came from Tony Blair.
37. *The Guardian*, 15 April.
38. Gould stood for the posts of both leader and deputy leader, whilst Beckett and Prescott stood as deputy leader only.
39. Poll of 5,000 party members in *The Guardian*, 16 June 1992, quoted in Stark (1996).
40. Continuing hostility amongst the trade unions was demonstrated by Composite 9 in 1992, which called for continued trade union involvement in all stages of the local selection process. This was supported, against the wishes of the platform, by 3,193,000 votes to 2,118,000.
41. 'Unions: time for reform, not divorce', *Tribune* 18 December 1992, quoted in Anderson and Mann (1997, p. 320).
42. For the last of these, see Chapter 8.
43. NEC Minutes, 24 February 1993.
44. This was effectively the 'soft' line that Solidarity had actively campaigned for over previous years – though others such as Spellar and the EETPU had pressed for full OMOV for selecting the leader.
45. *Financial Times*, 8 July 1993, quoted in Alderman and Carter (1994, p. 327).
46. At this time the standard annual membership fee was £15.
47. Papers prepared for the leader by Larry Whitty at this time set out the options for dealing with defeat, with the preferred option being to put the proposals to the conference again later in the week as a vote of confidence in the leader. See also Stuart (2005).
48. In fact the issue over which there was the greatest argument – local parliamentary selections – had little to do with the block vote. Officially GC delegates were not supposed to be mandated for selection meetings but to vote as individuals. Nonetheless the issue had become confused

in the public mind with trade union involvement in general, and thus the 'block vote'. Interventions like Jordan's simply fed this confusion.

49. It is worth noting that it was not only those who supported all-women shortlists and opposed OMOV who found themselves compromised by these arrangements. John Spellar, for example, who had long been one of the keenest campaigners for OMOV, was a passionate opponent of all-women shortlists and voiced his objections to the conference. He went on to back a campaign to try and reverse this policy the following year, as discussed in Chapter 5.

50. Other unions supporting included AEEU, COHSE, UCW, RMT, ISTC, TSSA. Those opposing also included GPMU, UCATT, NUM, FBU, ASLEF, NCU (*The Guardian*, 30 September 1993).

51. The information in this section is largely based on Alderman and Carter (1995).

52. Blair achieved 154 nominations, Prescott 46 and Beckett 42 (Alderman and Carter, 1995).

53. Blair's vote comprised 60.5 per cent of the votes of MPs and MEPs, 58.2 per cent of members' votes, and 52.3 per cent of trade union votes.

54. Originally the CLPD had sought an annual election taking place at the party conference. Later reforms moved the electoral college further and further away from this model, given the need for balloting, and made the process a longer and more expensive one.

55. This is by no means the only obstacle. Formally, under the 1993 rules, a challenger for the leadership must first be nominated by at least 20 per cent of the PLP. However, the decision of whether to go ahead with a contest must also be supported by a majority of the annual conference on a card vote.

4

Selection under Blair: The Fall and Rise of One Member One Vote

The adoption of OMOV at the 1993 conference marked the end of a long period of conflict within the party about selection mechanisms. The decisive shift between an old and a new style of party democracy with respect to candidate selection had now been taken. Or at least so it seemed. Certainly no such tense decision has been taken by the party conference, on any issue, since. However, subsequent years showed that controversy over internal selections in the party was far from over. During the next decade debates about systems for choosing Labour candidates for elected office continued, and at times returned to the national headlines. On occasion this was because of moves to further modernise the process. But at other times it resulted from attempts by the party leadership to retreat away from OMOV to more traditional methods when there were difficult decisions to be made

There were no major changes to the selection process between 1993 and the 1997 election, as the mechanism for selecting parliamentary candidates had now been agreed. However, after 1997 there were many innovations, largely in response to the new elected institutions created under the government's constitutional reform programme. The establishment of these new institutions, less high-profile than Westminster and based on different electoral systems, provided an opportunity to experiment with new methods of selection. The plethora of elections in short succession which occurred after 1997 also meant that these new methods could spread quickly, being tried in one context and then copied in others. Unlike the changes in the earlier period there was, however, no simple linear progression towards a new democratic principle. In part the changes were piecemeal, simply adapting the existing system to new circumstances. In part they involved a greater professionalisation of the selection process, so that it came to mimic more closely selections for senior jobs. But the period from 1997 also saw some reversals of the principles so carefully agreed in the early

1990s, with the leadership resisting OMOV, and particularly union balloting, at certain points. As a result activists on the left, also in a change to their previous position, came to embrace these principles.

After a difficult period in the late 1990s it seemed to be finally accepted that the principle of OMOV was not, after all, reversible. Attempts to restrict it were criticised by party members, the press and the public alike. Consequently a relatively stable settlement, with OMOV at its heart, was established in 2000. These developments demonstrated two particularly interesting things. First, that the OMOV principle was not as advantageous to the party leadership as had originally been assumed. And second, that the constraints on the leadership were such that it could not manage to reverse a principle that had become popular and widely accepted.

THE 1999 EUROPEAN ELECTIONS

One of the earliest controversies concerned selection of candidates for the European Parliament elections, which were held in 1999. Here the institution itself was not new, but constitutional reforms by the new Labour government created a need for change. The Parliament had last been elected in 1994 using the same 'first past the post' system that was traditionally used for Westminster. At this time Labour, benefiting from the Conservatives' unpopularity, had won 62 of the available 84 seats. In July 1997 the new government announced that the electoral system would be changed to a proportional one, to bring Britain into line with the rest of Europe. The combination of this change, and Labour's exceptional result in 1994, meant that the party stood to lose a large number of seats in 1999. This created a difficult environment for the selection of Labour's candidates.

The new electoral system abolished the existing single member constituencies and instead introduced party lists in Scotland, Wales and nine English regions. Previously, as for Westminster, Labour Party members in each European constituency had been responsible for choosing their own candidate. The new system disbanded party organisation at this level and instead required a selection process across whole regions. This was the first time such arrangements had been attempted in the UK. All of Labour's MEPs would be stripped of their seats and left to compete for positions on the party's electoral lists. Those securing positions at the top of the lists could be confident of retaining their employment. Some of those ranked lower would be almost certain to lose.

This situation understandably led to tension in the European Parliamentary Labour Party (EPLP) and faced the NEC with a dilemma. The selection system would need to be seen to be fair to existing MEPs as well as consistent with party democracy. These two principles were, however, not easily reconciled. The most obvious solution would have been for members across each region to be given the opportunity through an OMOV ballot to select and rank candidates for the lists. However, the EPLP lobbied heavily against such a system, as it would require potentially divisive campaigns between sitting MEPs within the party.

Unlike the selection system for Westminster, which was a regular focus of controversy at annual conference, selections for the European Parliament were more low-key affairs. Indeed OMOV had been introduced for these selections in 1991, two years before it was finally accepted for Westminster. In 1997 the annual conference simply delegated responsibility to the NEC for deciding the new selection system. After negotiation with the EPLP a consultation document was issued to the party in January (Labour Party, 1998). This proposed that members should be involved at the nomination stage by deciding in an OMOV ballot whether to nominate their sitting MEP, where one existed, to a central 'pool' of candidates. Members could also propose one additional male and one female candidate to the pool, as a third competing objective was to increase the representativeness of Labour MEPs.[1] But after this the involvement of grassroots members would end, and all later stages of the selection process would be run by the NEC. A small panel made up of representatives of the NEC and each regional party would draw up shortlists from the pool and rank candidates for the electoral lists.[2] All sitting MEPs were to be guaranteed a seat on a list (not necessarily in their own region) with additional seats filled by new candidates. However, in an attempt to boost gender and ethnic diversity, sitting MEPs would not necessarily win all the top places.

Although argued on the basis of necessity, and as a one-off process to deal with exceptional circumstances, these proposals were highly controversial in the party.[3] They introduced an unprecedented degree of centralisation, and the lack of member involvement in the final selection process was widely questioned. Of those responding to the consultation over half believed an OMOV ballot, rather than an appointed panel, should be used for selecting and ranking regional lists. Concerns were raised that such a panel would screen members politically, with those least sympathetic to the leadership liable to be excluded from winnable positions.[4] The NEC decided to approve the original proposals, however, with few concessions.

Another innovation in this process was the use of formal equal opportunities procedures. A 'job description' and 'person specification' for the job of MEP were drawn up, and an application form was structured around these, asking candidates to demonstrate their relevant knowledge and skills in areas such as campaigning, representation, problem solving and communication. The panels then used a scoring system to choose the successful candidates. In part this approach reflected the desire of party officers and the NEC to create a fair and open process. In part it was also a defensive move, given the judgement of the Leeds industrial tribunal in 1996 that candidate selection was a form of job selection (see Chapter 5). A transparent process would help to guard the party against legal challenges of sex or race discrimination by disgruntled candidates.

OMOV ballots to nominate to the pool of candidates took place in July 1998. 49 sitting MEPs indicated that they wished to continue to serve and won nomination to the pool.[5] The regional panels then met in September to interview those nominated and to draw up the final lists. This proved to be very controversial. Candidates were first asked to make a four minute presentation on why they would be a good MEP, and many new candidates were excluded at this point without being granted an interview. Some process of sifting was clearly necessary given the size of the pool. However, the form it took was brutal – particularly since all those who had reached this stage had already campaigned for and won an OMOV ballot in their area. Equally problematic was the second and final stage, which rested on those who survived the first round (including, by prior agreement, all sitting MEPs) being subjected to a ten minute interview in hostile 'press conference' format. These fourteen minutes determined where the panel placed candidates on the lists.

Given the competition between MEPs, these selections were bound to be difficult. They were made far harder by the party's stated objective of increasing diversity. These factors made it inevitable that many sitting MEPs were placed in unwinnable positions on lists. The most extreme example was in the West Midlands, where actor and gay rights activist Michael Cashman was placed at number two and a female candidate, Neena Gill, at number three, whilst two MEPs took the fourth and fifth places and failed to be elected. Several MEPs complained, privately or publicly, at the position that they had been allocated, and four chose to withdraw rather than enter the election in unwinnable positions. Christine Oddy MEP, who had been placed at number seven on the West Midlands list, lodged an appeal and ultimately resigned from the party to stand as an independent. The NEC insisted that all decisions had been taken on merit in difficult circumstances.

The results of the actual elections were even worse than the NEC had predicted. Labour won just 29 seats, of which 24 were taken by existing MEPs and five by new members (11 of these candidates were women). The size of the party's losses confirmed the NEC's claim that special procedures had been needed. However the process had caused significant resentment within the party, with concerns both about the central screening process and the backtracking on the OMOV principle. For the first time, those on the left of the party had found themselves backing OMOV, in preference to a more centralised system.

THE SCOTTISH AND WELSH ELECTIONS

At the same time that decisions were being taken about Europe, the party was also required to devise systems to select candidates for the new Scottish Parliament and National Assembly for Wales. Referendums to approve creation of these new institutions were held in September 1997, and the first elections were then scheduled for May 1999.

The new constitutional arrangements created a number of challenges for the party's traditional approach to candidate selection. Devolution within the state raised questions about devolution of decision making within the party, with its Scottish and Welsh Executive Committees eager to take on the traditional role of the NEC in overseeing candidate selection. In addition, the electoral system for the new institutions included not only constituency members, but also regional list members to create proportionality between the parties. A question therefore arose about how these list candidates would be chosen. Additionally the party faced questions over how the membership of the new institutions could be gender balanced and meet the aspirations of the 'new politics' that had been promised from devolution (Bradbury and Mitchell, 2001; Mitchell, 2000). The gender aspects of this question are primarily dealt with in the next chapter, but the desire for diversity and quality of candidates went further than this alone. There were concerns amongst the party leadership, and many in Scotland and Wales, that seats in the new institutions should not simply go to the 'usual suspects': sitting MPs, council leaders and senior union officials. This would not have provided the symbolic break from 'old politics' that devolution sought to achieve.

The NEC and senior head office officials were agreed on the importance of diversity of candidates, and were concerned that a devolved system within the party would not deliver this. Immediately following the devolution referendums, annual conference in 1997 agreed (as it had with respect to Europe) to delegate detailed decisions over the selection process to the NEC. This proved uncontroversial as these could be presented as second-order elections and, in any case, the bulk of conference delegates came from England. However, the Scottish party conference also decided to delegate details to Labour's Scottish Executive, having agreed some broad principles to be followed.

The NEC therefore established a 'selections taskforce' which drew up proposals, in consultation with the Scottish and Welsh parties. Joint meetings of the three Executives took the final decisions. This method of joint working – which ensured consistency but also significant central control – was continued into the selection process itself.

The new institutions created an opportunity to import a system that had long been used by Labour in local government but had been resisted for parliamentary selections: a panel of pre-approved candidates. There were at least three reasons why this became possible in the Scottish and Welsh context. First, it could be argued that, as an intermediate level of government, the devolved institutions had just as much to learn from local government procedures as from those for Westminster. Second, the creation of an approved panel, it was suggested, might help promote gender and ethnic diversity by providing constituencies with a balanced list from which to choose. Third, those forces, including some national trade unions, that were suspicious of an approved list for Westminster attached less significance to these selections. Unions generally did not have established policy regarding selections for the (previously hypothetical) devolved institutions.

Hence the principle that local parties would be required to select their candidates from an approved panel was agreed. Further, as it had been for Europe, the application process was professionalised, with a person specification and job description and a standard application form. Any individual member was free to nominate themselves for inclusion on the panel. In Scotland 534 applied to be considered for the 129-member Parliament; in Wales 438 applications were received for the 60-member Assembly (Laffin, Shaw and Taylor, 2004).

A selection board was established for each institution, comprising five representatives of the NEC, five members of the Scottish or Welsh Executive Committee, five 'independent' members (who should be 'prominent Labour Party members' from Scotland or Wales) and five non-voting 'advisers' with experience of selection processes. From this group individual interviewing committees were drawn. Members of the selection boards, on the advice of party officers, used the written applications to choose 326 applicants for interview in Scotland and 315 in Wales (Laffin, Shaw and Taylor, 2004). Such a huge volume of interviews was a major organisational task, but was managed with more sensitivity than had applied in the European case. Each applicant was required to make a five minute presentation, answer 25 minutes of questions and withstand a five minute mock press conference (Shaw, 2001).

At the end of this process 166 members were approved for inclusion on the panel of candidates in Scotland and 152 in Wales. The exclusion of so many – particularly in Scotland, where there were 129 vacancies to fill – proved controversial. The most high-profile casualty was Dennis Canavan, MP for Falkirk West, who subsequently resigned from the party and successfully fought the Scottish Parliament election as an independent. Ian Davidson MP was also excluded, as was Mark Lazarowicz, later elected as MP for Edinburgh North and Leith in 2001 (Shaw, 2001). In both Scotland and Wales there was an appeal process, and in Scotland this resulted in only one additional candidate (Susan Deacon, who went on to become a Scottish health minister) being included. In Wales there were 13 successful appeals (Bradbury et al, 2000).

Local constituency selections proved uncontroversial, with the exception of the 'twinning' process to ensure gender balance, discussed in the next chapter. These used the OMOV system that had been adopted for Westminster in 1993. The same principle was not applied, however, to the selection of candidates to the additional member lists. Here, as with respect to the list members for Europe, a very centralised process was established. The membership and ranking of the lists was decided by a selection board, although this time formal approval by a conference of constituency party representatives was also required. But the CLP represent-atives had no say in the order of the list and could only accept or reject it *en bloc*. The strongest argument for this approach was that it allowed the board to rebalance for any shortcomings (for example lack of ethnic diversity) amongst constituency candidates – although in reality Labour expected to win few seats from the lists. In two regions in Scotland and three in Wales agreement could not be reached with constituency representatives and lists had to be imposed. Consequently a survey of candidates found that around 80 per cent of respondents in both Scotland and Wales thought the process for selecting list candidates was undemocratic and unfair (Bradbury et al, 2000).

At the end of this process some of the conclusions already reached after selections for the European Parliament were confir-med. The notion of a panel of approved candidates had been accepted reluctantly, but the fact that it was strictly 'closed' was controversial. The centralised nature of the selection of list candidates was more controversial still – a situation only eased by the fact that few, if any, of these candidates were likely to win. It was becoming clear that there were limits to how far leaders could feasibly go in restricting members' rights over local selections.

In addition to selecting candidates for the Parliament and Assembly, devolution resulted in processes being adopted to elect the new positions of leader of the Scottish and Welsh Labour Party. The expectation was that those chosen would be the then Secretary of State for Scotland, Donald Dewar, and Secretary of State for Wales, Ron Davies. Election by the party would, however, boost their legitimacy and their profiles in the forthcoming election campaigns.

There was some debate initially about how the new leaders should be elected. One option would have been for the Labour groups in the new institutions to select their own leaders, as had applied in the PLP until 1981 and continued to apply in local government. However, a more high profile and more inclusive method was seen as desirable. Another option therefore was full OMOV ballots. However there was no precedent for such a process in these circumstances. Indeed since the 1970s the Scottish party's rulebook had referred to the election of the Scottish leader, stating that this would be carried out by the same method applying to the national UK leader. In 1996 the Scottish party conference voted on a new rule book which reaffirmed such an arrangement. The same system then went on to be adopted by the party in Wales.

In both Scotland and Wales the electoral college mimicked the national arrangements by giving one third of votes to the affiliates (mostly trade unions), one third to party members and one third to elected representatives. However, in other important respects the application of the arrangements differed from the national leadership college. As the selection of candidates was not yet complete at the time the leadership elections took place, the elected members section was included all members on the approved panel of candidates, as well as all MPs and MEPs sitting for Scottish/Welsh seats. In the constituency section CLPs cast block votes, which were normally based on decisions taken by GCs, rather than using OMOV. This was the arrangement that had applied in the national college prior to 1988. Similarly, there was no requirement on affiliated trade unions to ballot their members. Ballots had seemed unnecessary to the Scottish party, given that it was clear the election would be uncontested. The result of the exercise was simply that Donald Dewar was elected unopposed. There was less harmony in Wales, where Ron Davies was challenged for the leadership by Rhodri Morgan MP. However, the same system as used in Scotland was adopted. Whilst Morgan had significant support, Davies won all three sections of the electoral college, and secured 68 per cent overall to his challenger's 32 per cent (Flynn, 1999).

But this victory was to prove short lived. In late October 1998, barely a month after his election, Ron Davies resigned as leader of the Welsh party and Secretary of State for Wales after a mysterious 'incident' on Clapham Common. This threw Labour's devolution plans into unexpected disarray. Davies was replaced as Secretary of State by Blair loyalist Alun Michael MP. Michael had expressed no interest in standing for the Assembly, had not put himself forward as a candidate, and indeed the panel of candidates had closed. However, it quickly became clear that Tony Blair did not wish Rhodri Morgan to become Welsh party leader and hoped Alun Michael would displace him. Michael made a late application to the selection board, which reopened the panel in order to accept it. He did not secure selection in a constituency, however, and was instead placed at number one on the regional top-up list in Mid and West Wales (Flynn, 1999).

Although the election contest between Morgan and Michael in 1999 attracted considerable criticism for diverging from the OMOV principle it was in fact little different from that deployed the previous year, again being an electoral college of three equal parts. The two differences were that first, Assembly candidates now having been chosen, the elected members section of the college included only those actually selected, plus MPs and MEPs. Second, in the members' section the electorate was widened to an OMOV ballot. Although this seemed more likely to benefit Michael, and was thus open to criticism, it also represented a reversion to the accepted 1993 principle. In the affiliates' section there was (again) no requirement to ballot.

The obvious difference in this contest was that Alun Michael lost the members' ballot, but still won the electoral college overall. Rhodri Morgan gained 64 per cent of members' votes to Michael's 36 per cent. This focussed attention sharply on the democracy of the other sections. Amongst the affiliates the only major union to ballot was UNISON, whose members supported Morgan by a ratio of three to one. Amongst the unions that did not ballot was the AEEU, which had previously argued passionately for OMOV (see Chapter 3). It, along with the GMB and TGWU, voted for Michael. Consequently he won 64 per cent of the affiliates' section, which alongside 58 per cent of the elected members' section was enough to secure him the leadership (Flynn, 1999).

Although little had actually changed, Blair's intervention to strongly back Michael, coupled with the latter's lack of connection to the Assembly and his failure to secure the members' vote led to loud claims of 'stitch up'. There was widespread concern by members that their views were being overridden, fuelled by widespread criticism in the press. Once again it seemed that failing to apply the OMOV principle was a dangerous option for the leadership, and could come at a high cost. In this case the resentment caused was widely believed to have spilled over into the results of the election, in May 1999. Labour failed to gain the overall majority of Assembly seats that it had hoped for, and lost three of its previously safest seats:, Rhondda, Llanelli and Islwyn.

As a postscript it is necessary to note that Alun Michael resigned as First Minister in February 2000 and later stood down from the Assembly.[6] He was replaced as leader by Rhodri Morgan, but given that a new First Minister was needed immediately, Morgan was elected by a joint meeting of Labour Assembly Members and the party's Welsh Executive. He was later formally elected by the Assembly, but the electoral college procedure was not repeated. Similarly in Scotland the original conception of the electoral college had to be abandoned following Donald Dewar's sudden death in October 2000. The provisions of the Scotland Act required a successor to be in place within 28 days and Henry McLeish was thus elected at a joint meeting of Labour MSPs and the Scottish Executive (Mitchell, 2001). The electoral college was convened later to endorse his appointment. When McLeish himself was forced to resign the following year, Jack McConnell was elected unopposed to succeed him by a similar joint meeting. But this time there was no electoral college endorsement. The experiences in Scotland and Wales therefore raised some awkward questions, not only about the legitimacy of electoral college arrangements, but also whether they were practical when the party was in office.

SELECTING THE GLA AND LONDON MAYOR

The controversies over selections for the European Parliament and the Welsh party leader created new sensitivities. These were further aggravated by the process for choosing candidates for the next major new institution created by the government: the Greater London Authority (GLA). This was to comprise an Assembly and a directly elected mayor. The establishment of the GLA was approved in principle in a referendum in May 1998, with the elections due to be held two years later.

In fact the procedures to select candidates for the Assembly itself were relatively unproblematic. This matter was, again, delegated to the NEC, in consultation with the Greater London Regional Executive, and followed the precedent of the Scottish and Welsh selections. The joint Executives agreed the detail of the selection procedure and then shared responsibility for running it. There was a panel of approved candidates from whom local parties could choose, with applications to the panel being managed by a joint NEC/regional selections board.[7] The Assembly was to comprise just 25 members, with 14 representing large constituencies (each comprising roughly six Westminster seats) plus 11 elected from London-wide lists to ensure proportionality. To select the former, GLA constituencies were twinned on the Scottish and Welsh model.[8] Each London CLP could nominate from the approved panel, and those nominated formed the shortlist. The final selection of one male and one female candidate was made by an OMOV postal ballot. This process ran smoothly, although there were some initial concerns about members who had been excluded from the panel.[9] More problematic was the selection of the candidates for the list, which was done by the selection board with no reference to the membership. However, the opportunity was taken here to rebalance the absence of ethnic minority candidates in constituency seats, with black candidates in three of the top four positions.[10]

The most problematic part of the process related to the procedure for selecting the mayoral candidate. From the start it was likely that Ken Livingstone MP – former leader of the Greater London Council (GLC) abolished by the Thatcher government in 1986 – would want to stand. It was clear that his candidacy, given his left-wing credentials and difficult relationships with many colleagues, would not be welcomed by the leadership. But he was a popular figure in the party and made a strong start by publishing a personal manifesto for the job in August 1998 (D'Arcy and Maclean, 2000). Given how obvious it was that Livingstone would stand, the leadership committed a tactical error in not starting their search for a more sympathetic candidate far earlier. Instead broadcaster Trevor Phillips announced his candidacy in March 1999, followed by transport minister Glenda Jackson MP in July, minister for London Nick Raynsford MP in October and, a few days later, Secretary of State for Health Frank Dobson MP. Once Dobson had announced his candidacy, Raynsford and Phillips withdrew.

The expectation had been that the selection of the mayoral candidate would be by an OMOV ballot of London members. In June 1998 this proposal had been backed by the Greater London Labour Party conference. In May 1999 it had received ministerial support from Nick Raynsford in the House of Commons (Alderman, 2000; Shaw, 2001). However, there were concerns in leadership circles that even as big a figure as Frank Dobson would not be able to beat Ken Livingstone in a straight ballot, given Livingstone's head start in the campaign. An electoral college (supported in principle by some more traditional elements as it retained a clear trade union role) was thought likelier to favour Dobson. Consequently this mechanism was proposed by party General Secretary Margaret McDonagh to the NEC in November 1999. The left, which had by now been converted to OMOV, since it was resulting in support for leadership critics, tried to resist the electoral college system. But despite the protestations of their representatives on the NEC, this was the system chosen, rather than OMOV (Davies, 2001).

Two elements of the electoral college design were controversial. Like the national college it would be based on thirds, with a ballot of members making up one section. In the affiliates' section however, in a repeat of what happened in Scotland and Wales, there would be no requirement to ballot. The elected members' section, meanwhile, would include Assembly candidates, plus London MPs and MEPs. However this decision, whilst it might be appropriate when electing the national leader, made little rational sense for what was essentially a local government body. There was no clear justification for including MPs and MEPs in the college, when the group the mayor was most likely to work with was Labour councillors. The only possible logic for this construction was that the members included in the college were expected to support Dobson.[11] Thus with respect to both this and the affiliates' section it seemed that the electoral college had been designed specifically to deny Ken Livingstone the chance to stand as Labour mayor.

The other contentious point about the process was the use of a selection panel to vet candidates. This ran contrary to the wishes of the London conference, which had proposed that any candidate nominated by at least 10 CLPs should automatically gain a place on the ballot paper. This would have virtually guaranteed a place to Livingstone. However, the notion of a vetting panel was agreed by the Regional Executive in November 1998 and then endorsed by the NEC (D'Arcy and Maclean, 2000). The membership of this panel, agreed later, was to be five from the Regional Executive, five from the NEC and four 'independents'. Once the decision had been taken that there would be vetting, media and party attention focussed on whether it would be used to block Livingstone's candidacy. This controversy raged for months, with Livingstone suggesting that 'this is not my campaign to be mayor, it is my campaign to be allowed to stand'.[12] By the time the panel finally met, in November 1999, the leadership clearly thought it was not politically possible to block Livingstone in this way. Consequently there were briefings from Downing Street that Tony Blair was happy to see him included. However, at the interview itself the panel were not satisfied with some of his answers. Livingstone complained that 'I went in there knowing that the PM had decided I would be allowed to stand ... [but] they had developed a mind of their own' (quoted in D'Arcy and Maclean, 2000, p. 133). Only after a further interview two days later, and a statement from Dobson that he would withdraw if Livingstone was not shortlisted, was his candidacy accepted. This resulted in a shortlist of three: Livingstone, Dobson and Glenda Jackson.

The remaining difficulties with the selection focussed largely on two issues. One was access to membership lists, with complaints from other candidates that Dobson had been unfairly advantaged by being passed lists from head office, in contravention of the rules.[13] The other was the voting in the affiliates' section. Here several trade unions had been excluded for being in arrears with their payments to the London party, and there were suspicions that eligibility dates had been set selectively to exclude those supporting Livingstone.[14] The issue of balloting was also once again central to the controversy. However, given the growing sensitivities, most affiliates in this case had chosen to ballot. Of those that did, only two – socialist societies Poale Zion and the Fabian Society, each with a tiny proportion of the votes – supported Dobson. But he won the support of two larger affiliates that had not balloted. These were the South London Co-op and, again, the previously pro-OMOV AEEU (Alderman, 2000).

When the results were announced in February 2000 they showed the narrowest of victories for Dobson. Glenda Jackson was eliminated on the first ballot and once her votes had been redistributed he won 51.5 per cent to Livingstone's 48.5 per cent. But, like Alun Michael in Wales, Dobson had not won the support of grassroots members – gaining 40.1 per cent to Livingstone's 59.9 per cent of their votes. Given the huge controversy there had been over the selection methods, and Livingstone's perceived popularity, this was actually a remarkably narrow result – raising questions about whether Dobson would have had a better chance in a straight OMOV contest. In contrast to the situation in Wales, Livingstone had also won 72 per cent in the affiliates' section. Dobson's victory thus depended on the two affiliates that had not balloted (between them controlling eight per cent of the total vote), and his 86.5 per cent support in the dubiously-constructed elected members' section of the college (Alderman, 2000).

Once again, questionable democratic practices inside the party had got the leadership in trouble, and the difficulties over the selection process spilled over into the election itself. Having been denied the candidacy despite the support of a majority of members, Livingstone chose to fight the election as an independent. This resulted in his expulsion from the party. Nonetheless, his victory in the mayoral election was overwhelming. On the first ballot he won 40.5 per cent of the vote, whilst Dobson came third, behind the Conservatives, on 13.8 per cent. Many party members did not see Dobson as the legitimate candidate, given the outcome of the members' ballot, and either refused to campaign or even campaigned surreptitiously for Livingstone. Even before his humiliation at the polls Frank Dobson had admitted that the selection process 'could hardly have been handled any worse'.[15]

PARLIAMENTARY SELECTIONS

Although most changes to formal selection rules made after 1993 related to choosing candidates for other bodies, there were also some significant changes to the process for selecting parliamentary candidates. The basic structure of the OMOV ballot in local constituencies remained untouched, but some other elements first trialled in these other selections were imported.

The most important of these was the adoption, in advance of the 2001 election (and thereafter remaining in place), of a panel of pre-approved candidates. This was presented as an alternative to the traditional system whereby the NEC would endorse parliamentary candidates after they had been selected locally. The NEC's endorsement had usually been a formality, though at times it had led to difficulties when there were allegations of impropriety or candidates' unsuitability on other grounds.[16] Although these instances were few they could lead to public conflicts and embarrassment, given that the chosen candidate was by this time already publicly known. This applied most acutely in byelections, when the national media were focussed on the constituency, and the NEC was keen to see a candidate who would stand up to rigorous scrutiny. Thus the 1988 conference had agreed a rule change that required constituencies where there was a byelection contest to choose from a shortlist drawn up by the NEC.[17] This, alongside the later events in Scotland, Wales and London, had helped prepare the ground for introducing a panel at national level.

The idea of a pre-approved panel for all parliamentary selections had been around the party for some years. The consultation on parliamentary selection in 1990 had canvassed opinion on the idea, but the responses were split (Labour Party, 1990). The 1991 conference had then endorsed the principle, but it was not put into effect. In 1993 the idea was dropped by the NEC until after the next general election. Several prominent NEC members were uneasy about it, on the basis that a panel might exclude good local candidates from contesting their own seat if they had not had the foresight to apply nationally. The trade unions meanwhile suspected that a panel would interfere with their own processes for promoting favoured candidates.

The debate was reignited however in 1995 when the NEC received complaints that the selected candidate in Leeds North East, Liz Davies, should not be endorsed. Having carried out an investigation which considered her background as a councillor in Islington, and her association with the hard-left publication *Labour Briefing*, the NEC concluded 'that on the basis of her stated views and track record, Liz Davies is not a suitable Labour candidate' (Labour Party, 1995, p. 69). She was consequently blocked from standing for office.[18] This matter was the subject of a public and very acrimonious debate at that year's party conference. The proponents of a panel argued that the pain caused all round could have been avoided if the NEC's role was to vet candidates before, rather than after, they had been through the local selection process.

The question was thus returned to after the 1997 election, as part of the overall review of the parliamentary selection process. By this point the use of panels had already been relatively easily agreed for the Scottish Parliament and Welsh Assembly although, as we have seen, their operation was in practice controversial. The compromise proposal from the NEC's selections taskforce was that an 'open' panel should be introduced, whereby aspirant candidates would be encouraged to apply but not required to do so. If a member not on the panel sought selection in a constituency they would not carry the 'mark of approval', and the CLP would thus risk greater danger that they failed to get post-selection endorsement by the NEC. Additional incentives would include the circulation to candidates on the panel of information about vacancies and invitations to training events. This compromise met some of the aspirations of those who had championed a 'closed' panel, but also dealt with the concerns of their opponents. The trade unions were reassured by the fact that they would be allowed to run parallel selection processes, with their own panels of approved candidates given equal status to that of party. As the panel was 'open' this avoided allegations, such as those that had occurred in Scotland and Wales, that it could be used to bar members on grounds of their political

views. With these concessions the policy was agreed by the conference in 1998.

The panel process helped introduce the same professionalised
approach to Westminster selections as had been already introduced
elsewhere. The party produced an application pack for aspirant
candidates, including a job description, person specification and
standard application form. The required qualities included experience in the party, strategic thinking, advocacy and campaigning
skills.[19] Interviews were to be carried out by a three person panel,
which in each case comprised a member of the NEC, member of the
relevant Regional Executive, and an 'independent' and experienced
member of the party. Forms were initially marked blind by two
assessors, with only those scoring above a minimum standard
invited for interview. Those passing this hurdle then attended a 20
minute interview and completed a written test. Marks from these
three elements were combined to give a final score which
determined whether the applicant was accepted to the panel.

This was a new departure in comparison to previous application
procedures. As with other post-1997 selections it represented an
attempt to apply equal opportunities procedures and profess-
ionalise the process. However, the panel arrangements remained
flexible and in practice have had limited impact on the type of
candidates selected. Despite the initial suspicions, the panel in its
present form would be an ineffective political screening tool. The
volume of applications (around 1,300 prior to the 2001 general
election) and brevity of interviews mean it would be difficult to
identify politically troublesome candidates, and – despite the
original aspirations of some – the strict marking system did not
provide for this. In any case members rejected by the panel continue
to be able to seek selection in constituencies, and all candidates still
require post-selection endorsement by the NEC. The new system
thus offers little protection to the Executive, or to local parties and
candidates. The NEC can still refuse endorsement to any candidate,
even if they have already been 'pre-screened'. But in practice the
fact that candidates have already been through one 'approval'
process probably makes them more difficult to block. Indeed in one
case for the 2005 election the NEC even chose to endorse a
candidate in a safe Labour seat who had been refused for the
party's own panel, but had won a place on a panel run by one of its
affiliates.[20]

Another area where the NEC has not regained its old authority over the selection process concerns the reselection of MPs. Mandatory reselection was a core demand of the CLPD in the 1970s and its agreement in 1980 marked a significant shift of power to activists (as described in the previous chapter). Although this power has since been modified, it has not been completely reversed. The first change came in 1982, when conference agreed that constituencies which had a sitting MP could if they wished draw up a shortlist of one, comprising only the MP. In 1991 a 'trigger' mechanism was agreed whereby local party members would be balloted on whether a full reselection should be held. The CLPD vigorously opposed this change, on the basis that it effectively required members to cast a vote of no confidence in their MP, rather than making reselection a routine matter. Nonetheless the mechanism was approved by the party conference. In 1993, in part due to boundary changes (meaning that some MPs' seats had significantly changed) there was a return to the previous mandatory rule. One MP was deselected before the 1997 election.[21] In recent years a compromise has been developed, whereby the MP is considered automatically reselected if he or she receives a majority of the total nominations. This also has resulted in some deselections.[22] A modified form of mandatory reselection, balanced by OMOV, has thus become an established part of local selection procedures.

OMOV'S RETURN, 2001–04

The controversy over the selections for Europe, the Scottish Parliament, Welsh Assembly and GLA were widely seen to have damaged the party. Critical stories in the news media about 'control freakery' and 'stitch ups' fuelled cynicism amongst the membership, with evidence of members refusing to participate in election campaigns, or withdrawing their support altogether. This atmosphere also influenced public perceptions of the party and, many believed, contributed to Labour's poor results in these elections. Although Tony Blair's preferred candidates had been selected as Welsh leader and London mayoral candidate, the price paid had therefore been very high. Meanwhile OMOV, whilst it had been initially viewed with scepticism by many on the left of the party, had become a touchstone – seen by activists as far preferable to selection outcomes decided by trade union leaders or elected

Labour representatives, either of whom were potentially receptive to pressure from the party leader to support particular candidates.

The need to rebuild confidence in the selection process was thus widely recognised, particularly after Labour's humiliation in the London mayoral election of May 2000. Following this, Downing Street consented to a review, to be carried out by the NEC's Organisation Committee. The results of a consultation with the party were reported to the annual conference in autumn 2000 in the document *21st Century Party*. This set out four principles for future selections, proposing that these should:

- 'be consistent, transparent and fair
- encourage equality of opportunity, increasing the number of women and ethnic minority candidates
- ensure accountability of elected representatives
- be clear, simple and easy to administer' (Labour Party, 2000, p. 40).

The document proposed that OMOV would be the norm for selections, including for Westminster, the European Parliament, constituency representatives in the devolved institutions, and directly elected mayors. For 'major selections' – of the party leader, deputy leader, Welsh and Scottish party leaders – an electoral college would continue to be used. But affiliates would be required to ballot and split their votes accordingly. These proposals therefore took the party back to the basic principles agreed in 1993, but applied them across the board to the new constitutional arrangements. The exception would remain the selection of candidates for top-up lists in Scotland, Wales and London, who would continue to be chosen by a board that was 'representative of stakeholders', rather than by an OMOV ballot (Labour Party, 2000, p. 48). This was the only element which could be seen to be open to leadership manipulation. As an improvement on the practice of previous years, these principles were broadly welcomed. Thus a rule change was agreed by the conference in 2001 stating that OMOV 'shall be adopted in all selections where reasonably practicable, including those where an electoral college is used'.

For the second elections in Scotland and Wales, which took place in 2003, the changes had little impact in practice, as most candidates simply fought their existing seats and the leaders in both cases remained unchanged. The same applied to members of the Greater London Assembly. The major changes were seen in the selection of

Labour's candidates for the second London mayoral election and the next European Elections, both held in June 2004.

The London mayoral selection remained dominated by the personality of Ken Livingstone, and the ability of the party to find a candidate who could defeat him now he had become established as a popular independent mayor. Livingstone's preferred solution was that he should be readmitted to membership of the party and fight the election as a Labour candidate. However, this not only contravened the party's rules (since members who had stood for election against the party were barred for a period of at least five years), it was also against the express wishes of the party leader. Blair had campaigned vigorously against Livingstone ever since he had first sought the Labour nomination in 1998; and once elected, Livingstone had consistently challenged the government over matters such as the Public Private Partnership for the London tube. When his application for readmission was considered by the NEC in July 2002, members were thus under considerable pressure from Downing Street to deny him membership. His application was narrowly rejected, by 17 votes to 13.

This same NEC meeting agreed the selection process for Labour's candidate. Despite the earlier commitment to use OMOV for mayoral selections, the rules were sufficiently general to allow an adapted electoral college to be adopted. This time the discredited elected members' section would be omitted, and instead the college would comprise two equal halves: one for party members, to be run by OMOV, and the other for affiliates, who were required to ballot and cast their votes proportionately. This was a curiously pragmatic solution with no obvious precedent, denying any special role to London Assembly members. Whilst a 50:50 college had earlier been favoured by some (notably John Smith) for electing the leader, the unions would have been the partner to have lost out. However, with no suggestion of bias to suit a particular candidate, this was accepted by the London Labour Party in a relaxed way.

The ballot itself was held in October 2002 and there were three contenders: Labour's deputy mayor Nicky Gavron, former Sports Minister Tony Banks MP, and Bob Shannon, a trade union official. Although not formally a contender, Livingstone's presence dominated the contest, as Gavron was seen to be close to him whilst Banks was overtly hostile. Even more than during the previous selection the need to reach the roughly 40,000 London Labour Party members, plus members of affiliated organisations, was essential to the candidates. As far as possible they sought coverage in the *Evening Standard* and other London media, as well as targeting members directly. To avoid a repetition of previous problems candidates were provided with membership lists. This potentially enabled them to set up telephone banks to contact members, as well as circulating leaflets and letters.[23] However this was an expensive process and Gavron's campaign cost £41,451 – around half of which was spent on mailings.[24] She won in both sections of the electoral college, with a total vote of 52.2 per cent.[25]

The spectre of Ken Livingstone could not, however, be banished, even after the selection contest was over. Controversy continued about his possible readmission to the party, particularly as Labour continued to do badly in London opinion polls. Throughout the latter months of 2003 there were regular news stories, apparently based on Downing Street briefings, that Blair now wanted Livingstone back in the party. This matter was thus put again to the NEC in December 2003. Nicky Gavron had been persuaded to withdraw her candidacy in favour of Ken Livingstone, and did so on the day of the meeting. Once again under pressure from the leader the NEC reversed its previous decision and this time happily voted to accept Livingstone's application, by 25 votes to 2. Tony Blair had in one respect got his way, but only through finally accepting a candidate that he had earlier vigorously opposed.

The ironies of the situation did not, however, end there. London members, having chosen their candidate in a democratic process, were now stripped of that candidate and instead asked to accept the leader's choice – albeit that this was the candidate many of them had wanted in the first place. To lessen the blow the NEC agreed to run a confirmatory ballot of members and affiliates using the same 50:50 electoral college that had been used in 2002. However, by consent of both the NEC and Ken Livingstone, affiliates would not be required to ballot. Livingstone won 93.9 per cent of votes cast, including 100 per cent of trade union votes.

The selection of Labour's European Parliamentary candidates was carried out to the same timetable as the London mayoral selection. In a reversal of the 1999 procedure, the final ranking of regional lists was now to be by an OMOV ballot. With the traumatic change in the electoral system passed, this was a far easier process.[26] However, it did retain a significant amount of central control. A closed panel of interested candidates was established, with interviews conducted by selection boards created at a regional level. These selection

boards were also responsible for shortlisting candidates to go
forward to the final ballot. Nominations of both sitting MEPs and
new candidates were invited from constituencies. Those MEPs
nominated were then guaranteed the top seats on the list in their
region, with new candidates to compete for the lower ranking
positions. The role of the OMOV ballot was therefore to rank the
sitting MEPs (where there was more than one in a region) and
separately rank the new candidates. As in the London mayoral
selection, campaigning for this ballot presented candidates with a
major organisational and financial challenge. New candidates were
primarily competing for unwinnable positions, yet to maximise
their chance of success they needed to circulate literature to large
numbers of members in the region. In London, the largest region,
the cost of circulating a leaflet to all members was roughly £15,000.[27]
Those candidates who did not circulate such literature came bottom
in the members' ballot.

EVALUATION

More than a decade after the historic 1993 decision to adopt OMOV,
Labour's selection processes appear to have reached a more or less
stable settlement. As in the 1980s the balance of control tipped
temporarily – this time to the leadership, that time to the activists –
but a natural system of rebalancing led to a process that both sides
eventually seemed able to live with. The main selection processes
since 1993 are summarised in Tables 4.1 and 4.2. The changes that
have taken place contribute to an increasing convergence between
the three main British parties over selection processes – a factor
which may further add to their stability.[28] However, the electoral
college remains a uniquely Labour phenomenon that continues to
reflect the party's traditional federal structure.

Developments in this period within the Labour Party demonstrate some of the same features discussed in the previous chapter.
Again, developments were gradual, with a principle conceded in
one site of negotiation going on to be applied in others. The import
of the electoral college for leader into the new arrangements in
Scotland, Wales and London is an example of this phenomenon, as
is the creeping use of panels of approved candidates. In some cases
this is an example of pragmatism – if a system has been shown to
work then it can be reapplied. But there are also frequent examples
of precedent being cited by the supporters of a particular reform. It

generally proved hard to resist a principle once it had been conceded in another forum.

The biggest and most robust principle has of course proved to be that of OMOV itself. Once members had been given control over the selection of candidates they soon became reluctant to give it up – indeed the pressure has been for it to be extended. This has continued to undermine the principle of representative democracy in the party, with a growing emphasis on the rights of the individual member.

Table 4.1: Processes for selecting Labour candidates since 1993

	A. Parliament	B. European Parliament	C. Scottish Parliament/ Welsh Assembly	D. Greater London Assembly
Approved panel	To 1997: none Since 1998: open panel (self nomination)	Closed panel (self nomination)	Closed panel (self nomination)	Closed panel (self nomination)
Nomination	By branches and local affiliates	By CLPs, from names on panel	Constituency: by branches and local affiliates, from names on panel List: none	Constituency: by branches and local affiliates, from names on panel List: none
Shortlisting	By local General Committee	By regional selection board	Constituency: as A List: As B	Constituency: as A List: As B
Final selection or ranking (in case of lists)	At all-member meeting (with limited postal votes)	For 1999: by regional selection board For 2004: by postal OMOV ballot	Constituency: as A List: by regional selection board	Constituency: as A List: by regional selection board

One of the most interesting features of the period since 1993 was the almost complete reversal of attitudes by many in the party towards OMOV. Initially favoured by leaders who wanted to circumvent activists and sought involvement of less active members whom they believed would be more compliant, OMOV did not perform as expected in some settings (see particularly Chapter 7). It thus came to be viewed by the leadership with increasing suspicion. At the same time it became a cause increasingly backed by those elements on the party's left who had initially most opposed it. Activists defended the principle against trade union incursion and centralised panels. Meanwhile Tony Blair, who had been one of OMOV's most hardline proponents up to 1993, came to see the benefit of the traditional 'old Labour' fix of the trade union block vote when there were candidates he wanted to see elected. In contests where affiliates were not required to ballot, his most loyal supporters in this endeavour proved to be the AEEU, one of the unions that formerly most stridently supported OMOV. This demonstrates the extent to which all groups tended to act instrumentally – supporting the system that they thought was most likely to deliver their own desired outcome. Both leader and activists were willing to abandon previously valued democratic principles if this suited their immediate needs. The Ken Livingstone saga also provides some nice examples. Livingstone abhorred stitch-ups – except, that is, where they would deliver him the candidacy he wanted.

Despite the growing scepticism of the leadership the OMOV principle proved itself in this period to be almost irreversible. The leader's attempts to use electoral colleges to deliver 'reliable' candidates repeatedly ended in trouble. In the light of Blair's conduct the media, and through them the public, expressed sympathy with activists' claims that the principle of OMOV should be defended. This became a major issue in the electoral campaigns in Wales and London and was seen to damage the party's popularity. It also resulted in a withdrawal of support by many activists, when the leadership needed it most. The later reversion to the OMOV principle under these pressures demonstrated the constraints on leadership power, including the influence of actors outside the party on debates about its internal democracy.

Whilst Labour's founding principle of representative democracy has been severely questioned in this period by the acceptance of OMOV, to a lesser extent so too has the principle of federal decision making. The use of electoral colleges for choosing individual party leaders has come to appear increasingly fragile, and the difficulties encountered in Wales and London may presage other future problems. In these examples the electoral college was controversial in itself, but this reached crisis point when the results in its different sections were in conflict. In particular there were protests about candidates' legitimacy when they had not won the support of a majority in the members' section (just as there had been in the late 1980s with respect to the local electoral college). Such a situation has not occurred at the national level since the deputy leadership election of 1981, when Tony Benn won amongst CLPs but lost in the other two sections of the electoral college. However, since this predated the OMOV rule, the CLP vote could be considered to some extent unrepresentative. Were such a result achieved today the legitimacy of trade union involvement, in particular, might well be brought into question. A close result in the future would therefore probably result in pressure from members to switch to a pure OMOV system. A sudden change of leader in office – as occurred in Scotland and Wales – might on the other hand lead to pressures for a quick election by the PLP. [29]

Table 4.2: Processes for selecting Labour leaders since 1993

	A. National leader	B. Scottish / Welsh leader*	D. London mayoral candidate
Nomination	By members of PLP	Self nomination	Self nomination
Vetting panel?	No	No	Yes
Electoral college	College of thirds comprising: - MPs and MEPs - affiliates, balloting compulsory - OMOV ballot of members	College of thirds comprising: - MPs, MEPs and MSPs/AMs (or candidates) - affiliates, balloting not compulsory - block votes of local parties (1999 in Wales: OMOV ballot)	2000: college of thirds comprising - MPs, MEPs and GLA candidates - affiliates, balloting not compulsory - OMOV ballot of members 2002: college of halves comprising - affiliates, balloting compulsory - OMOV ballot of members

* But note that these procedures were not followed in the special circumstances in 2000 and 2001 – see page 77.

Another important change illustrated by this chapter is the extent to which the party has become less rule based, with fewer detailed decisions on organisation debated at the annual conference. The process after 1997 became much more difficult to influence, as decisions were largely delegated to the NEC. This represents a major change compared to the very public discussion of OMOV up to 1993. The closed nature of the decision-making process offered few opportunities for the kind of groups that had lobbied at earlier stages to gather support for particular positions. Had the debates been more public some of the positions adopted, such as trade union votes without balloting, or the selection of list candidates by closed selection panels, might never have been agreed.

A new principle that came to be applied in this period was that of equal opportunities, with professionalisation of the selection process and attempts to score candidates against set criteria using modern personnel recruitment methods. This was in part a response to the new legal environment, described in the next chapter. There were some attempts to pass these methods down to local parties, although probably with limited success. The extent to which the qualities needed in a candidate can be minutely specified remains dubious, when one of the strengths of parliaments and assemblies is the diversity of their membership and the many different roles that their members may choose to pursue.

Although the OMOV process has come to be valued by party activists, it has not been without problems. It was followed by a loosening of the rules with respect to candidates' access to membership lists and ability to circulate literature, as in practice these have proved difficult to police. This has sharply raised the cost to candidates of competing in selection contests, particularly across large geographic areas. This raises questions about equal opportunities, and about the ability of members to identify any outstanding candidates. As NEC member Eddie Haigh presciently suggested to the conference in 1989: 'With the introduction of one member one vote the scope for members with financial resources to mount a concerted campaign for their selection could well be a threat to the basic democracy of the party. Candidates must be selected on merit and not on their ability to produce glossy literature' (Labour Party, 1989, p. 145-6). The danger of these biases is growing, particularly in contests covering entire regions, where postal OMOV has been used. In these cases the problems identified early on by the CLPD (now thoroughly committed to OMOV) of media influence in internal party selections are also a potential problem. Despite all the flaws of the systems used to select list candidates to date, a system based on a transparent representative principle would probably be fairer to less telegenic or less wealthy candidates than is OMOV. These are issues that deserve further research, and raise difficulties that Labour, and the other British parties, have yet properly to address.

Notes

1. Just 13 of Labour's 84 MEPs at that time were women. However, following the party's industrial tribunal defeat in 1996 over quotas for selection (see Chapter 5) it was not felt possible to restrict local parties to nominating only new *female* candidates. It was the addition to the pool of the large number of new candidates – half of them men – that caused many of the difficulties that followed.
2. These panels were in practice dominated by representatives of the national party. Each comprised five NEC members, three members appointed by the relevant Regional Executive Committee, one national trade union representative, one ethnic minority member and the General Secretary.
3. See Wring, Baker and Seawright (2000).
4. In particular it was later noted that only three of the 16 MEPs who had signed a statement in 1995 criticising Tony Blair's decision to rewrite Clause IV went on to obtain winnable seats (Shaw, 2001).
5. Most of the remainder had decided to retire or leave the parliament voluntarily rather than compete in the selection process, although there were also two (Ken Coates and Hugh Kerr) who had resigned from the party in December 1997, before the process began.
6. See Bradbury and Mitchell (2001), Osmond (2000). The fact that Michael was forced out was generally seen as linked to dissatisfaction with the previous leadership contest and poor results in the Assembly elections. Osmond points out that 21 of the 28 Labour Assembly members had been Morgan supporters.
7. The use of an approved panel in fact had precedent for such elections, not only because the GLA was considered as an extension of local government, but also because a similar system had previously been used for screening Labour's candidates for the GLC.
8. See Chapter 5.
9. One notable case was Lee Jasper, who went on to become a race adviser to Ken Livingstone. However, his exclusion could be justified on the simple grounds that he did not have the requisite 12 months' party membership.
10. Trevor Phillips, David Lammy and Jeanette Arnold were at numbers one, three and four respectively.
11. Not least because within the elected members' section how individuals cast their vote would be publicly recorded, as it was in the leadership electoral college.
12. *Evening Standard*, 8 Feb 1999 – quoted in Alderman (2000, p. 746).

13. For details see D'Arcy and Maclean (2000); Davies (2001).
14. These included the RMT, ASLEF and MSF. The latter launched a formal legal challenge, but lost.
15. *Scotsman*, 21 Feb 2000 – quoted in Alderman (2000, p. 737).
16. In the 1950s the NEC regularly chose not to endorse candidates, generally those from the left. The sensitivities this caused, coupled with the growing strength of the left on the NEC, led to a less interventionist system from the mid 1960s onwards – see Shaw (1988).
17. See Shaw 1994. Though note that the rules far earlier had given the NEC extra powers with respect to byelection candidates, even including the choice of the candidate – see McKenzie (1963, pp. 551-2).
18. Ironically, Liz Davies was later elected to the NEC – see Chapter 7.
19. Shaw (2001) has criticised this process for not putting emphasis on Labour MPs' scrutiny role, including their scrutiny of Labour governments. However, whilst dedication to independent-minded scrutiny is undoubtedly an important attribute in MPs, it is doubtful whether the party's selection arrangements have ever sought to encourage it.
20. Linda Riordan was a member of staff of the left-wing MP for Halifax, Alice Mahon, and won the selection contest to replace her when she retired. Riordan had won endorsement from the Co-operative Party (affiliated to Labour), despite having been rejected for the party's own panel. The June 2004 meeting of the NEC voted to let her stand nonetheless.
21. David Young in Bolton South East.
22. In 2003 members in Tooting voted to open up the selection procedure to other candidates and MP Tom Cox withdrew from the contest. In 2004 Jane Griffiths was deselected in Reading East.
23. The number of mailings candidates were allowed was limited. No such limits applied, however, to local parliamentary selections in the run-up to the 2005 election.
24. I am grateful to Nicky Gavron for having provided this figure, based on her official declaration of expenses submitted to the party.
25. This figure follows Bob Shannon's elimination from the ballot in the first round. Tony Banks achieved 44.6 per cent.
26. Though the number of British seats did decline from 84 to 78 as a result of European enlargement.
27. This is an approximate cost, based on printing a colour leaflet, purchasing envelopes and stamps, and buying labels from the party. In practice some candidates sent out their leaflets jointly to cut costs.
28. Both the Conservatives and Liberal Democrats already used OMOV for local selections, and centrally approved panels of candidates (Norris and Lovenduski, 1995). Similarly, in 1998 the Conservatives followed Labour by widening selection of their leader beyond the parliamentary party (Kelly, 2003). Though see below for their 2003 contest.

29. This is exactly what happened to the Conservatives in 2003 when Iain Duncan-Smith was replaced by Michael Howard. Despite the earlier commitments to membership ballots, the contest was managed so that only one candidate emerged from the parliamentary party. This ensured that no ballot was necessary.

5

Women in the Party: The Quiet Revolution

One of the most remarkable changes to Labour's organisation during the 1990s was the increased representation of women at every level of the party. This had a profound impact both on Labour's culture and its external image. Nothing was more symbolic of the party's 'newness' than the image of Tony Blair as prime minister with the massed ranks of 101 Labour women MPs in May 1997. Yet the reforms that brought this situation about had not been championed by Blair, nor indeed by Neil Kinnock. Both leaders had been distinctly lukewarm about the proposals for women's quotas which transformed the face of the party (though John Smith was far more positive).

This chapter traces the changes with respect to women's representation in the party from the early 1980s. At this time feminist activists aligned with the party's left put women's representation onto the agenda, protesting at Labour's traditional masculine ethos. The organisational changes that they demanded were largely resisted by the party leadership, as they would have benefited the left. Nonetheless activists did succeed in getting a measure requiring women on parliamentary shortlists voted into the party's rules for the first time. Subsequently a broader coalition of women, with a strong base in the trade unions, gathered support for a radical package of internal party quotas. Given the lengthy disputes with women on the left this was seized upon as a compromise and accepted almost immediately. This then created an environment from which increased women's representation in elected office – a far more challenging objective – could more effectively be agreed. Continued pressure from women in the party, many of whom now held senior positions, crucially coupled with the perceived electoral benefits of fielding women candidates, led this principle also to be agreed. It then went on to become firmly established, and applied in new forums such as the Scottish Parliament and National Assembly for Wales.

It was thus women activists who took the initiative for pressing increased women's representation. Although the original protagonists achieved few of their demands, and were initially sceptical of some of the solutions that came to be agreed, their actions helped set off a chain of events that fundamentally changed the party.

WOMEN IN THE PARTY IN THE 1980S

Henry Drucker (1979) provided a classic and well-respected account of Labour's ethos. However, as Sarah Perrigo has pointed out, this analysis was blind to one central feature: the party's masculine culture. As she suggests, the traditional model of the Labour activist was 'the male unionised industrial worker' (1995, p. 408). The party had been built by and closely modelled on the organisation of the trade unions, which were themselves overwhelmingly male. Although it had a separate women's organisation (descended from the pre-1918 affiliate the Women's Labour League), women remained poorly represented in the party's main structures even by the 1970s (Hills, 1981). And despite Labour's record for women's parliamentary representation being proportionately better than that of the Conservatives, defeat in the 1979 general election resulted in a drop from 18 Labour women MPs to just 11.[1] Meanwhile the new Conservative leader, Margaret Thatcher, though not sympathetic to feminist demands, helped boost the 'women friendly' image of the new party of government.

Many on the party's left were already sympathetic to the demands of the feminist movement, but the drop in Labour women MPs at this election put the issue of women's representation more firmly on the agenda. In 1980 the CLPD established a 'Women's Action Committee' (WAC), arguing that 'extending democracy within the party meant nothing ... if it could not be extended to the large body of women effectively disenfranchised and largely excluded from the party's powerful policy and decision-making bodies'.[2] The organisation was formally founded jointly by Vera Derer (wife of CLPD founder Vladimir Derer) and Frances Morrell. It quickly became a magnet for feminist women in the party and included, for example, Rhona Brankin, Harriet Harman, Clare Short and Glenys Thornton amongst its early members. For many years WAC's key organiser was Ann Pettifor. In 1983 it took on an independent existence, though remaining affiliated to the CLPD. Until becoming associated with the 'hard' left in the later 1980s, the organisation also worked co-operatively with many women in the LCC.

The Women's Action Committee adopted three central demands, which it sought to progress through the party. The annual women's conference, which by the early 1980s had come to be dominated by the feminist left, was used to put these onto the agenda. Two demands related to the rights of the women's conference itself, and were aimed at strengthening not only women but also the left. WAC argued (as had the women of the right when they dominated it in the 1970s) that the women's conference should have the right to place a number of motions on the main annual conference agenda. They also proposed that the women's section of the NEC, originally a concession to the Women's Labour League when it merged with the party, should be 'reclaimed' by women and elected at the women's conference. Instead since their creation under the 1918 constitution these NEC seats had been elected by annual conference as a whole – a body that was overwhelmingly male and dominated by the trade unions. On this latter point WAC was reviving a demand which had been first made by women in the 1920s, but never achieved.[3] Since then the women's seats on the NEC had come under threat. The party's 1968 Commission of Enquiry into organisational matters had proposed their abolition, and this was repeated in several key submissions to the 1980 Commission.

WAC was successful in getting its claims onto the main conference agenda on an almost annual basis throughout the 1980s, using the tactic of model resolutions.[4] However, although their proposals won support amongst many constituency activists they were consistently opposed by the NEC, and defeated by the votes of the trade union majority. It was natural for trade union delegates to want to protect their rights to vote for the women's seats on the Executive, but in this period the matter also had a special significance. These five seats were proving central to the fightback by the right of the party against left dominance on the NEC. Election by conference of women such as Gwyneth Dunwoody – a right-winger who was unsympathetic to feminist demands – to the women's section was seen as an affront by WAC women. However it was crucial to the right's success in winning back control of the Executive from 1981. Thus when WAC sought to 'discredit the process of men electing women to advance the interests of men', this was an argument about women's representation and rights tinged with a significant dose of factionalism.[5] Consequently leadership loyalists were determined not to bend to the demand. Given the current make up of the women's conference, surrendering control of the women's seats would guarantee the election of candidates from the left. Similarly, if the leadership conceded that the women's conference should place items on the annual conference agenda this would be likely to result in greater numbers of hostile resolutions.

These two demands, and the leadership response to them, illustrate the central dilemma at the heart of WAC, which never resolved whether it was above all an organisation promoting left or women's interests. This dilemma, which caused conflicts within the organisation's membership, was at its clearest when organising 'slates' for internal elections. Here some WAC activists urged support for women over men on principle, even if they were drawn from the right of the party. Others would argue that a candidate's politics was more important than their gender. Just like the CLPD, and indeed more so, WAC faced conflicts between organisational demands and affinity to a particular policy agenda. In turn the organisation's association with the left, and increasingly the 'hard' left, caused suspicion amongst leaders, who could thus dismiss its claims as motivated by a desire for factional advantage.

The conflict is clearly illustrated by WAC's third demand, which turned out to be its most successful. Since its inception the organisation had argued that, in order to redress the shortfall in women's representation in the House of Commons, the party's rules should be amended to require that all parliamentary shortlists include at least one woman, where a woman had been nominated by a local branch or affiliate. This demand was widely supported by women in the party as a moderate and badly needed step towards increasing the proportion of Labour women MPs – just 4.1 per cent in 1979 (see Table 5.1, page 110). At this time affirmative action, aside from the five reserved seats on the NEC, was not part of the party's culture. However WAC and the CLPD, inspired amongst other things by recent experience in the United States, sought to put it on the agenda.

In 1982 the demand for 'one woman on a shortlist' reached the floor of conference, but was opposed by the NEC. Replying for the Executive, Gwyneth Dunwoody argued that whilst constituencies were of course to be encouraged to include women on shortlists, it was not desirable to require them to do so. The proposal was heavily defeated.[6] Although plainly about women's representation, there were also factional undertones to the proposal as – importantly for some in the CLPD who were sympathetic to the hard left – it could help protect the opportunity to deselect right-wing MPs. Mandatory reselection of MPs before each general election had been a key CLPD achievement in 1980 (as discussed in Chapter 3), yet had been resisted by the leadership and the PLP. The following year it emerged that some local parties were avoiding full reselections by drawing up shortlists of one, comprising of only the sitting MP. At the 1982 conference the right managed – against opposition from the CLPD – to get agreement to a rule change confirming that this practice was acceptable. This significantly weakened the mandatory reselection rule. Requiring inclusion of at least one woman on every shortlist, however, would potentially prevent the practice in the vast majority of seats where the sitting MP was male. If this could be achieved it would open the door for left-wing women, in particular, to challenge the incumbency of right-wing men. Once again there were both factional and gender advantages for WAC in pursuing this proposal.

After 1982 the demand was to surface repeatedly at annual conference. Pressures in the trade unions (discussed further below) made them increasingly reluctant to be seen to block women's representation. They were also subject to vigorous internal campaigns by WAC supporters, who could work through the unions' own women's organisations to get their claims onto the agenda. In 1983 a resolution supported by WAC called for a working party to be set up to consider 'mandatory inclusion of members of disadvantaged groups on parliamentary shortlists wherever such members apply'.[7] Given promises by left-winger Jo Richardson MP on behalf of the NEC that such a group would be established, the movers of the resolution agreed to remit. But with no proposals brought by the NEC to the 1984 conference, the principle of one woman on a shortlist was again pressed to a vote. Again it was defeated.[8] The proposal was also defeated in 1985, despite the NEC having now changed its position and urged the conference to support it.[9]

By the 1986 conference sufficient support had been built, and the principle of one woman on every shortlist was finally accepted by both conference and the NEC. However, when a raft of changes to selection procedures were put to the 1987 conference (as discussed in Chapter 3) the proposal had not been implemented to the satisfaction of women activists. The package retained the right to draw up shortlists of one in seats with sitting Labour MPs, and only if there were several people on the shortlist would the 'one woman' requirement apply. This resulted in noisy protests from women delegates, which were widely reported in the press.

Thus by 1988 the one woman on a shortlist principle had become the source of significant tension, and model resolutions circulated by CLPD and WAC demanded immediate rule changes to put it into effect. A total of 27 CLPs submitted resolutions on this subject to the 1988 conference. Consequently a composite resolution was debated demanding 'one woman on every parliamentary shortlist, where a woman has been nominated'.[10] Although the NEC recommended rejecting the proposal, many trade unions now had policy to support it, and the resolution passed on a show of hands. In an unusual twist the NEC had thus been defeated on the same policy twice in three years – once for supporting it and the second time for opposing. A rule change was reluctantly tabled and supported by conference later in the week. This achievement was celebrated by many women from all wings of the party as a major victory.[11] However, it was particularly celebrated by the left, as the mandatory reselection principle had been reasserted. For the same reason it was resented by many on the right. Although the rule potentially allowed female candidates to challenge any sitting male MP, they would have little chance unless backed by hostile elements in the constituency. This implied that challenges would be mostly by the left on the right. By this time WAC itself was more sympathetic to the hard left. It circulated materials encouraging women to put themselves forward, stating that right-wing MPs with restrictive attitudes to abortion would be prime targets for deselection.

WAC had thus successfully forced the party's first positive action mechanism for women in selection. This was a significant achievement. However, the measure did not provide the parliamentary breakthrough that its supporters had hoped for, as discussed below. The factional element to the change also helped harden the attitudes of some on the right of the party, already far from enthusiastic, towards future positive action. Although many moderates saw justice in the proposals, the politics of the women's conference and of WAC activists meant that others increasingly associated greater women's representation with advances for the hard left.

During the 1980s the dynamics of the women's conference were increasingly seen as problematic by moderate and right-wing elements in the party. Whereas the conference had previously been dominated by older women from the trade unions, and had been a bastion of the traditional right, the influx of largely younger feminist women, many of them middle class, changed its complexion completely. Conflicts between these groups of women had led to a decline in attendance by the trade unions and increasing ascendancy of WAC supporters and women from the 'ultra' left, including Militant. The informal nature of the conference structure exacerbated this trend. Unlike annual conference, where trade unions were holders of up to 90 per cent of the vote, decisions at the women's conference were taken on a one delegate one vote basis. The growing numbers of left-wing women from the constituencies thus quickly outvoted the more traditional elements. In turn the lack of formal structure meant the decisions of the conference could easily be dismissed as unrepresentative by the trade union majority at annual conference, allowing its recommendations to be ignored.

By the mid 1980s moderate women in the trade unions were determined to see change, and tensions reached a climax at a particularly acrimonious women's conference on the Isle of Bute in 1986. At this point the unions offered an ultimatum: the women's conference must either change or be abandoned, as they could no longer see a benefit in participating. Consequently the 1986 annual conference agreed, on a resolution from GMB APEX, to consult on its system of voting.[12] A consultation paper was issued, with changes brought to annual conference in 1988. These created a new structure of voting at the women's conference in which constituencies had 45 per cent of votes, trade unions 50 per cent and other affiliates five per cent. The effects of this change were threefold. First, it moderated the conference and required greater negotiation between trade union and feminist women. Second, as a result, it legitimated the conference and made its decisions more difficult for the leadership to ignore. Third, as Minkin (1992) has pointed out, the new women's conference voting structure created a precedent for the smaller proportion of trade union votes which would later be adopted by annual conference itself (see Chapter 8).

FIRST STEPS: QUOTAS WITHIN THE PARTY

The first major programme of structural reform for women, which the leadership came to support, was the package of quotas within the party's internal organisation. Rather than aiming at strengthening the traditional women's organisation as a separate structure, as WAC had wanted, or immediately getting women into elected public office, this programme sought to guarantee women's presence throughout the mainstream structures of the party. It was this plan that, once proposed, was rapidly taken up – in part to defuse the long running conflicts described above.

There were a number of influences leading to the proposal of the quota programme, well summarised by Clare Short (1996), who was chair of the NEC's women's committee from 1990 to 1996. One was changes taking place in the trade unions, which were adjusting to structural changes in the economy. Women's participation in the labour market had already long been growing when the Thatcher governments of the 1980s oversaw a sharp decline in manufacturing jobs, largely held by men, and growth in service sector jobs, increasingly taken by women. Between 1979 and 1992 the number of male trade union members almost halved, whilst the number of female members remained stable.[13] In this climate it became important for the unions to shake off their traditional male-dominated image and re-evaluate their strategies to appeal to women workers. As early as 1975 the public sector union NUPE had introduced reserved seats for women on its executive, and by the early 1980s other unions were starting to consider similar action. All of this changed both the makeup and the attitudes of the trade unionists who were active in the party. A second significant influence was the practice of socialist and social democratic parties overseas, many of which were experimenting with quotas for women. The Socialist International Women, of which Clare Short became a vice president in 1992, circulated details of these experiments and actively sought to encourage change within its member parties.

The third crucial factor, which increasingly concerned party leaders from the mid 1980s, was the image of the party amongst women voters. In 1985 a Fabian pamphlet on *Winning Women's Votes* drew attention to the 'gender gap' whereby women in the electorate consistently voted Conservative in greater numbers than men. It showed that the Conservative lead over Labour amongst women had been eight per cent higher than that amongst men at the 1983 election, and a similar gender gap of nine per cent had existed in 1979 (Radice, 1985). Women voters thus became a key target group for Labour, in its fight to win back electoral ground from the Conservatives. By 1987 the party was taking active steps to appeal to women by, for example, giving women politicians a more visible role in its campaigns. At this election the gender gap almost disappeared. However, research afterwards by Labour's Shadow Communications Agency showed that women continued to view Labour as the most male-dominated of the political parties, and that even many women who shared Labour's values did not transform this support into votes. The research also showed that both male and female voters thought highly of women politicians (Hewitt and Mattinson, 1989). This suggested that there was nothing to lose and everything to gain from changing Labour's image to give women a more prominent role.

At the same time the factional battles with WAC over the role of the women's conference were continuing. WAC was not, in its early years, particularly supportive of the principle of internal quotas. In 1983 it rejected a proposal to campaign for a 50 per cent quota on the constituency and trade union seats on the NEC, preferring to seek greater control over the existing women's seats (a policy more likely to benefit the party's left). The quota proposal had been supported by the LCC in its submission to the 1980 Commission of Enquiry. WAC did, however, seek greater representation for women amongst delegates to annual conference, including on trade union delegations.[14]

The issue of internal quotas first formally reached Labour's agenda thanks to links with the Socialist International Women. In the summer of 1988 the organisation's General Secretary, Maria Jonas, was invited to speak to the Labour women's conference. Her presentation, focussing on the quota policies recently agreed in sister parties in Germany, Canada and Norway, captured the imagination of delegates. At that year's annual conference WAC organised a fringe meeting to which women from the German SPD were invited to speak, and from this point the organisation formally adopted a policy of supporting quotas. The more moderate LCC also started to actively campaign for quotas at around this time. In practical terms the work of women in existing positions of power in the party and trade unions was also vitally important in getting the policy agreed. A group of women who were women's officers of their respective unions (and responsible for implementing quotas there) started to meet regularly behind the scenes with the party's women's officer, Vicky Phillips, and to build support in the unions for change.[15]

A package of quotas had many attractions. For activists motivated by a desire to improve women's representation (rather than necessarily seeking factional gains) it promised far greater advances than had previously been proposed. For leaders it promised a new party image and greater appeal to women voters. Importantly it also offered the chance to calm the battles with WAC, without conceding to their demands. Indeed in the conflict between leaders and activists it offered yet more. Requiring fair representation of women amongst branch and constituency officers, on constituency General Committees and amongst conference delegates would help break up the power bases of the remaining hard left by bringing many new and less active members into positions of influence. This could potentially have profound effects (as discussed for example with relation to annual conference in Chapter 8). Some indeed proposed further changes that would disadvantage these groups. The LCC's 1989 commission on party democracy suggested that quotas should replace the party's traditional women's organisations which were 'prey to factional groups who use them as [a] vehicle for putting a particular line' (1989, p. 3). The commission's report suggested that a 40 per cent quota for women at all levels of the party would end the need for a women's organisation with decision-making power. In its place informal women's networks for campaigning and training purposes might be created. Although these proposals were rejected, it was likely that the party's traditional women's organ- isation would be weakened in any case, if quotas were introduced. Some saw this as an added advantage.

Despite its potential benefits the package of internal quotas that was later implemented was not actively promoted by the leader- ship. On the NEC Neil Kinnock, along with many on the traditional right, remained wary of positive action. Senior party staff including General Secretary Larry Whitty and Director of Organisation Joyce Gould were, however, actively supportive. There was thus a certain amount of covert cooperation between those inside and outside seeking change. Once the women's conference had been reformed it could be used to progress these demands, and from this point things moved quickly. The 40 per cent quota principle was first agreed by the newly reformed conference in 1989. It was then supported by six resolutions submitted to that year's annual conference. The composite resolution that resulted called for 'urgent reforms', claiming that greater representation of women would 'not be achieved by exhortation'.[16] In practical terms it asked the NEC to bring forward proposals for a quota system, including a minimum of 40 per cent women on all party bodies and delegations. It also called for action to promote women as parliamentary candidates. In debate it was noted that quotas were already in use in other European parties and their effects were likely to prove popular with voters. Despite the NEC's reluctance to initiate reform, it was prepared to accept the principles of the composite, and this went on to be passed by a show of hands.

A number of observations are worth making about why this change happened so fast. First, as already noted, there was an active network in the unions working to build support for reform, backed by key staff at the party's head office. Second, by using resolutions they managed to 'bounce' the NEC and union leaders into supporting change, when these groups had not necessarily had the time to think through the consequences fully. Third, the earlier actions of WAC, in particular, had been essential in readying the conference for these debates. In the early 1980s there had been concerns that mechanisms to promote women's representation would amount to 'tokenism', and numerous voices had been raised in opposition. However, in later years it was merely the practicality of the mechanisms that were contested, as the principle had come to be conceded. Thus when a more practical set of proposals was presented, the conference readily accepted them.

The 1989 decision meant that the NEC was duty bound to consult the party on possible changes. A consultation document was drawn up by the NEC women's committee and circulated in February 1990. The number of responses was modest in comparison to consultations on other key organisational issues. But of the 74 constituencies and branches that replied only 14 expressed opposition to quotas. The 1990 women's conference then offered an opportunity to test the mood of the trade unions, with the result that most specific proposals for quotas were supported. There was backing for quotas on the NEC, amongst officers of local parties and delegates to annual conference, on local General Committees, and on all new bodies, such as the proposed National Policy Forum. These responses put further pressure on the NEC. Such an overtly feminist agenda however remained a cultural challenge for an Executive where only six out of 29 members (five of whom sat in the existing women's section) were women. Further external pressure from groups such as WAC and the LCC remained important. A Fabian pamphlet by two reformers was also published in advance of the forthcoming annual conference, setting out the case for 40 per cent quotas (Brooks and Eagle, 1990).

The NEC's document to the 1990 conference noted that women saw Labour as the most male dominated party, and this was likely to be costing votes. Increasing women's representation was thus presented as part of the party's electoral strategy (Labour Party, 1990). The document did not go as far as reformers had proposed, but did recommend strict quotas on the new policy bodies (see Chapter 6), and a phased programme for increasing women's representation amongst the NEC's own membership. The detail of quotas throughout the rest of the party was again left to resolutions – an unusual route for such a major reform.[17] This meant the NEC retained a largely reactive rather than proactive role. Party staff and women in the unions helped ensure that there was a long and detailed composite resolution for the conference to consider, which was again moved by the GMB. This instructed the NEC to bring forward proposals for 40 per cent quotas nationally, 50 per cent quotas in local parties and 'a phased programme over the next 10 years or three general elections so that at least half the Parliamentary Labour Party should be women'.[18] These principles were accepted by the NEC and went on to be supported by a show of hands. Only a tiny number of delegates voted against the proposals, and there were no speakers against.

Although the NEC had caused some delay to the process the implementation of detailed rule changes, at the 1991 conference, was rapid when compared to some other major reforms.[19] And the changes agreed were wide ranging. On the NEC itself two of the 12 trade union members and one of the seven constituency members were required to be women by 1993. This would rise to three and two respectively in 1994 and four and three respectively in 1995. If insufficient women were amongst the highest ranking candidates, those with the most votes would be considered elected. In local parties the changes required two out of four elected officers in each branch and three out of seven in each constituency to be women, along with 50 per cent of delegations to general committees. Parties sending one delegate to annual conference were required to send a woman at least every other year, whilst parties sending more than one delegate were to apply a quota of 50 per cent. Where such quotas could not be met, positions were to be left vacant. Trade union delegations to annual conference were also required to include women, in at least the proportions in which they were represented in the trade union's membership. This required majority female delegations from unions such as COHSE and

NUPE, whilst leaving traditional male unions such as the NUM largely unaffected. Again these detailed proposals attracted no hostile speakers when discussed in 1991, and in a card vote were supported by 98 per cent of those taking part.[20] This demonstrated that the overwhelming majority of constituencies, as well as unions, backed the changes.

This was a very significant raft of changes, which was followed in 1992 by a tidying up exercise to extend quotas to other bodies that had been overlooked. The impact of the changes is difficult to measure fully, but has certainly been profound. The effects of greater women's representation at annual conference are discussed in Chapter 8, and may well have influenced the outcome on women's representation in parliament, as discussed below. On the NEC the impact was also highly significant. The number of women on the Executive rose from just five out of 29 members in 1991 to a high of 18 out of 32 in 1998. This was a rapid change for a body where by 1990 there had still never been a single woman elected in the trade union section, and only four women had ever been elected in the constituency section.[21] In 1996 Clare Short concluded that quotas had 'changed the atmosphere of the NEC', making it 'more friendly and collaborative' (Labour Party, 1996, p. 56). And the change in the Executive's balance was certainly to prove influential in the decisions taken later, with respect to women's representation in elected office, as described below. In local parties quotas theoretically ended the exclusion of women from positions of influence. There was some grumbling from constituencies, but it would appear that most largely adhered to the new rules. Given that women continued to carry the majority burden for childcare and other domestic responsibilities they almost certainly remained underrepresented as active participants. However, quotas forced local parties for the first time to go out and actively encourage women members to take part if they did not want positions to go unfilled.

The principles laid down in the reforms of the early 1990s continued to be adhered to when later organisational changes were introduced. Most notably, the Partnership in Power proposals that formalised the role of the National Policy Forum and changed the structure of the NEC maintained the strict pattern of 40 per cent quotas. Although the changes introduced in 1991 maintained the five separate women's seats on the NEC (against the recommendations of some, such as the LCC) the reforms of 1997, as discussed in

Chapter 7, abolished these seats, replacing them with an increased quota on all other sections. This finally ended a 15 year argument about how they should be elected.[22] Since 1991 there have also been significant changes to the women's conference and other aspects of the women's organisation, discussed at the end of the chapter. Although not a direct target of the quota reforms, the women's organisation has been significantly weakened by the mainstreaming of women's representation throughout the rest of the party.

THE PARLIAMENTARY BREAKTHROUGH: ALL-WOMEN SHORTLISTS

Whilst the transition to quotas within the party structures was made remarkably smoothly, the same cannot be said of the adoption of positive action for selection of parliamentary candidates. First put on the agenda through the one woman on a shortlist demand in the early 1980s, with more radical and urgent action called for after the disappointing results for women at the general elections of 1983 and 1987, change only occurred after long struggles and continued to be resisted even when adopted as policy.

Those seeking to learn from overseas parties in improving women's representation through quotas also hoped to do the same in ensuring women were selected for parliament. However, the British electoral system created a major obstacle. Whilst parties in other countries that elected their parliaments using list systems (such as Sweden and Norway) could simply require a certain number of women to be included on each list, in Britain each local party picked one single candidate.[23] Measures that reserved a portion of places for women on shortlists were no guarantee that they would be selected, whilst tougher measures *requiring* local parties to select women implied significant central interference. The only thing that could absolutely ensure that parties selected women would to require at least some of them to select from 'women only' shortlists.

This measure was first proposed in the mid 1980s by women on the party's left. From 1985 WAC circulated materials encouraging local parties to voluntarily adopt all-women shortlists for their own parliamentary selections. This initiative was largely unsuccessful, and following disappointment at the number of women selected the organisation wrote to the party General Secretary urging that all-women shortlists should apply in the remaining selections.[24] The

NEC, however, was unsympathetic. At the 1985 party conference the seconder of the resolution on one woman on a shortlist stated her regret over its timidity, and suggested that the more effective method would be to require all-women shortlists in all seats with retiring Labour MPs.[25] However at that time even one woman on a shortlist proved too radical a proposal for conference to accept. And WAC itself was not strongly focussed on the policy, with its main energies going into the battle over one woman on a shortlist, and its other two organisational demands.

Table 5.1: Labour women candidates and MPs 1974–2001

| | Women candidates | | Women MPs | | % Candidates |
	No.	%	No.	%	elected
1974 (Oct)	50	8.0	18	5.6	36.0
1979	52	8.3	11	4.1	21.2
1983	78	12.3	10	4.8	12.8
1987	92	14.5	21	9.2	22.8
1992	138	21.8	37	13.7	26.8
1997	158	24.6	101	24.2	63.9
2001	140	21.8	95	23.0	67.9

Source: Amended from Norris and Lovenduski (1993), Eagle and Lovenduski (1998).

As shown in Table 5.1, the 1987 general election saw the number of women Labour MPs more than double, but women's representation in the PLP remained a disappointing 9.2 per cent. The next year the one woman on a shortlist policy was agreed. This, however, was only ever likely to have limited impact. It did not actually require any women to be selected, and those activists involved in nomination and shortlisting meetings were still likely to be overwhelmingly male. In 1988 a new organisation, Labour Women's Network, was set up by a group of women wanting to offer training and practical support to others seeking selection on a strictly non-factional basis. Thus women were offered new forms of encouragement, but they were given no guarantees of success.

In the late 1980s interest in all-women shortlists became more widespread, as concern grew about selections for the 1992 election. In 1989 the LCC's commission on party democracy proposed that local parties should be encouraged to adopt all-women shortlists for this election, but noted that this would probably fail and need to be followed by mandatory all-women shortlists in a proportion of seats (LCC, 1989). In December that year General Secretary Larry Whitty wrote to all constituencies recommending that they 'consider' using all-women shortlists, and citing evidence that increasing women's representation would be popular with voters.[26]

However, the results of this effort were disappointing. By 1990 most selections for safe seats were complete, yet only one constituency had chosen to adopt an all-women shortlist (Brooks and Eagle, 1990). Increasing numbers of activists (including Brooks and Eagle) therefore came to call for compulsion. This mood affected the 1990 conference, where the GMB's resolution on women's representation (referred to above) committed the party to a gender-balanced PLP within three general elections. This resolution, described as 'bloodless' by the CLPD, specified no precise mechanism but required the NEC to bring forward proposals. By this time WAC and the CLPD had adopted firm support for all-women shortlists, accepting that the one woman on a shortlist initiative had failed to show results. Model resolutions circulated by these groups from 1990 onwards proposed that all Labour seats where the MP was retiring, and all seats in byelections, should be required to select from all-women shortlists. The NEC women's committee also expressed its concern at lack of progress, although its own proposed solution was somewhat more moderate. In April 1991 it issued a consultation document to local parties suggesting that all-women shortlists should be imposed on sufficient seats to ensure that the target proposed by the GMB would be met. But local parties were not comfortable with the idea of imposition from the centre, and 73 per cent opposed this recommendation. The NEC thus put no firm proposals to the conference in 1991 – to the anger of many women activists. WAC had succeeded in getting 11 constituencies to submit its model resolution on compulsory all-women shortlists in Labour-held seats, but the resulting composite was lost on a show of hands.

The results of the 1992 election for women were mixed. Once again there had been an increase in the number of women candidates selected (up from 92 to 138), and the number of Labour women MPs had almost doubled, to 37. However, most of these women were elected in the most marginal seats, and just two of Labour's 20 retiring MPs had been replaced by women. As a result, women still made up just 13.7 per cent of Labour MPs. Far more importantly the election had been lost, and the gender gap in voting had reopened. Whilst the Conservatives had only a four per cent lead amongst men, they had a 10 per cent lead against women (Stephenson, 1998). A common claim became that 'if women had swung to Labour in equal numbers with men in 1992, Labour would have won the election' (Short, 1996, p. 19). The analysis of the defeat put a great deal of focus on the need to connect better with women voters. Increasing Labour's representation in parliament was seen as a crucial part of this goal.

The argument over all-women shortlists thus resumed at the 1992 conference. The NEC women's committee had continued to pursue options for change, but no proposals were made by the Executive. There were 17 resolutions based on the WAC proposals and a composite to this effect was debated. The mover taunted the NEC's lack of action, asking whether the commitment to greater women's representation had been no more than 'an election gimmick'.[27] However, when pushed to a vote, the proposal was again heavily defeated.[28] A second composite, calling for proposals to be brought forward to the next year's conference, was remitted to the NEC for further consideration.

This was a difficult situation for the NEC to negotiate. There was resistance to compulsion from the constituencies, but the voluntary route had largely failed. Meanwhile, there was growing anger amongst women activists. Many senior figures saw greater women's representation as essential to changing the party's image, and to winning women's votes next time round. In this environment a compromise proposal was drawn up by the same group of trade union women who had pressed for quotas, and who now sat on the reformed NEC women's committee, working with women's officer Vicky Phillips and committee chair Clare Short. They were fortunate that the new leader, John Smith, was firmly convinced of the need for positive action in a way that Neil Kinnock had never been, and Smith attended crucial meetings to demonstrate his support for the group's work (Short, 1996). Thus in June 1993 the NEC agreed the principle that for the next election all-women shortlists should be required in 50 per cent of seats where Labour MPs retired, but also in 50 per cent of other seats that the party hoped to win. This would be organised on a regional basis, with officers from the relevant constituencies brought together to agree, where possible, which seats would use all-women shortlists. The system was designed to be flexible enough to accommodate local circumstances (such as a strong male candidate who had fought the seat before), but also strict enough to guarantee progress. It did not go as far as the WAC demand of all-women shortlists in all vacant Labour seats, and could thus be presented as a compromise.

At the conference in 1993 the rule changes to implement this policy formed part of the wholesale package of reforms to internal selections and elections, discussed in Chapter 3. The most contentious item in this package was the move to OMOV for selection of parliamentary candidates. However the all-women shortlist policy was also highly controversial, as demonstrated by the previous opposition in the constituencies. The new composition of conference – now feminised as a result of the quotas agreed in 1991 – seems likely to have increased support amongst delegates. But potentially critical to the outcome was the fact that OMOV and all-women shortlists had been drafted together as one rule change for parliamentary selections. This meant that the keenest supporters of one could not oppose the other. As the opposition to OMOV was concentrated in the unions, and the opposition to all-women shortlists was largely in the constituencies, this strategy could also avoid one of these blocks visibly imposing an outcome on the other.

By the time of the conference women in all the main trade unions had worked hard to secure formal support in their organisations for all-women shortlists. This allowed the officers drafting the rule change to take a calculated gamble that treating the two issues jointly would maximise support for both. Like debates about OMOV the discussion about women's representation in parliament had now been going on for many years, and positions had become increasingly fixed. The 1993 conference provided the last opportunity to change the policy before selections began for the next general election, expected in 1996. The decision taken by some trade unions (see Chapter 3) to switch their votes to support OMOV, or to abstain, on the basis of their support for women's representation was not, therefore, as some have suggested, a purely 'spurious argument' (Rentoul, 2001, p. 213). Ironically given the conjunction of issues, one of the few speakers against all-women shortlists was right-winger John Spellar (by this point MP for Warley West), himself central to the OMOV campaign. But despite the risks the gamble paid off. Along with OMOV, all-women shortlists narrowly passed into the party's rules.

Even once agreed, the policy was still constantly challenged. Regional 'consensus' meetings in general ran relatively smoothly, helped by the fact that half of the constituency officers attending these meetings were women, as a result of the earlier quotas. In only one region was there no agreement, and an all-women shortlist had to be imposed by the NEC on the constituency of Slough. Elsewhere constituencies which already had a favoured woman candidate, or where members were open minded, were generally accommodating. However, the policy was consistently attacked in the tabloid press, and by a small group of hardcore opponents in the party. The *Daily Mail* ran a regular 'quota watch' column, monitoring selections and seeking to ridicule candidates chosen from all-women shortlists. Campaigners in the party, including John Spellar and others from the hard right who had most opposed quotas and WAC, formed an organisation entitled 'Labour Campaigners for Real Equality', which sought to reverse the policy.[29] The conference in 1994 considered critical resolutions, including one moved by Slough CLP, whose delegate complained that all-women shortlists 'squeezed through almost unnoticed on the back of OMOV' (Labour Party, 1994, p. 109). At this point the new leader, Tony Blair, who had never been particularly comfortable with the policy, was tempted to let it drop. He was, however, put under heavy pressure from his supporters in the LCC, as well as the now greater numbers of women from the PLP and NEC, to stand firm. Having not won over their sceptical leader, the opponents' resolution was lost on a show of hands after a tense conference debate. For the moment, all-women shortlists were safe.

The policy was dealt a fatal blow, however, when in 1995 two male party members took the party to court on the basis that all-women shortlists were contrary to anti-discrimination law. Peter Jepson and Roger Dyas-Elliot had been refused access to two seats because the constituencies concerned had been designated for all-women shortlists. They argued that this exclusion was contrary to the Sex Discrimination Act 1975 because selection as a candidate should be considered equivalent to providing a qualification for employment. This was a potential threat that the party had been aware of, but on balance it had been advised that the policy was legally sound. However other legal experts, including Lord Lester of Herne Hill – who had been involved in the original drafting of the Act, disagreed and said so publicly. These arguments were played out through the press and in July 1995 an exasperated Blair stated that, whatever the outcome of the court case, the policy would be dropped after the next election.[30] The following January the Leeds industrial tribunal found against the party, arguing that the constituencies concerned had indeed acted in a discriminatory way.[31] This was a major blow and a public embarrassment. Supporters of the policy argued that the party should appeal the decision to a higher court. However, if this had upheld the tribunal's view the ruling would have had general application – rather than just applying in these isolated seats. It could thus have threatened the 35 women already selected under all-women shortlists. This, coupled with the impending general election, the media controversy, and Blair's unease, persuaded the NEC that all-women shortlists should be dropped. By this time relatively few selections were outstanding. The policy had largely had its effect.

The impact of all-women shortlists was clearly seen in the 1997 general election result, when a record 101 Labour women were elected. This was almost three times the total in 1992. Analysis showed that without all-women shortlists few of these gains would have been made (Eagle and Lovenduski, 1998).[32] The result brought women's representation in the Parliamentary Labour Party to 24 per cent – a very noticeable transformation. The policy of higher visibility for women also seemed to have paid dividends, as the gender gap had once again closed. One of the most memorable images of the election was of prime minister Tony Blair with his new women MPs. This became symbolic of the party's modernisation, and was even celebrated by the *Daily Mail*, despite its earlier hostility to the policy.[33] Thus Clare Short's prediction to the party in the midst of the conflicts that 'after the election you will all be very proud of the result' (Labour Party, 1995, p. 115) had proved to be correct. Yet whilst the all-women shortlist policy was supported by many 'modernisers', Blair himself had been a reluctant participant in reform.

CREATING 'NEW POLITICS': SCOTLAND AND WALES

After the 1997 election attention soon turned to the appropriate processes for selecting Labour candidates for the new Scottish Parliament and National Assembly for Wales – as discussed in Chapter 4. Questions about women's representation were absolutely central to these debates.

There was a long-standing commitment to ensuring fair women's representation in the devolved institutions. As early as 1990 Labour's Scottish conference had passed a resolution saying that the design of the new parliament should ensure that 50 per cent of seats went to women. This commitment reflected the proposal of the Scottish Constitutional Convention (comprising representatives of the Labour, Liberal Democrat and Green parties, alongside others from civil society) which was published in the same year. In Scotland in particular, fair levels of women's representation were seen as a key part of delivering a 'new politics' distinct from that at Westminster.[34] In 1995 Labour and the Liberal Democrats publicly signed an 'Electoral Agreement' which was incorporated into the final report of the Scottish Constitutional Convention. This confirmed that the electoral system for the parliament would be an additional member system (AMS) – combining constituency seats with 'top up' lists to ensure proportionality. It also committed both parties to 'select and field an equal number of male and female candidates ... [and] ensure that these candidates are equally distributed with a view to the winnability of seats' (SCC, 1995, p. 23).

In Wales the plans for the Assembly were less well advanced, and the commitments to women's representation always less firm. But after the Welsh Labour Party first adopted the policy of an elected Wales-wide body in 1992, it agreed that the Assembly should have 40 two-member seats, based on Westminster boundaries, and that each seat should elect one male and one female representative. In 1996 these proposals were dropped in favour of a similar AMS system to that proposed in Scotland, with 40 constituencies and 20 top up seats. Although it was now less clear how it was going to be delivered, the commitment to fair women's representation in theory remained.

Throughout Labour's quota debates in the early 1990s regular reference was made to the need to ensure that the devolved institutions were fully representative of women. The prospect of devising a mechanism for new bodies with no incumbent candidates was less intimidating than that of achieving change at Westminster. However, after the industrial tribunal defeat in early 1996 doubts began to set in. At that year's conference an NEC statement issued in response to the ruling offered a promise of equality in the devolved bodies as compensation to those who were disappointed by the abandonment of all-women shortlists. But within the confines of the law it was not clear how this was going to be achieved.

In 1997 the NEC set up a 'women's representation taskforce', to investigate this question, which worked with the newly established 'selections taskforce'. As described in Chapter 4, this latter group already faced a dilemma over the extent to which decisions about the selections should be devolved within the party itself, to the Scottish and Welsh Executives.

The proposal that emerged from the taskforces was one devised by women in the Scottish Labour Party. This was to 'twin' neighbouring constituencies, requiring each pair to jointly select one woman and one man. For the purpose of the selections the constituency memberships would merge into one selectorate, and draw up one male and one female shortlist. Members would then have two votes, one for a woman and one for a man. Once one candidate of each sex had been chosen there would be a discussion over who represented each of the twinned seats. This system avoided the problem inherent in all-women shortlists, where men were excluded from certain selection contests altogether. But it was still potentially open to challenge by a disgruntled candidate. Other proposals, however, such as using the top up lists to rebalance any gender bias in the constituencies, could not promise success. Labour knew that it would elect most of its members in constituency seats, and therefore this was where women's representation needed to be achieved.

The principle of 'twinning' was agreed at the 1997 annual conference, with responsibility for drawing up the detail delegated to the NEC.[35] Speaking for the NEC Mary Turner promised that the devolved bodies would 'be the first democratic structures in British history to be fully representative right from the start' (Labour Party, 1997b, p. 79). Rhona Brankin, then the Scottish representative on the NEC women's committee, claimed that Labour's 'plans for a Scottish Parliament and a Welsh Assembly will create a new kind of politics', and that equal representation for women and men was central to that ambition (Labour Party, 1997b, p. 81). The conference, most of whose delegates came from England, found the proposals uncontroversial.

But the approach was by no means secure. While the Scottish Labour Party was relatively united on the question of women's representation, the Welsh Labour Party was resistant to a rigid mechanism – especially one devised in Scotland and passed down by London – being imposed. And there were grave concerns about the potential legal difficulties that could be encountered. When the bills to create the new institutions passed through parliament the government resisted amendments by Labour women backbenchers to clarify the legality of positive action, on advice of its own law officers (Russell, 2000). There were concerns that a legal change might put the UK in breach of European law, although leaving the law unchanged left Labour as a party open to challenge. Combined with discontent in Wales, and likely press hostility, this created powerful pressure on the leadership to resist positive action for women. But there were equally powerful factors creating pressure in the opposite direction.

One of these was the results of earlier positive action mechanisms. Women were now well represented on the Scottish and Welsh Executives and formed a majority on the NEC. The women in parliament were also now a large and effective lobby, led on this occasion by the Minister for Women Joan Ruddock, herself originally from Wales. A second factor was the desire to live up to the promises that devolution would bring a new style of politics. At Westminster, nothing had been more symbolic of this than high representation of women. Male-dominated institutions in Scotland and Wales had the potential not only to tarnish Labour locally, but also to dent the party's 'modern' image at the national level. And selecting women was also a means of ensuring that the new institutions were not simply filled with 'the usual suspects' from parliament and local government, most of whom were men. As in the party generally, fair representation for women was a way of injecting new blood into the system.

Additionally, very public promises had been made (particularly in Scotland) that women would be well represented. The leadership faced the wrath of both the Scottish Labour Party and, potentially, the Scottish electorate, if this promise was broken. The proportional electoral system made it particularly important that Labour maximise its electoral support. Its main challenger the Scottish National Party (SNP) – a party which had previously been led by a woman, and had a high proportion of women MPs – was doing well in the polls and was ready to capitalise on any weakness. For these largely electoral reasons the Scottish leader Donald Dewar concluded that the twinning plan must be adopted, and recommended this to Tony Blair. Well organised pressure had been necessary, however, as neither man was an instinctive supporter of positive action.

This decision having been taken, the problem remained getting it implemented in Wales. Here the potential for a largely male body was even greater than in Scotland. Prior to 1997 only one of the 40 MPs in Wales was a woman. This had increased to four only as a result of three selections from all-women shortlists. It was therefore firmly believed that positive action in Wales was necessary in order to deliver representation for women in the Assembly.

By maintaining strong central control over the selection process the NEC was able to pressurise the Welsh party into applying the same system that had been agreed for Scotland, in the name of uniformity. However, there was much resistance from Welsh const-ituencies. Concerns on the Welsh Executive led to a consultation paper on twinning being issued, and constituency responses were completely split. A campaign for twinning, headed by Welsh women MPs and MEPs with assistance from Welsh General Secretary Anita Gale, and strong backing from party head office, worked hard to maximise support. Other leading figures, including the Secretary of State for Wales, Ron Davies, let it be known that they were opposed to the twinning plan. The final decision was taken at the Welsh Labour Party conference in May 1998, where the General Secretary Tom Sawyer and Deputy Leader John Prescott urged the delegates to support twinning. The mechanism was approved, with support of just 51.95 per cent of conference votes.

The implementation of twinning was not entirely straightfor-ward. In Wales there was continued resistance from some constit-uencies and some twinned arrangements had to be imposed. There were also suggestions of a legal challenge, but this did not materialise. Some women reported very unpleasant experiences during selections (Gill, 1999). However the result of the policy, after the election in May 1999, was as its proponents had wished. In the Welsh Assembly women made up 54 per cent of the Labour group, and in Scotland the equivalent figure was 50 per cent. This contrib-uted significantly to these new institutions being established with overall women's representation of 40 per cent and 37 per cent respectively.[36]

WOMEN'S REPRESENTATION BECOMES MAINSTREAM

The results of the Scottish and Welsh elections, well received by the press and public, marked a breakthrough for women in elected office. Just as quotas had done throughout the party, mechanisms to ensure that women were chosen as Labour candidates came to be seen as effective and increasingly uncontroversial.

The procedure agreed between the NEC and the London Labour Party for selections to the Greater London Assembly in 1999 used the same twinning arrangement as had applied in Scotland and

Wales, and this caused no difficulties. In May 2000 a Labour group of four women and five men was elected. More problems attached, however, to the appropriate procedure for the next Westminster elections. Some hoped that the breakthrough that had been achieved in 1997, and its positive reception, would provide sufficient encouragement for CLPs to select women without compulsion. In any case, all-women shortlists had been ruled out and there was no other mechanism that could guarantee success. Twinning was impractical since it was based on neighbouring constituencies, whereas vacant winnable seats for Westminster were few and far between. In these circumstances the taskforces and the NEC arrived at a compromise. This would require all constituencies to select from gender balanced shortlists, comprising 50 per cent women and 50 per cent men. As with twinning, branches would be required to nominate one woman and one man, but at the end of the process only one candidate would be selected. This was accepted easily, but proved to be ineffective. Only one in five new candidates selected for the 2001 general election was a woman, and this proportion dropped to just one in ten in safe Labour seats. In both cases this was actually a worse performance than the party had achieved in 1992. At the election itself the number of Labour women MPs fell, from 101 to 95. It seemed clear that the cultural change some had hoped for had not occurred, and compulsion continued to be required.

As had happened in 1979, this result spurred the party into action. By now, however, the mainstream nature of women's claims to representation meant change came from the top. Pressure by women in parliament to amend the law with respect to selection of candidates had continued, and now paid dividends. In July 2000 ministers accepted an amendment tabled at the National Policy Forum in Durham stating that legal change would be considered. A commitment to this then appeared in the 2001 election manifesto, and the Sex Discrimination (Election Candidates) Bill passed rapidly into law in February 2002 (Childs, 2003). This allowed political parties to use positive action in selection where women were underrepresented – enabling Labour to act, whilst not forcing action on any other party.

The Labour Party's response to this change was to revert to the only mechanism that had been shown to work for Westminster – all-women shortlists. This was agreed by the NEC in 2002. In order to see any real improvement from the current level of 23 per cent women in the PLP, the policy was to be applied strictly. Under the new proposals MPs would be required to announce their intention to retire by December 2002. A percentage of these seats would then be subject to all-women shortlists, with decisions on a regional basis, dependent on the proportion of existing women MPs.[37] Where MPs announced their retirement after the deadline (which was certain to be common), *all* seats would be subject to all-women shortlists, except in 'special circumstances'.

The change in culture over the previous decade, illustrated by this reform, was remarkable. Compared to the controversies of earlier years, this rigid policy was passed unanimously by the NEC. It was then approved by the 2002 conference with barely a comment. The contrast to the furore over the application of all-women shortlists in half the available seats from 1993 to 1996 could hardly have been more stark. Indeed the policy now embraced by the NEC bore strong resemblance to that of the (by now largely inactive) WAC in the early 1990s: all-women shortlists in all retirement seats. This change of mood may be explained by many factors. The most obvious was the changing attitude towards women's representation within the party, brought about in large part by previous victories for women. However, the quiet acquiescence of conference and the NEC in this decision was also symptomatic of a generally more compliant party, and a decline in influence of activist groups.

By the December 2002 deadline, 16 Labour MPs had announced their retirement. Of these, 12 constituencies (75 per cent) were designated by the NEC to select from all-women shortlists. Later decisions were delegated by the NEC to a 'late retirements panel', and despite the apparent rigidity of the procedure several open shortlists were allowed.[38] And despite wide acceptance of the all-women shortlist principle, consent was not universal. In Blaenau Gwent in Wales (a constituency that had been strongly opposed to twinning) the officers of the local party refused to co-operate with the selection when it was designated for an all-women shortlist. The Wales Labour Party managed the shortlisting process and the candidate – Maggie Jones of the NEC – was chosen in a ballot of local members in December 2003. She however faced threats that the local Assembly member would resign from the party and stand against her as an independent candidate.

THE IMPACT OF QUOTAS ON THE WOMEN'S ORGANISATION

By the early 1990s the impact of quotas throughout the Labour Party was already being felt in profound ways, and changing the culture of the party. Whereas in traditional areas such as Wales and the North East of England women had previously been very dependent on the separate women's organisation to get their voices heard, the new rules required that women be strongly represented in the mainstream structures of branches and constituencies. Women were also guaranteed representation at the party's annual conference for the first time.

It had not been the explicit intention of the quota policy to undermine the traditional women's organisation. Proposals that the organisation should be dismantled when quotas were introduced had been rejected. However, the mainstreaming of women's representation throughout the party inevitably weakened the organisation over time. From the party's inception women's sections at branch and constituency level, and women's 'councils' which could span broader areas, had provided essential forums for discussion, campaigning and social activity amongst women excluded from the party's main structures. At national and regional level women's conferences offered opportunities to gain political experience and put women's issues onto the agenda. However, as women's representation in the rest of the party blossomed, fewer women populated these traditional structures. In 1979 there had been 970 women's sections registered with head office, by 1992 there were 650 and by 1997 there were just 200.

The first major change to the women's organisation in the 1990s was to the national women's conference. As discussed above, the voting structure of this conference was changed in 1988. In 1993 it was agreed to experiment with replacing the usual resolution-based women's conference with an informal training event. The first such conference was held in Southport in 1994. It was based on the political education model, largely comprising policy seminars and skills workshops, offering training for example in public speaking, being a councillor or seeking selection as a parliamentary candidate. Despite protests from the stalwarts of the traditional women's conference about its lack of decision-making power, the event was well attended and feedback was positive. The NEC thus decided to make it biennial, alternating with the traditional conference. But in fact the last ever resolution-based conference was held in 1995, and a switch to annual training conferences was then agreed by the NEC. In 1997 the women's training conference was held jointly with the youth conference, and from then on all national conferences other than the main annual conference (i.e. youth, women, European, local government) were held together to cut costs. This joint event has now become the annual 'Spring Conference', of which specific events for women form an increasingly small part.

A major review of the women's organisation was precipitated by the Partnership in Power process in 1997. It was widely anticipated at the time that Partnership in Power would dismantle and stream-line the party's formal structures at a local level (see Chapter 9). However, the project's taskforces were secretive, and those outside the core circle were unsure what to expect. Given its declining membership, its historic association with the hard left, and previous proposals that it should be disbanded, the women's organisation of the party seemed likely to be under threat. In this situation its senior figures sought to pre-empt change in order to protect the organisation's most valuable features. In early 1998 the NEC women's committee and national women's officer initiated a consultation on the future role of the women's organisation after quotas (Labour Party, 1998a). Amongst respondents there was support for more training, mentoring and informal networking for women to complement the work of the mainstream party (Labour Party, 1998b). These results were palatable to the party's modern-isers, and a raft of reforms were proposed to the 1998 conference. These abolished women's councils, and women's sections at branch level, and instead created constituency-wide women's 'forums' which retained some formal powers. Regional women's committees and conferences would be restructured and a new NEC women's committee would have a smaller core membership, drawn from the (now greater numbers of) women on the NEC.

These changes sought to create a more focussed and flexible organisation, to complement the use of quotas throughout the party. They protected the immediate future of the organisation though ironically (as discussed in Chapter 9) the broader restructuring of local parties never came about. But the women's organisation has nonetheless continued to be weakened. By 2005 the NEC women's committee no longer existed in any real sense, having been subsumed into a more general 'equalities' structure. As already discussed, the national women's conference had also all but disappeared. Thus the tradition of a separate women's organisation, dating to the party's 1918 merger with the Women's Labour League, had all but come to an end.

EVALUATION

The reforms to improve women's representation throughout the Labour Party comprise some of the most remarkable changes to the party's organisation in recent decades. Yet they are often passed over in discussions about organisational change in the party. In part this is because they were agreed with relatively little fuss. In part it is because their success resulted in no simple shift of power from one recognised group of interests to another (for example from activists to leadership or left to right). However, these changes have undoubtedly led to a major shift of power within the party from men to women. Their overall effect has been to contribute profoundly to a change in the party's culture.

The dynamic of change bears similarities to that of reforms discussed in other chapters, in that it resulted at least as much from pressure from the grassroots as from the initiative of leaders. The exception was the package of internal quotas, which was not that demanded by activists (or even a halfway compromise), but an alternative that allowed these demands to be sidestepped completely. Feminist women, mostly aligned with WAC and the CLPD, had campaigned for changes that would have given factional advantage to the party's left. The leadership, whilst not sympathetic to these demands, conceded that women's representation was important electorally and this made it an increasingly high priority. An alternative package was crafted by a 'progressive bureaucracy' of women in the trade unions and in senior office in the party, at times acting covertly to avoid opposition from senior men. These proposals, successfully agreed as a result of campaigns within the unions, went on to be accepted by the leadership and were radical in their effects.

Although activist women were not responsible for the package of internal quotas, they were central to achieving other reforms. It was they who put the proposal of one woman on a shortlist onto the conference agenda, forcing this into the party's rules after seven years of debate, against the NEC's wishes. It was they, also, who first raised the suggestion of all-women shortlists, and who pressed this proposal repeatedly in the late 1980s and early 1990s. The annual debates at the party conference, and growing awareness in the constituencies of the injustice of women's underrepresentation, can largely be traced to the campaigns of WAC. These prepared many in the party mentally for the bold decisions that were later to be taken. The campaigns also helped radicalise women in the trade unions. However, the real breakthrough in terms of parliamentary selections came only after internal party quotas had been agreed. As women populated the constituencies and the party conference in greater numbers, all-women shortlists became possible. Similarly, once quotas fed through to better representation in the PLP and NEC, there were new women ready to lobby for progress in the devolved institutions.

The creation of new bodies, inside and outside the party, was also central to the ability to improve women's representation step by step. For example, the new National Policy Forum could be approved in 1990 (and implemented in 1993) with a 40 per cent quota from day one. Likewise the new Scottish Parliament and National Assembly for Wales, with no incumbent members, provided opportunities for reaching record levels of women's representation in elected office.

The changes to women's representation within the party and in elected office have been crucial to its conception as 'new' Labour. The image of the parliamentary party, the NEC, the party conference and Labour groups in the new devolved institutions, is startlingly different to that of the traditional Labour Party described by commentators such as Drucker (1979) and Minkin (1980, 1992). Yet women's quotas were never part of the project of either of its famously modernising leaders. Indeed both Kinnock and Blair were resistant to moves towards positive action, and proponents of change worked around rather than with their leaders to achieve it. Instead it was others at the top of the party, often seen as more traditional – John Smith, Larry Whitty, Clare Short, senior women trade unionists and senior head office staff, along with activists in groups such as WAC and the LCC – whose conception of party modernisation included a new deal for Labour's women members. Only the timing of Blair's announcement of 'new' Labour has led these changes to be seen as synonymous. The election of Labour's 101 women MPs – the product of the all-women shortlist policy that Blair was deeply uneasy about – helped to cement this association.

A further link between 'new' Labour and women's representation comes as a result of the turnover in personnel that flowed from reserved seats for women. In local parties, at conference, on the NEC and finally in the devolved institutions, rules requiring women to hold a proportion of seats denied representation to the 'usual suspects'. As men overwhelmingly held such positions in the past, the enforced entry of women into these arenas necessarily created a party with new personnel bringing new ideas and attitudes. This was anticipated by some of those championing quotas in the early 1990s as a beneficial side effect. In fact its impact, combined with other changes, has been greater than could have been imagined. The replacement of a large cohort of activists with a new cohort of previously less active members helped provide opportunities for further profound organisational and cultural change. Although not prominent in the demands of 'new' Labour's most vocal advocates, a transformation in the levels of women's representation was thus central to building a new party.

Notes

1. This reflected the party's overall loss of seats, from 319 to 269. The Conservatives elected just eight women out of their total 339 MPs.
2. WAC leaflet, 1983.
3. Instead the women won the minor concession that the number of seats in the women's section should increase from four to five (Graves, 1994). Their campaign was later echoed, more successfully, by the Constituency Parties Movement, which won the right for CLPs to elect their own representatives on the NEC in 1937 (Pimlott, 1977).
4. Compared to the six resolutions on the women's organisation submitted to annual conference from 1974-81, there were 74 such resolutions between 1983 and 1985 alone (Wainwright, 1987).
5. WAC leaflet, 1984.
6. Composite 37, defeated by 1,095,000 votes to 5,720,000.
7. Composite 28.
8. Composite 58 was defeated on a card vote by 1,386,000 to 5,078,000.
9. Composite 35 was defeated on a card vote by 1,731,000 to 3,875,000.
10. Composite 2.
11. Speakers in favour had included Harriet Harman MP, then a member of the parliamentary frontbench.
12. During this period many key resolutions on women's representation, and other organisational matters, were moved by sections of the GMB. As the union had several sections it was entitled, unlike most other unions, to submit more than one resolution to the annual conference. It thus had the capacity to submit proposals on women's organisation without sacrificing the right to submit resolutions on industrial policy.

It was also close to Larry Whitty, who used to be an officer of the union.

13. In 1979 there were 9.5 million men in trade union membership, and 3.9 million women. By 1992 there were just 5.5 million men and 3.6 million women (Wrigley, 1997).

14. Annual General Meeting minutes, 1981 and 1983. There was at the time considerable overlap between these organisations, however. Several key CLPD members, including Frances Morrell who was also active in the LCC, sat on a commission in 1980 which proposed replacing the women's section of the NEC with quotas on the trade union and constituency sections – see Burnell (1980).

15. These women included Angela Eagle (COHSE), Maureen Rooney (AEEU), Bernadette Hillon (USDAW), Maureen O'Mara (NUPE), Anne Gibson (MSF) and Margaret Prosser (TGWU). When the NEC women's committee was reformed in 1989 to include six trade union women elected at the women's conference, these women took up the seats.

16. Composite 54, moved by Newham North West and seconded by the GMB.

17. There were 17 resolutions submitted on this subject in total. As well as one from the GMB these included proposals from COHSE and NUPE, and various constituencies.

18. Composite 9.

19. See for example the discussion of the struggle to change the share of conference votes held by the trade unions, in Chapter 8.

20. The rule changes were approved by 4,850,000 votes to 114,000.

21. These were Barbara Castle, Joan Lestor, Jo Richardson and Audrey Wise.

22. Or indeed a 70 year argument, if the efforts in the 1920s are included.

23. For a discussion of the links between women's representation and electoral systems internationally see for example Norris (1996, 2004).

24. *Tribune*, 5 July 1985.

25. Louise Christian of Streatham CLP.

26. This proposal would not however apply to seats with a sitting male MP, as he would be entitled to an automatic place on the shortlist.

27. Valerie Wise speaking for Preston CLP, moving composite 2 (Labour Party, 1992, p. 184).

28. By 4,382,000 to 936,000.

29. See McDougall (1998).

30. 'Women only shortlists are cut short by Blair', *The Guardian*, 26 July 1995.

31. For a fuller description of the Leeds industrial tribunal decision and surrounding issues see Davis (1995), Russell (2000), Russell and O'Cinneide (2003).

32. Ironically the party's landslide victory had reduced the proportion of women elected below what it might have been. Labour had won many

seats unexpectedly and in these seats, where all-women shortlists had not applied, 55 out of 66 candidates were men.

33. On 8 May 1997 the *Daily Mail* proclaimed that 'At last, the mother of Parliaments will cease to be predominantly a men's club', saying 'this newspaper warmly welcomes the decisive and long overdue increase in the number of women MPs'.

34. For discussion of women's role in the 'new politics' see for example Breitenbach and Mackay (2001), Brown (1996, 1998). For a fuller discussion of women's representation amongst all the parties in the Scottish Parliament and National Assembly for Wales see Russell, Mackay and McAllister (2002).

35. This approach was necessary as the referendums to approve the new institutions had only been held in September, but candidates for the 1999 elections needed to be selected before the 1998 conference.

36. Other parties all did less well at selecting women. The SNP achieved 43 per cent representation and Plaid Cymru (using positive action) 35 per cent. In Wales the Liberal Democrats elected three women and three men, but in Scotland (despite having signed the electoral agreement) they achieved only 12 per cent women's representation. The Conservative group in the Scottish Parliament was 16.7 per cent female and in Wales was 100 per cent male. For an account of selection procedures and debates in the other parties see Russell, Mackay and McAllister (2002).

37. As Labour's representation in 2001 remained at a high water mark, only seats with Labour MPs retiring were seen as winnable. Amongst other seats the previous policy of 50/50 shortlists continued to apply.

38. The 'special circumstances' clause was originally intended primarily for seats where there might be a strong male ethnic minority candidate. However, it was open to interpretation by the panel. By February 2005 there had been 32 'late' retirements, and 24 of the constituencies concerned (75 per cent) had been required to select from all-women shortlists.

6

Making Policy

One of a political party's most central roles is the formulation of policy programmes for government. Within Labour this process has also often been one of the most controversial. In contrast to the other main British parties Labour was founded on the basis that party policy was determined by its members, brought together in an annual conference, rather than by the party's parliamentary leaders. Between conferences the responsibility for policy fell to the National Executive Committee (NEC), which produced policy statements that the conference would be asked to agree. When the trade union majority in the conference and NEC was amenable, the leadership could thus comfortably secure its policy positions. As McKenzie (1963) documented, this was the case through much of Labour's history. However, as outlined in Chapter 2, consensus broke down from the late 1950s onwards, as the left gained strength and there were increasing policy differences between the unions and the party frontbench. This created growing conflicts between the parliamentary leadership, responsible for implementing and publicly defending policy, whilst having no formal role in creating it, and the extra-parliamentary party.

The NEC and annual conference are discussed in Chapters 7 and 8 respectively. First this chapter reviews the changes to the formal policy process, and in particular the new structures introduced to consider policy between conferences. These responded to the leadership's desire to ensure that conflict was minimised, and also to some extent to the demands of grassroots activists for more access to policy debates. The arrangements increasingly institutionalised links between the parliamentary and extra-parliamentary party over policy matters, and changed the role of the NEC in particular.

These moves began after Neil Kinnock took over as leader in 1983, and led to the initial establishment of the National Policy Forum in 1993. Until 1997 the traditional role of annual conference was unchanged. However further reform then followed, under the auspices of Partnership in Power. The first half of the chapter traces the entirety of these changes, from their inception in 1983. The second half looks at the operation of the current policy-making procedures in practice, and what general conclusions can be reached about their impact.

In assessing the changes to Labour's policy process a central question is whether these strengthened or weakened the power of the party leadership. Is the new 'partnership' between leaders and the extra-parliamentary party a real one, and to what extent is one partner more dominant than before? As this chapter shows, the answers to such questions are not wholly straightforward, especially given that the proposals implemented were not all ones that the leadership itself had originally pursued. As many of the proponents of change had sought, the new policy process significantly widened membership participation and discussion beyond that which had gone before, and created a more rational process that was more difficult for leaders to dismiss. It is undoubtedly true that the reforms also increasingly formalised the leadership's control over policy formation. However, these were also powers that it, in practice, already largely held.

KINNOCK AND THE POLICY REVIEW

Neil Kinnock took over the leadership after one of the most painful episodes of conflict in the party's history between the parliamentary and extra-parliamentary wings over policy. During the 1960s and 1970s there had been growing anger on the left at the extent of the parliamentary leadership's control over policy, culminating in great anger about the 1979 manifesto.[1] This was followed by the CLPD's attempt to guarantee more control to the NEC, and by the famously left-wing manifesto of 1983.[2] Kinnock inherited a situation where he wished to review the content of policy in order to increase Labour's electoral appeal. But he also sought to change the process of policy-making, to re-establish a greater sense of partnership between the parliamentary and extra-parliamentary parties.

Between conferences policy matters had traditionally been handled by the NEC, which prepared detailed documents on which much conference debate would focus (see also Chapter 8). For this purpose there were two main NEC committees – the Home Policy Committee and International Policy Committee – each of which oversaw a series of subcommittees. Crucially the Home Policy

Committee had been, since 1974, chaired by Tony Benn. The political control of the NEC and its committees resulted in many decisions that were unwelcome to the party's leaders. But the gains made by the right in NEC elections from 1981 enabled important changes to be made, including the ending of Benn's tenure as chair in 1982 (Golding, 2003).

In 1983 Kinnock was able to convince the NEC to change the system itself. These changes broke down the traditional barrier between the parliamentary and extra-parliamentary parties and 'accorded the front bench (for the first time in Labour's history) an institutionalised role in the Party's policy-making machinery' (Shaw, 1994, p. 111). NEC subcommittees were replaced by joint NEC / shadow cabinet structures, overseen by a joint Policy Co-ordinating Committee. The new policy committees comprised equal numbers from the two bodies, and were also able to co-opt other members and advisers.[3] This eased policy responsibility away from the NEC – an extremely important change given the party's traditions. However, it was achieved by negotiation within the NEC itself, rather than by formal amendment to the party's rules.

Agreement was reached to revise the system further after the 1987 general election defeat. At the suggestion of Tom Sawyer, Deputy General Secretary of NUPE and then chair of the Home Policy Committee, Kinnock launched the Policy Review.[4] As before, the intention was not only to pursue new policy directions, but also to change the format and culture of decision making. As the document put to the 1987 conference suggested, policy making needed to be less adversarial and involve 'the widest possible range of individuals and organisations, inside and outside the party' (Labour Party, 1987b, p. 8).

The new system maintained the principle of joint policy structures. A series of Policy Review Groups were established, each with joint convenors, one from the NEC and one from the shadow cabinet. The convenors were chosen by Kinnock, and with them he agreed the membership of the groups (Minkin, 1992). Due to the preponderance of MPs on the NEC, parliamentarians were in a minority on just two of the seven groups (Taylor, 1997). The new system also shifted responsibility for servicing policy groups to the leader's office, away from the party's policy department (which had gained a reputation for being too close to Tony Benn). This was made possible by recent increases in parliamentary allowances, enabling Kinnock to have 12 staff – six of them working on policy –

where his predecessor Michael Foot had only had five.[5] The combination of these factors resulted in a further shift in power from the
extra-parliamentary party to the leader and the PLP. Critics complained that 'the review was controlled step by step by the leader's
office' and that 'policy formation by a small inner circle of unelected
advisers surrounding the leader ... became custom and practice'
(Heffernan and Marqusee, 1992, p. 114).

As well as bringing senior figures together in new forums to
agree a more moderate policy platform, a secondary intention of the
Policy Review was to involve more people inside and outside the
party in a more deliberative system of policy discussion. One
vehicle was the 'Labour Listens' campaign, described by Kinnock at
its launch as 'the biggest consultation exercise with the British
public any political party has ever undertaken' (quoted in Shaw,
1993, p. 114). This programme included public events inviting input
from groups and individuals outside the party, with the media also
present. Being a rather confused mixture of PR exercise and
consultation, Labour Listens was widely considered an 'embarrassing flop' (Shaw, 1993, p. 114). The programme's original plan to
consult with party members was a particular failure. It was difficult
to reach beyond the activists on the GCs, but the leadership were
nervous about involving what it saw as an unrepresentative group.
In any case there was an almost complete lack of experience, both at
the centre and the grassroots, in running a consultation exercise of
this sort. Information was circulated to local parties, but Policy
Review Groups were unsure how to respond to submissions, and
plans to hold a 'national policy forum' to discuss each of the policy
areas were abandoned (Shaw, 1993; Taylor, 1997). Tom Sawyer
reflected that '[t]he party just isn't in a position to handle proper
membership participation in policy making' (quoted in Hughes and
Wintour, 1990, p. 101).

In some ways the Policy Review did, however, offer new access
for members. The documents it produced for consideration by
annual conference were circulated some months in advance,
allowing local parties and affiliates to discuss them. Previously
delegates had arrived at conference to find large indigestible NEC
policy documents on their seats.[6] However, the early availability of
documents seemed simply to feed resentment amongst activists that
there was no mechanism by which these could be amended. Such
documents had always been non amendable – with the exception of
a single experiment in 1953.[7] But when Tony Benn had controlled

the committee that drafted them, the results were generally pleasing to activists on the left. With control of the process now returned firmly to the leadership, and given the change of policy direction over issues such as defence and nationalisation, resentment grew amongst many in the constituencies.

THE ESTABLISHMENT OF THE NATIONAL POLICY FORUM

The submission to Labour's 1980 Commission of Enquiry from the party's own staff had drawn attention to many weaknesses of the traditional policy process. This noted that 'policy statements are drawn up by NEC subcommittees with little communication with other sections of the party; the views of the individual membership carry little weight at conference; there is little opportunity for discussion of policy outside debates on resolutions in branches or at conference'. At the end of the first period of Kinnock's leadership these central problems had still barely been addressed. Meanwhile the new system had formalised input from the shadow cabinet into the party's policy bodies, but the policies that had resulted were causing much unease in the party, as became particularly apparent from 1988 onwards.

There had long been interest by some in the party in exploring more radical reforms to the policy-making process. Proposals to rationalise the piecemeal system of resolutions that set much of the conference agenda, and bridge the gap between these and the 'take it or leave it' policy documents that came from the NEC, had been made by those on both the left and the right of the party since at least the 1970s. The head of the party's Research Department, Geoff Bish, with the support of Tony Benn, was among those proposing that the development of the party's 'policy programme' by annual conference should be made more transparent. In the late 1970s the idea of a 'rolling programme' of policy making to replace the current system gained ground.[8] At this time Larry Whitty, then Research Officer for the General and Municipal Workers' Union (GMWU) but to become the party's General Secretary in 1985, was exploring the model used in the Swedish Labour Party. Here there was an annual policy-making conference, but this considered statements on which there had been extensive prior consultation with members (Linton, 1985).

Many such suggestions were made to the party's Commission of Enquiry in 1980, but had not been acted upon. The submission from the party's Research Department suggested that, as in the 1953 experiment, policy documents should be amendable by the conference. One way of achieving this would be through allowing local parties and affiliates to submit amendments, with a system of 'compositing' similar to that which had traditionally existed for resolutions. An independent commission established to respond to the Commission of Enquiry, which included a number of key CLPD activists, suggested similar arrangements, including creation of an elected committee that would sift amendments from local parties and propose composite forms of words.[9] The GMWU's submission set out Whitty's proposals, suggesting that a new body representative of the whole party should be created to oversee a rolling policy programme. Meanwhile the submission from the right-wing group the CLV proposed that the number of policy areas to be discussed at the conference each year should be limited, and it might break into smaller groups to discuss policy in detail. A common theme in all of these proposals was that there should be more involvement by grassroots members in policy discussion throughout the year, with documents circulated in draft by the NEC sufficiently in advance of the annual conference. In various forms all of these ideas later went on to be adopted.

In 1988 dissatisfaction with both the Policy Review process and the old conference system reached the conference floor through a model resolution circulated by the LCC. This group had always supported establishing a stronger culture of policy discussion in the party, and from 1985 onwards became the main proponent of new policy structures and a more 'deliberative' or 'participative' approach. Composite 3 was moved at the conference by LCC executive member Peter Hain, for Putney CLP, and seconded by the organisation's chair Paul Thompson, of Lancashire West.[10] It picked up a number of points from the earlier proposals, including 'a "rolling programme" whereby policy can be integrated in an overall context and regularly presented to Conference for agreement or amendment', with a priority ballot to decide subjects for debate.[11] Hain spoke critically about both the traditional compositing process and the unamendable nature of policy documents. The NEC asked for the resolution to be remitted, and this was agreed. Consequently an NEC consultation with the party was begun.

By the time the consultation paper was issued, shortly before the 1989 conference, tension was rising about the problems with the Policy Review process. Although there had been promises that conference decisions would be taken into account in drafting documents, those published diverged from conference policy on touchstone issues such as unilateral nuclear disarmament and the repeal of anti trade union legislation. The CLPD had thus circulated a model resolution which supported making policy documents amendable by conference, and proposed that resolutions took precedence over documents where there was a clash.[12] A total of 46 resolutions were submitted to the conference on this matter. The consultation paper on the policy process, prepared by Larry Whitty, thus sought to calm these concerns, as well as addressing the proposals made by the LCC the previous year. In so doing it built on the principles of the Policy Review, but also the various earlier proposals, including those Whitty had drafted when at the GMWU. The document noted that so long as conference considered both detailed documents and resolutions the result could be 'unclear, internally inconsistent, and sometimes actually contradictory' (Labour Party 1989a, p. 6). A rolling policy programme, with documents subject to amendment at each conference, was among the proposals. Under this model new 'policy commissions', building in wider representation than the existing Policy Review Groups (for example through seats for regional parties and local government) could receive amendments between conferences and decide which to incorporate directly into the programme, and which should be subject to separate conference debate. In designing such a system the document emphasised that Labour could draw from the experience of other European socialist parties, including those in Sweden, Denmark, Germany and Spain, whose systems it summarised for discussion.

At the 1989 conference itself the shortcomings of the policy-making process were a major subject of debate. A commission set up by the LCC to progress its own proposals had complained that 'Policy making in the party is really the preserve of the front bench and the policy researchers', whilst '[i]ndividual and affiliated members of the party have almost no opportunity for involvement' (1989, p. 7). It emphasised the need for a less confrontational and more deliberative model, with greater involvement of members between conferences.[13] Clearly discontent was reaching dangerous levels in the unions, as well as the constituencies, as demonstrated by the relatively narrow margin with which the composite resolution based on the CLPD's proposals was defeated.[14]

Another resolution at the conference was moved by the GMWU's successor union, the GMB. This broadly backed Whitty's proposals. It agreed that there should be greater participation in policymaking and new policy commissions to manage consultation with the party. It also proposed alternative methods of dealing with conference resolutions and amendments. Moving the resolution, John Edmonds described the existing compositing arrangements as 'so democratic in concept but so very defective in practice', complaining that a system 'designed for the 1920s' was 'wilting under the television lights of the 1980s' (Labour Party 1989, p. 139). Despite concerns from some delegates that the resolution sought 'to close down the Labour Party as we know it', it was passed on a show of hands.[15]

Responses to the NEC's consultation showed that there was 'clear majority support for some form of more radical approach to policy making involving wider participation by all elements within the party and the production of a clear and definitive programme of party policy' (Labour Party, 1990d, p. 2). Three quarters of constituencies responding favoured instituting a rolling programme, and there was significant support for conference being able to amend policy statements. The CLPD's submission had expressed concerns that the proposals were 'designed to restructure the party so that the balance of power may be permanently tipped in favour of the parliamentary leadership' (CLPD, 1989, p. 1). However, even this group conceded that the proposal of a rolling programme was 'attractive' and 'would produce a greater clarity and continuity in Labour's policy making' (p. 15).

Thus whilst there was support for change to the policy process, this was by no means driven from the top. In many ways the leadership was on the defensive, as a result of frustrations with the Policy Review. Key figures such as Neil Kinnock, Tom Sawyer and Charles Clarke (Kinnock's chief of staff) wanted to build on the momentum and more consensual style of the Policy Review process, whilst calming the anger that clearly existed. Their concern in particular was that the process should be formally changed before Labour entered government, to avoid clashes between the cabinet and the party of the kind that had occurred under past administrations. Meanwhile there was broad consensus in the wider party that a new process was needed to deal with the weaknesses of both the old system and the Policy Review. The settlement that ultimately emerged was therefore a compromise. The NEC's proposals, for which Whitty had secured soft left support, were set out in the document *Democracy and Policy Making for the 1990s* (see Chapter 2). These were presented to the 1990 conference, for implementation after the general election – widely expected in 1991.

This document stated the desire to build on many aspects of the current system, and emulate overseas experience, to try and create a more 'deliberative' and 'representative' process providing 'a policy programme which is a clear and authoritative statement of party policy at any given time' (Labour Party, 1990a, p. 1). At the heart of the system would be a two-yearly cycle of discussions, with constituencies and affiliates able to submit resolutions in the form of amendments to the programme. New policy commissions would manage documents and amendments, and a National Policy Forum (NPF) of 150-200 members would oversee the whole system. The NPF would significantly broaden involvement in oversight of the policy process including (in addition to the trade unions and the NEC) representatives of the party's regions, socialist societies, PLP, European Parliamentary Labour Party (EPLP) and local government. It would also have a strict quota for women. Each constituency party would be able to submit two amendments annually to the programme, whilst regional conferences were each to be able to submit five. The creation of a more representative intermediate organisation would allow some filtering of these proposals, as the handling of hundreds of amendments at conference itself was considered 'impracticable' (Labour Party, 1990a, p. 133). The policy commissions and NPF would thus decide which proposals should be accommodated within the programme and which would be put to votes at conference as 'minority options'. Circulation of documents early in the summer would allow local parties to digest and discuss these, before delegates arrived at the conference.

These were bold proposals, which potentially loosened the control of the NEC (and thus, generally, the party frontbench) over policy documents. However, despite the attempts to reach compromise, the proposals proved controversial. The CLPD, in particular, feared that the new system spelled the end of conference resolutions, and that the National Policy Forum would be dominated by an elite. The 1990 conference nonetheless took in-principle decisions to support the package. Speakers from the platform were keen to allay activists' concerns that they would lose powers and to emphasise that the sovereignty of the annual conference would not be eroded. Closing the debate on behalf of the NEC, Tom Sawyer stressed that 'you will be able to come here and turn down the reports of the policy commissions ... you will also be able to come here and turn down any amendments or any alternative proposals' (Labour Party, 1990c, p. 7). Sympathetic commentators contended that 'the rolling programme, far from centralizing power with the leadership, would actually grant to party activists – and ultimately, individual members – a democratic policy oversight which they ha[d] hitherto enjoyed only in their imagination' (Hughes and Wintour, 1990, p. 199). Given the previous lack of control by activists over policy, and the leadership's determination to retain the power it had, there turned out to be elements of truth both in this and the CLPD's predictions.

The 1990 blueprint, however, was never implemented. After the 1992 election defeat the urgency of preparing for government had disappeared, and the whole package came under pressure. The 1992 conference thus accepted a proposal from the NEC for a smaller National Policy Forum than previously proposed, comprising just 81 members.[16] As a result of nervousness, both by the leadership and its opponents, no change was now made to the way in which constituencies formally contributed to the policy programme. This avoided leaders having to give up their control over documents, but also placated the concerns of the CLPD about local parties' ability to submit resolutions to conference.[17] However, policy submissions and discussion in the wider party would be encouraged.

The new National Policy Forum met for the first time in May 1993, and elected Tom Sawyer as its chair.[18] This meeting considered three documents, on economic policy, Europe, and constitutional reform, and elected representatives to the five policy commissions. However, the Forum's relationship to the policy process remained unclear. Its members complained that documents reached them in largely finished form and that there were few opportunities for influence. In any case the last word over content still rested with the NEC. Nonetheless the Forum did come to find a role as a semi-formal sounding board for documents drawn up by the policy commissions (that is, in practice, by shadow ministers). It adopted a consensual style, copied from the Swedish model, which used workshop sessions to discuss documents in detail, and never resorted to votes. This, and the quota guaranteeing women's representation, created a very different atmosphere to that at traditional party meetings. The Forum's less confrontational and more deliberative approach allowed shades of opinion to be expressed, and promoted informal negotiation between its members and members of the frontbench, which both sides found rewarding. Yet it remained a shadowy body which raised suspicions amongst party members, who had little contact with its deliberations. The controversy was muted, however, by the fact that the Forum now held little real power. The involvement of conference in the policy-making process, including its inability to amend policy documents, remained completely unchanged. In practice the NPF simply added a new and more representative layer of oversight to the drafting of policy documents, which were previously produced by even smaller and more elite groups.

FLIRTATIONS WITH DIRECT DEMOCRACY

The party that Tony Blair took over in 1994 therefore had a fledgling new system of policy making which had been untested under the pressures of government, and fell well short of the original ambitions of those who had proposed it. In order to have a major impact on the party's policy-making culture, the system would require much further development. The new leader arrived, however, with his own ambitions for broadening participation in policy decisions, through 'direct' democracy. Since his time on the review group on trade union links in 1992 (see Chapter 3) Blair had advocated the involvement of all members in major policy decisions through one member one vote (OMOV) ballots. This proposal, reiterated during his leadership campaign, would, he argued, make policy making more representative. It was also suggested that it would create added incentives for Labour supporters to join the party.

Such a proposal was, however, widely criticised by those on the soft left who had supported more deliberative methods, as well as by the hard left who defended the old conference system. In 1993 NEC and shadow cabinet member Clare Short had suggested that it was 'absolutely crass and stupid' to suggest that you could write 'a long and detailed policy document ... then say "Are you in favour, yes or no?" and call that a rational, intelligent policy-making process' (quoted in Rentoul, 2001, p. 215).

The idea received its first partial test after Blair indicated to the 1994 conference that he wanted to change Clause IV of the party's constitution.[19] This was a risky move through which the new leader hoped to demonstrate decisively that the party had changed. However, he had discussed it with neither the shadow cabinet nor the NEC (Gould, 1998). A consultation was started after the conference, with documents sent to local parties and affiliates, and articles in the all-member *Labour Party News*. But a campaign against change was launched in January by a group of 20 Labour MEPs, and a survey by *Tribune* suggested that most local GC delegates were opposed (Thompson and Lucas, 1998). It was in this context that a decision was taken to urge local parties to ballot all of their members on their preference between the old clause and the proposed alternative. Where constituencies balloted, results were overwhelmingly supportive of Blair: of 470 CLPs, 467 voted for change (Judge, 1999). This effect was reinforced by the fact that the only trade union to ballot, the UCW, recorded 90 per cent support for change. Meanwhile many other unions that did not ballot, including the TGWU, UNISON, RMT and GPMU chose to vote for the status quo (Panitch and Leys, 1997). The trade unions had 70 per cent of the votes at the conference called to make the final decision, and although the new clause passed by a two-thirds majority, just 54.6 per cent of union votes were cast in support of change, compared to 90 per cent of the votes of CLPs (Shaw, 1996). This behaviour 'incensed' Blair, strengthening his commitment both to OMOV and to changing the unions' role (Gould, 1998, p. 230).

The chance to try the pure plebiscitary model came in 1996 when it was decided to publish a draft election manifesto. This was a further symbolic opportunity for the leader to demonstrate the party's support for his perspective. The document was first debated and voted on (with unanimous support) by the 1996 party conference. But it was decided to also put it out to a full ballot of the membership. Such an approach was unprecedented, raising questions about both the authority of the conference and the role of trade union affiliates. The opportunity to vote yes or no to a detailed document also presented just the problems that Clare Short had warned of, and caused some unease. Some speakers at the conference, defending the new policy-making process negotiated over previous years, warned Blair that grassroots members 'do not want just passive consultation. We want direct participation.'[20] However, given the proximity of the election the process won general support. In the event 95 per cent of members participating voted for the draft.

Despite the desires of some to use membership plebiscites as a regular form of policy consultation, this exercise has not been repeated. The experiment was not only controversial and expensive, but it also demanded significant effort. The 61 per cent turnout in 1996 had only been achieved after a concerted telephone canvassing operation from head office. In a briefing to journalists later that year it was alleged that Stephen Byers – then a close Blair ally – had floated the idea of using the ballot method to gain members' support for ending the union link immediately after the general election (Anderson and Mann, 1997). However, no such threat was carried through (not least because the party continued to rely heavily on trade union funds). In any case, by 1997 the leadership had come to see some of the benefits of more traditional forms of decision making. As discussed in Chapter 4 with respect to selections and Chapter 7 with respect to the NEC, OMOV ballots were not always the moderating influence that had previously been imagined. Indeed once Labour was in government it was the traditional left that called (presumably with its tongue firmly in its cheek) for consultative ballots on issues such as the choice to go to war in Iraq.

THE PARTNERSHIP IN POWER REFORMS

There were therefore problems for both leaders and members with the plebiscitary model. In any case even its most enthusiastic supporters realised that member ballots could not provide an immediate replacement for the policy-making system that remained in the rulebook, based on conference and the NEC. Following defeat in 1992 the package drawn up by Larry Whitty and others had never been fully implemented, and even then the final proposals had dodged some difficult questions. Although the new NPF had met eight times before the 1997 election, it had no formal policy-making power and did not even exist in the party's rules. Meanwhile the power and procedures of annual conference remained unchanged. Attention thus soon returned to how the process should be reformed to ensure a constructive relationship between the frontbench and the party under a future Labour government.

The vehicle for further change was the Partnership in Power process. Following Whitty's departure as General Secretary in 1994 this was one of the key tasks that Blair passed to Tom Sawyer, who was appointed as his successor. At the heart of Partnership in

Power, as described in Chapter 2, was a desire to ensure that fractures did not appear between the party and the government as had happened in the past. Nothing was more central to this than attempting to manage the policy process differently. The consultation document issued to the party early in 1997 acknowledged that devising a platform of credible policies was 'the first goal of any modern, democratic political party' (Labour Party, 1997, p. 6). Policy making touched the work of all four of the project's taskforces, on the party–government relationship, the NEC, conference and local parties.

Although there was much agreement on broad principles, the details of the changes that might be introduced were hotly contested, both within the taskforces and in the party at large. Some on the inside saw this as an opportunity to implement the more participative and deliberative model of policy making that had previously been discussed but never brought to fruition. Others, still nervous of the politics of activists and the trade unions, wanted to use reform to formalise the leadership's control. These tensions existed throughout the negotiations. With many of the same actors having been involved in the earlier process the first task was, in the words of one, to 'dust down' the documents from the Kinnock/ Whitty era. But there was also a strong desire to present an initiative that was 'new' to the outside world, to continue to build confidence that the party had changed.[21] And although much relied on the earlier proposals, Blair was more determined to be bold in breaking with traditions than Kinnock wanted, or perhaps felt able, to be. At this point there were no particular activist pressures, in the way that there had been in 1989. The leader was in a powerful position and there was now less need to compromise.

Some elements of the new package were simply inherited from the previous proposals. There would still be something called a 'rolling programme' of policy making, but this was no longer conceived as a continuously evolving text. Each policy document would be discussed over two years, with the first year involving wide consultation and debate about principles and the second year concentrating on the detail. The entire policy programme would be completed in this way over three years between general elections, with two overlapping cycles. The National Policy Forum and policy commissions would remain central, and have the responsibility for receiving submissions from local parties and affiliates. But the difficult question remained over the powers of annual conference to amend policy. The most radical of those involved in the taskforce discussions, including some close to the leader, believed that policy documents emerging from the NPF should continue to be non-amendable, and that the process of submitting resolutions to conference should be ended. However, it was completely infeasible to get this agreed by annual conference, not least because the trade unions would never accept it. At the other extreme the CLPD continued to propose that amendments to documents be submitted and composited at the conference. However, this had already been dismissed as impractical, and would cede far more control to local parties than the leadership was willing to countenance. In any case the compositing system was one of the aspects of the current process that was most widely mocked.

In the end two compromises were reached. First, an agreement was made that the NPF and policy commissions would be empowered, as had originally been proposed, to present alternative policy options on which conference could vote. The document debated at the 1997 conference made clear that '[w]here the NPF was unable to reach a consensus view it would be the responsibility of the NPF to include alternative proposals representing different constituencies of opinion within the forum and the party as a whole' (Labour Party, 1997a, p. 15). Thus 'annual conference would for the first time have the opportunity to debate and vote on alternative positions within policy statements' (Labour Party, 1997a, p. 7). This principle, which had been agreed by conference seven years before, was necessary to win the support of major unions to the package, as well as that of some taskforce members. It promised to deliver, in a managed way, the amendable policy documents that activists had long called for.

The second compromise was a more fundamental breach with the rolling programme principle, but also proved necessary to win trade union support. As the programme was to focus on future policy it was conceded that there would also be a small amount of space left on the conference agenda to debate 'contemporary issues'. Each CLP and affiliate would be entitled to submit one resolution which addressed issues that were 'not substantially addressed in the ongoing policy work of the NPF and organisational and cam-paigning work of the NEC and which therefore would not other-wise be addressed on the conference agenda' (Labour Party, 1997a, p. 16). A ballot would be taken at the opening of conference to prioritise between these issues, although only a few would be debated. The retention of some right to submit resolutions direct to the conference was seen as an important 'safety valve' which would ensure that the policy process remained responsive to the wider party. The compromise was hard fought and agreed only shortly before the final documents were drawn up. It helped stifle the protests by those such as the CLPD that Partnership in Power was destroying the rights of local parties. But it was almost certainly not what Blair wanted.

These two concessions somewhat calmed the fears that Partnership in Power would mark the end of conference's traditional role as the final arbiter of policy. A warning shot had been fired at the 1996 conference, in a composite moved by the party's largest trade union affiliate the TGWU which expressed concern that conference was 'in danger of losing its status' and that it must remain central to the policy process.[22] The final document promised that the new system would be 'more deliberative and extended ... without detracting from the sovereign powers of annual conference' (Labour Party, 1997a, p. 6). However the compromise that had been reached with the unions was distinctly shaky. Rather surprisingly given the centrality of 'alternative positions' to the package, the exact mechanism for agreeing these was not spelt out or voted into the party's rules. Likewise the number of contemporary resolutions to be timetabled for debate was left to the discretion of the Conference Arrangements Committee.[23]

Also central to selling the proposals to the membership was the extent to which they promised to broaden participation in policy discussions throughout the party. Although this had formed part of the rhetoric of previous packages, relatively little had been achieved in practice. As Tom Sawyer acknowledged in his conference speech in 1996, '[t]he National Policy Forum has been a success ... for the people involved. It has not been a success for the thousands of people who are not involved, many of whom are not absolutely certain what goes on there' (Labour Party, 1996, p. 220). The reforms promised a more representative National Policy Forum, and a system of local policy forums for discussion of policy documents. Policy commissions would invite submissions from local parties, members, affiliates and outside organisations, which would in theory inform the drafting of documents. Reports of the submissions received would be passed to the NPF and used, where necessary, to construct the alternative positions that conference would later consider.

These carefully crafted compromises were probably as much as the party could bear, even in the euphoric glow of victory in which the proposals were considered at the 1997 conference. Consultation on the package had been left very late, and spanned the election period itself. Of the 842 responses received, only 31 per cent actively supported a rolling programme, though substantially fewer were opposed (Labour Party, 1997a). In the constituencies a concerted campaign of resistance was mounted by the CLPD and other groups. A new organisation, Labour Reform, established in 1996, took on a co-ordinating role amongst the sceptics. A model resolution was circulated calling for delay, and some 50 constituencies submitted resolutions to this effect to the 1997 conference. Opponents noted with irony that the document promising amendable policy documents was itself being put to conference on a non-amendable basis (though supporters also suggested that the shambolic process for compositing resolutions on the subject also illustrated why this system should be dropped). The debate attracted contributions from many involved at earlier stages. Peter Hain, elected to parliament in 1991 and now a Welsh Office minister, urged support for the rolling programme he had proposed in 1988. Larry Whitty, now Lord Whitty, emphasised the continuity from the 1990 package, though noting that the proposals had now 'been somewhat overspun as a centralising process' (Labour Party, 1997b, p. 23). The composite resolution which called for delay was supported by 43 per cent of CLP votes, but was easily defeated by the votes to the trade unions. They had already won their concessions, and with these in place the NEC's document passed by a show of hands. Rule changes formally cemented the NPF and new conference process, but left much of the detailed design to the NEC.

The proposals created a larger National Policy Forum to that established in 1993, but with a similar structure. The biggest change was to expand the seats available to CLPs and regional parties, who now made up 72 of the 175 members (41 per cent of the total). The separate women's section was abolished (as happened simultaneously to the women's section on the NEC – see Chapter 5) but a women's quota of roughly 40 per cent applied to all sections. This left the trade unions as the under-represented group. However, given the concessions they had won over the powers of annual conference, coupled with their ability to organise on the Forum (as discussed below), union influence remained significant. Overseeing the whole process would be a new Joint Policy Committee (JPC), with equal numbers of representatives from government and the NEC, and there would be a new set of policy commissions.[24] Both of these built on the structures created by Kinnock.

The new system could thus be seen to a large extent to be a development of the previous arrangements. The joint involvement of the PLP and extra-parliamentary party in policy making had now finally been put into the rules. In such a partnership the front bench – particularly when the party was in government – was always likely to be dominant. But the NPF was now bigger and more representative, with clearer methods of election. Policy commissions were also to be given a more representative membership and greater visibility. The system finally promised the elusive prize of documents that conference could amend. It also promised proper consultation throughout the policy cycle, which had never before been achieved. However, the price paid by local parties and affiliates in terms of control of the conference agenda had been high. From now the number of issues submitted through resolutions directly to conference and going on to be debated would, in practice, be reduced to four. This put a far greater emphasis on the importance of the NPF, and its ability to reflect and champion the party's views.

THE NEW SYSTEM IN PRACTICE 1997–2001

The new National Policy Forum was put together immediately after the 1997 conference. The original membership is shown in Table 6.1. Members of each section were to be chosen by those they represented, by a variety of means. Hence MPs and MEPs elected their members by ballot, as did Labour councillors. Trade union representatives were chosen collectively by the trade unions (with no balloting required). Regional representatives were to be chosen by regional conferences and, in a curious twist given earlier commitments to OMOV, constituency representatives were to be chosen by a ballot of constituency delegates at annual conference. This mechanism – which had been dropped for NEC elections in 1993, in favour of OMOV – had not been popular in the constituencies themselves when the consultation had taken place.[25] The leadership's decision represented one of the first reversals of the OMOV principle, and demonstrated party managers' growing realisation that conference delegates might prove easier to control.

There was significant interest in the new NPF amongst party members at the outset. The attention that had focussed on the new arrangements led to a lively contest for the first constituency seats, with many candidates putting themselves forward. Results were announced in January 1998, and in that same month the new NPF met for the first time. In the absence of policy commissions and documents this was primarily a business meeting. Robin Cook MP (who had chaired the old NPF since 1994) was elected as chair and Ian McCartney MP as vice chair. Members then approved detailed procedures that had been recommended by the JPC, including a timetable of work and proposed structure of policy commissions. There were to be eight commissions, each broadly shadowing one or two government departments, with equal numbers of representatives from government, the NEC and the NPF.[26]

Table 6.1: NPF membership as agreed by 1997 conference[27]

	Total	Women's quota	How elected
CLPs†	54	18	Conference delegates
Regions†	18	9	Regional conferences
Trade unions	30	15	'Agreed formula'
PLP	9	4	MPs
EPLP	6	3	MEPs
Government	8	3	Appointed
Local government‡	9	4	See note below
Socialist societies	3	1	Conference delegates
Co-op Party	2	1	Co-op NEC
Black Socialist Society	4	2	Black Socialist Society
NEC	32	12	All members, ex officio
Total	175	72	

† CLP representatives to comprise five plus one youth representative from each of nine regions, regional representatives two from each region. Quotas are two per region for constituency representatives and one for regional representatives.
‡ Comprising four from the Local Government Association Labour Group and one from its Scottish equivalent, elected by these groups, plus four for the Association of Labour Councillors, elected by all Labour councillors.
Source: Labour Party (1997a).

It was agreed that three documents, on Health, Welfare, and Crime and Justice, would be circulated in the first year of the programme for consultation. This would be followed in the second year by six further documents. The full timetable for both policy cycles is shown in Table 6.2. The new NPF also agreed to adopt the same Standing Orders as its predecessor. These stated that the Forum's main business was to be taken in small workshops, which would seek where possible to reach consensus views. Notes taken in the workshops would be brought together into one set of comments on each document, to be discussed in a plenary session. Whilst the chair or 'facilitator' of each workshop was generally an NPF member, the note taker was a member of staff from the party's Policy Unit. The process therefore sought to emphasise points of consensus between workshops, but did leave much to the discretion of party staff. This was a regular source of friction with those Forum members who felt their views had not been accurately reported.

Table 6.2: Timetable for policy documents 1997–2001

	First cycle 1997-99†	Second cycle 1998-2000‡
NPF agrees first year document	May 1998	Jan 1999
First year document circulated	June 1998	Feb 1999
Comments due	Dec 1998	Sept 1999
NPF agrees second year document	Jan 1999	Dec 1999
Second year document circulated	Feb 1999	Jan 2000
Comments due	April 1999	March 2000
NPF agrees final document	July 1999	July 2000
Final document circulated	Aug 1999	Aug 2000
Conference votes on final document	Sept 1999	Sept 2000

† First cycle documents: Health; Crime and Justice; Welfare.
‡ Second cycle documents: Industry, Culture and Agriculture; Education and Employment; Economy; Democracy and Citizenship; Britain in the World; Environment, Transport and the Regions.

Policy commissions included the relevant ministers within their membership, with one of these acting as joint convenor. Although responsibility for drafting documents for approval by the NPF officially lay with the commissions, in practice this was controlled by ministers and special advisers – who had policy knowledge and access to specialist information – working in collaboration with party staff. Practice between commissions varied widely, but the job of non government members was generally just to comment on and approve these drafts, often to short timescales and in meetings that were ill attended. Nonetheless, complaints about such matters by policy commission members appeared merely to echo those made by members of similar policy groups in the Kinnock era and before.[28]

Once documents were approved by the NPF, they were circulated for wider consultation. At this point all groups – and indeed individuals – were invited to comment, but particular emphasis was put on creating 'local policy forums', open to all members and run along the same deliberative format used at national meetings. After the first documents were circulated, in June 1998, 45 such forums were co-ordinated by head office and regional office staff. These ran on a similar model to the national meetings, and ministers and NPF members from the region were encouraged to attend. Originally it was intended to hold such meetings at each consultative point in the cycle. However, they proved extremely resource intensive and still could reach only a fraction of the national membership. Over time discussion became increasingly concentrated in more traditional forums – regional conferences, workshops at national conferences, and within CLPs.

Perhaps the most difficult question within the process remained how differences of view were to be reflected. At all stages, locally and nationally, the procedure encouraged consensus. However, inevitably conflicts remained. The views of those consulted in the party, and on the NPF itself, were bound to sometimes be critical of the government line. The new arrangements had promised that conference would be the final arbiter, but had not specified how alternative positions would be arrived at.

The suggestion in the original 1990 proposals, echoed in the Partnership in Power consultation document, had been that the policy commissions would draft alternative positions, on the basis of submissions received. As the commissions handled both the submissions and the drafting of documents, this would seem a logical approach. However, it would require staff to prepare text that contradicted government policy, and ministers to approve it. This proved too great a cultural challenge. Thus the JPC – in effect the co-ordinator of the process, under strong guidance from staff at head office and 10 Downing Street – proposed that the responsibility for inserting alternative views should be passed to members of the NPF. This would require the NPF's last meeting in the second year of the cycle, when the documents were finalised for annual conference, to devise the policy options. The JPC thus proposed that documents drafted for the meeting would include only the government-approved line, but that NPF members could table amendments to reflect views held in the wider party. The JPC would then decide which amendments were acceptable.

Workshops at this final NPF meeting of the cycle would then focus largely on amendments. NPF members who submitted amendments would have an opportunity to discuss them with ministers and attempt to negotiate mutually acceptable forms of words. Final decisions would be taken in votes by the whole NPF at the end of the weekend. Any amendments achieving majority support at this point would be incorporated in the documents. Amendments not achieving a majority but supported by a quarter of Forum members present (or at least 35 members, if attendance was low) would be included as a 'minority position'. On these issues conference would have the final choice.

This system created a number of problems. For the first time it turned the NPF meeting into an adversarial process, with members set up as potential opponents of the official line. It no longer acknowledged that differences of view over policy were inevitable, instead generating pressure on NPF members not to 'rock the boat'. The emphasis was on negotiating away conflict amongst a relatively small closed group, with any concessions by ministers not visible to the wider party. In effect the pressure remained to create non-amendable documents for consumption by conference.

The NPF met regularly between 1997 and 2001 to consider documents at different stages of preparation, and to discuss how to run the policy process. It generally sought to reflect views heard in the wider party, insert perspectives based on Forum members' own experiences, and amend errors and omissions to make documents palatable for consultation. However, it was at the final stages of formally agreeing and amending documents that the Forum became the particular focus of attention. The following sections review these final meetings during both cycles in the 1997-2001 parliament, before returning to assess the success of the process as a whole.

The first cycle

The final meeting about the first round of documents was held in Durham in July 1999. This discussed documents on Health, Welfare, and Crime and Justice. Dealing with amendments was a new experience for Forum members, ministers and party staff alike. The mechanism adopted required each amendment to be submitted in advance, and to be backed by the signatures of eight Forum members. This created a challenge, as papers were circulated only around a week in advance, and members were scattered throughout Britain. Amendments also had to reflect opinion expressed in the consultation. To aid this judgement, documents compiled by party staff summarising the roughly 300 submissions received were circulated to NPF members. By the deadline 215 amendments had been submitted by 28 members of the Forum.

Dealing with these amendments was a big logistical task. All were typed for circulation at the pre-Forum JPC, and later at the NPF meeting itself. Following recommendations from the staff (in close consultation with ministerial offices) the JPC decided which amendments would be endorsed. Those members who had submitted amendments that were not endorsed were then invited to individual meetings with relevant ministers at the start of the Forum meeting. At these meetings, also attended by Policy Unit staff and special advisers, the proposer of an amendment could withdraw it, or negotiate new words with the minister. If agreement could not be reached the amendment would remain 'non endorsed' when the workshops began. As an illustration, 113 amendments were submitted on the Welfare document, of which eight were considered not to reflect the consultation, leaving 44 that were endorsed by the JPC and 67 that were not endorsed. Of these 67, mutually acceptable words were agreed at the start of the Forum meeting on 20, a further 32 were withdrawn, and just 15 therefore remained for decision at the end of the weekend.

Changes negotiated through this process included a commitment to block commercial planting of genetically modified crops until there was evidence that they were not environmentally damaging, a commitment to ensure that Private Finance Initiative (PFI) projects in health offered value for money, and pledges on tackling domestic violence. Many other amendments covered smaller matters of wording and presentation. The biggest issue of the weekend concerned restoring the link between increases in the state pension and earnings growth, which had been broken by the Thatcher government in 1980. This was a touchstone issue for many in the party and had been raised widely in consultation responses on the Welfare document. It therefore formed the substance of numerous amendments. However, ministers argued that a commitment to restore the earnings link would be too costly, and that any additional spending on pensions was better targeted at the poorest pensioners. Intense negotiations with trade union representatives over the weekend on this and other issues resulted in an agreed statement that government would launch a 'national debate' on welfare policy, and seek to ensure that a 'rising Basic State Pension ... will remain the foundation of pension provision' (Labour Party, 1999a, p. 85-6). In return for endorsement of this single amendment, 14 others by the trade unions were withdrawn, and ministers won trade union support for their positions across the board. In the closing plenary union representatives therefore voted against all outstanding amendments, including those from constituency representatives on the earnings link. Despite the belief by some members of the Forum that such a controversial issue was just the type of subject appropriate to leave to conference to decide, no outstanding amendment won more than 16 votes in the closing plenary. Most of these came from supporters of the left-wing 'Grassroots Alliance'. Pleas for unity by the platform had impressed trade union and constituency representatives alike, and resulted in the first cycle of documents being completed without any alternative positions. Conference would therefore, as had always previously been the case, be presented with documents on a take-it-or-leave-it basis. This was just the outcome that some of those closest to Blair had wanted but, given the commitments made when Partnership in Power was agreed, it led to controversy.

The second cycle

The second such meeting was held in Exeter a year later. Although the system had been tested once, this meeting represented a greater challenge. There were six, rather than three, documents to consider and NPF members were now clearer about what was expected. The new process was suffering credibility problems because of the lack of alternative positions from the first cycle, and this caused many members, and some ministers and party staff, concern. Due to the previous difficulties of submitting amendments, changes to the Forum's standing orders had been negotiated so that only two signatures were needed and members received documents two weeks in advance. However, unlike previously, no summary was circulated of the submissions received, in part because there had been more than a thousand of these and the task had become infeasible for the policy staff to manage. Instead NPF members were advised to visit their regional offices if they wanted to view the submissions in full.

On this occasion there were 658 amendments proposed. Of these, 30 were ruled out of order and 213 were endorsed in advance. A further 229 were accepted after negotiation with ministers and 148 were withdrawn. At the end of the weekend 38 amendments remained non endorsed.

Amendments negotiated at the Forum covered a wide range of issues. For example, in part due to the active organisation by the Labour Party's affiliated environmental pressure group, SERA, concessions were won on ending 'fuel poverty', recognising the unsustainable nature of current levels of traffic growth, and promoting organic farming and renewable energy sources. On the Democracy and Citizenship document words were accepted stating that government would consider changing the law to allow positive action for women in elected office (later acted upon, see Chapter 5). An agreement was also brokered between supporters and opponents of changing the electoral system for the House of Commons. This recommitted the party to a referendum before any change took place, and promised a review of the systems currently in use across the UK. It went on to form the basis of the words in the 2001 manifesto.

A number of issues were successfully negotiated with the trade unions over the weekend. These included reviewing the exemption for transport workers from the EU Working Time Directive, a commitment that public service reform would not rely on a 'two-tier' workforce with different terms and conditions of employment, and a commitment that the Low Pay Commission which monitored the national minimum wage would be made permanent. The way in which these negotiations were conducted however angered many members of the Forum, who felt excluded. Senior trade unionists were generally absent from the workshops, with wording of key amendments discussed in parallel private meetings and not available to the full Forum until the final plenary meeting. Through this process the trade unions demonstrated their continuing collective muscle, which far exceeded the ability of the disparate constituency representatives to negotiate collectively, despite their far greater numeric strength. Negotiation over such workplace issues had always been central to the party–union relationship and to winning trade union support for leadership policy platforms, traditionally at conference (Minkin, 1980; 1992). In many ways the NPF just provided a new site within which these negotiations could take place, but at the same time made this more visible to activists. These members were dismayed by what they saw, though they none-theless largely welcomed its results.

One issue on which the trade unions were not satisfied at Exeter was pensions. Following the agreement at Durham there had been no significant progress on the part of government. Attempts to amend the Economy document to reflect union concerns were ruled out of order, as under the 'rolling programme' discussions about an issue included in the previous year's document were considered closed. However, ministers were forced to promise a statement to conference on these issues, including the earnings link. The inability to satisfy union discontent ultimately led to a conference defeat, as discussed in Chapter 8.

At the close of the Exeter meeting there was less certainty about the outcome of votes than there had been the previous year. At the final plenary two of the 38 non-endorsed amendments won majority support and were incorporated into the documents. One gave a vague pledge to review the use of standing charges by utility companies. The other, more specifically, promised to lower the minimum age to stand for elected office (for example, as a local councillor or MP) from 21 to 18. Notably this was not acted upon by Labour in the 2001 parliament, despite occasional reminders from Forum members. Most remaining amendments were defeated, with many falling just short of the required 35 votes. These included, for example, proposals to end the charitable status of private schools, to raise the National Insurance upper earnings limit and to end the PFI.[29] The Grassroots Alliance group formed a core of support for these amendments, but were joined by some other members, inclu-ding some trade union representatives.

At the end of the weekend seven amendments had won over 35 votes but fallen short of an overall majority, giving them 'minority position' status. These positions were as follows:

- To extend the Sure Start scheme into the next parliament.
- To extend the New Deal for Schools into the next parliament.
- To commit to basing education funding on a block grant.
- To consider introducing personal penalties for directors of polluting companies.
- To consult on lowering the voting age to 16.
- That elected members should make up the majority in a reformed House of Lords.
- To introduce the Automatic Train Protection safety system onto all rail lines rather than just high-speed lines.

Some of these positions were relatively uncontroversial, and indeed there was suspicion that opposition to them had been engineered by party staff specifically to ensure that there were alternative positions left for conference to consider. However, others were not evidently welcomed. The rail safety amendment, proposed by the rail unions RMT and TSSA, had been won with support of other union representatives. The proposal on votes at 16, though later to be floated by government as a possible policy, was won with support of youth and other constituency representatives against the wishes of the platform, as was the amendment on Lords reform. This latter was probably the most genuinely controversial alternative position to reach the conference agenda, and was vigorously opposed at the NPF meeting by Home Secretary Jack Straw.[30]

Problems with the system

The National Policy Forum arrangements formalised sites for deliberation on policy detail within the party's structures, bringing together party members and government ministers, and resulting in some genuine negotiation. However, they also had a number of significant weaknesses. These may be considered under four main headings.

Member participation

Although the new arrangements sought to break with the past by involving members throughout the party in debating the content of policy statements, this succeeded only to a limited extent. In part this can be attributed to resource constraints both at the centre and in local parties. But it also had cultural roots, including the continued mutual distrust between members and leaders.

Local parties were provided with draft documents and invited to comment, but suffered a number of problems. Timetabling could be difficult, with only two months to comment at some stages and nine documents issued simultaneously at one point. The organisation of local meetings proved resource intensive and ideally demanded skilled facilitators, often not available locally. Meetings also needed to accommodate members with very mixed skills and levels of knowledge about policy. Arguably this required political education alongside policy discussion, but this suggestion was often resented by the membership. To avoid some of these problems regional offices, also with limited resources, organised the first local policy forums. Seyd and Whiteley found that these were 'a success for the participants, since most enjoyed the experience. However, only a minority among them believed such forums to be influential' (2002, p. 24).

By creating the impression that local discussions would directly influence policy the party set high expectations. The reality, local parties found, was generally that their comments were sent into a void and they had little idea of the result. The party's Policy Unit, comprising no more than 10 staff, did not have the capacity to respond to every submission. Indeed, as the level of submissions steadily rose it is doubtful whether they even had the capacity to read them. Meanwhile, links between NPF members and local parties were often poor. Constituency representatives on the NPF were volunteers with limited resources. Their visibility was low and they were thus often not invited to local meetings. This meant they arrived at NPF meetings with patchy knowledge of the views from their region and (with the exception of the papers circulated before the Durham meeting) were not informed of this by others.

Problems such as these fuelled suspicion by local members that the consultation process was a front. This was aggravated by the virtual boycott of the system by left groups in the party, which either had so little faith in it or so few resources (or both) that they did not seek to organise responses to consultation documents as they had previously organised resolutions to conference. Some moderate groups, such as SERA, did use the system successfully. But generally the lack of organised voices resulted in a disparate cacophony that could all too easily be ignored. As one CLP complained, 'There was a strong perception that although the party paid lip service to taking the views of ordinary members into account, in practice the structure is designed to make it difficult for a constituency to advance a view which is different from the policy line which has already been set by the party leadership.'[31]

Internal democracy

The National Policy Forum has also suffered from some problems of its own internal democracy. Following the initial rush in 1997, interest in standing for the Forum rapidly declined, as the processes for gaining nomination were difficult to negotiate and it returned to relative obscurity. By 2000 only 41 people stood for the 27 constituency places available, leaving several of these uncontested. Election by conference delegates was far from inclusive, as it did not engage directly with members or constituencies. It was also restricted to those constituencies that sent delegates to conference (sometimes as few as one in three in Scotland). Although hustings were held for the first elections in 1998 this process was never repeated and delegates were instead asked to decide on the basis of short written statements. There were regular allegations that party staff sought to influence delegates' votes, and similar claims were made within the Forum with respect to elections to policy commissions. Given the potential influence of Forum members in deciding the wording of policy documents, particularly once they had been given the job of proposing and voting on amendments, the temptation to interfere was obvious.

As mentioned above there were also concerns about the powers of party staff to set the agenda through the reporting of workshops, and these were duplicated to some extent with respect to regional staff at local policy forums. Summarising the views of over 100 members in a few pages was a challenge at best, and claims that this was not done impartially were common. Similarly, concerns about the running of policy commissions have already been mentioned. And whilst in principle these bodies had responsibility for dealing with submissions from the wider party, in practice the volume of submissions made this difficult.

One of the intractable weaknesses with the democracy of the Forum is the strength of organised rather than unorganised voices. The trade unions, whilst formally only 17 per cent of members, have significant influence due to their ability to organise collectively.[32] This is backed up by their seats on the NEC/JPC, their vote share at conference and their financial contributions. In contrast, constituency and regional representatives, whilst having 41 per cent of NPF votes, do not naturally adopt collective positions and have failed to organise as a group. Indeed smaller groups such as the local government representatives (crucially also resourced by full time paid officers outside the Forum, unlike the constituencies) formed a more effective collective lobby. The left-wing Grassroots Alliance also sought to organise collectively, but its numbers were small and its initiatives always strongly resisted by the leadership.

Partnership with government

The original vision of the new policy process was to create a partnership between party and government that would allow different perspectives to be discussed and accommodated. Meetings of the National Policy Forum and policy commissions certainly facilitated this to some extent. NPF members (albeit not always well connected to grassroots members) had direct access to lobby ministers, and deals were struck as a result. The process – sending ministers to local meetings as well as to the Forum itself – was unprecedented, and kept government to some extent in touch with the concerns of the party. Yet government remained very much in the driving seat.

This power relationship between government and party over policy occurs naturally as a result of the former's far superior access to resources, and ultimate responsibility for implementing decisions, and had always created tensions in the party. However, some weaknesses crept into the new 'partnership' which could have been avoided. One difficulty was the structuring of policy commissions to shadow Whitehall departments, giving one lead minister effective control. This created barriers to discussing cross-cutting issues and reinforced rather than diluted the 'departmentalitis' that can afflict government itself. Problems occurred in particular with respect to economic issues – affecting all policy areas, but closely guarded by Treasury ministers within the economic policy documents. In addition the drafting of documents by special advisers within departments discouraged consideration of issues not already on departmental agendas. This second significant agenda-setting power militated against policy innovation from the grassroots, and increased the indirect influence of the non-partisan civil service above that of the more value-driven politics of party members. Finally, there was a mindset that sought to negotiate away differences for fear of generating 'splits'. This was a reversal of the more pluralistic approach originally envisaged, which sought to recognise that the party inevitably included a range of views. Containing differences within the NPF itself was somewhat artificial, and meant that arguments could fail to be made by ministers in the wider party.

The relationship with government raises the question of how the new policy machinery would operate in opposition. Without the resources of the civil service, shadow ministers would be far more reliant on expertise that could be drawn in through the NPF process. This system operated relatively effectively in some areas under the original NPF from 1993. The policy commission on the environment, for example, included various specialists from external pressure groups who worked successfully with shadow ministers and other Labour members. Although the new system was designed specifically for government, a return to opposition might, ironically, see a more balanced partnership in operation.

Accountability of policy outputs

The ultimate test of the process is the quality of its outputs, and the extent to which they both reflect the views of the party and go on to form the basis of government action.

We have seen that in the early stages the promised alternative positions did not materialise. So much did the arrangements encourage consensus between those present at NPF meetings, and create procedural and psychological barriers to dissenting positions, that concerns of the wider party were often stifled. Even in the second round alternative positions did not reflect the big questions facing the party, and NPF members chose to negotiate compromises rather than present opposing views to conference. Whether conference *should* have the last say on policy is another question, but the failure to live up to promises made about the new process caused frustration and disillusionment amongst activists. A particular difficulty was the lack of transparency of policy commissions, with submissions from local parties not published or even publicly summarised. As Peter Hain observed later, the process lacked an 'audit trail' (2004, p. 30). Members were unable to trace what had happened to their submissions, and could not view those coming from other local parties and affiliates. This was in stark contrast to the old conference system, where resolutions and amendments guaranteed each CLP two published statements each year which were circulated widely inside and outside the party. The changes thus limited the opportunities for 'horizontal' communication between local parties of the kind that had previously existed (Shaw, 1994, p. 120). Then members may have been denied formal power, but at least they were guaranteed 'voice' (Hirschman, 1970), which in turn created a degree of leverage.

The goal of the process in terms of outputs was to form the basis of the policy that would be presented in the next general election manifesto. This in itself caused friction, as members were generally more interested in discussing contemporary controversies. However, there were also concerns about the extent to which the manifesto reflected positions negotiated at the NPF, and this went on to produce tensions, as discussed below. Shaw (2002) argues that there was only modest sign of influence by the party in the 2001 manifesto. An analysis by two Forum members, Daniel Zeichner and Anne Campbell MP, noted, for example, that the government's future plans for the National Health Service, published after the NPF's own health document, included various controversial issues that the party had not discussed (Campbell and Zeichner, 2001). There is some evidence, however, that the Policy Forum process had a more gradual and indirect impact on the party's policy agenda. The leadership sought to convince doubters by producing lists of government policies for which it ascribed the initiative to the NPF. But the extent to which this was really the case is largely immeasurable. For example the proposal to reduce the voting age to 16 was brought to the NPF by Daniel Zeichner, on behalf of the Eastern region, following discussion at a local policy forum. It went on to be debated and ultimately rejected by conference in 2000. The proposal was later the subject of much national debate and came close to being adopted as government policy in 2004. The extent to which the Policy Forum had influenced government, rather than the same external forces influencing both, is difficult to assess. However, it is likely that Labour's new structures played at least some role in alerting ministers to issues such as this.

REFORM, RERUNNING AND REVIEW

The National Policy Forum process in the 2001 parliament was characterised by much continuity, but also a weakening of some of the original principles, and a growing scepticism which led to a review. This was due to be discussed at the 2005 conference, expected to fall on the far side of a general election.

After the 2001 election dissatisfaction focussed particularly on the divergence of government policy from that discussed at the NPF, which had supposedly set the agenda for Labour's second term in office. Two of the most controversial policies pursued by the new government, both resulting in large parliamentary rebellions in the House of Commons, had not been the subject of consultation and had not appeared in the manifesto. The proposal to create 'foundation' hospitals, governed locally and with new financial freedoms, had not even been hinted at in the NPF document on Health agreed in 1999. The proposal to allow universities to charge students 'top-up' fees had been explicitly ruled out in the 2001 manifesto, and it was alleged that the policy had been changed without agreement by either the cabinet or the PLP.[33] These policies raised serious questions about the credibility of the NPF process – but also far bigger questions about the leadership's commitment to consultation in general.

Table 6.3: Timetable for policy documents 2001–2005*

	First cycle 2001-04†	Second cycle 2002-2004‡
NPF agrees first year document	Feb 2002	Nov 2002
First year document circulated	Mar 2002	Jan 2003
Comments due	Oct 2002	Oct 2003
NPF agrees second year document	Mar 2003	Nov 2003
Second year document circulated	May 2003	Jan 2004
Comments due	Oct 2003	May 2004
NPF agrees final document	Mar 2004	July 2004
Final document circulated	Aug 2004	Aug 2004
Conference votes on final document	Sept 2004	Sept 2004

* This reflects the revised timetable agreed in July 2002 and followed for consultation. However, plans were then changed so that only five documents (on Reconnecting People with Politics; Britain in an Interdependent World; Building Prosperity for All; Improving Health and Education; Creating Sustainable Communities) would be discussed at the 2004 conference.
†First cycle documents: Britain in the World; Democracy, Citizenship and Political Engagement; Welfare Reform; Health; Trade and Industry.
‡ Second cycle documents: Crime, Justice and Citizenship; Economy; Education and Skills; Quality of Life; Transport, Housing, Local Government and the Regions

After the 2001 election the process itself underwent a series of changes, agreed by the JPC with nominal input from NPF members. In November 2001 policy commissions were re-established largely as before, and the NPF agreed that there would be five documents discussed in the first cycle (2001–03), and five in the second cycle a year later. However, it was subsequently proposed by the JPC that both cycles would run until 2004, with all ten documents to be discussed at conference that year. This raised concerns on several fronts. One was the ability of the NPF, conference and party staff to cope with 10 documents simultaneously. Another was that the 2004 conference, relatively close to the general election, would feel constrained in its ability to express opposition, whilst earlier conferences would have relatively little to discuss. In December 2003 the JPC proposed a partial solution to the first of these problems by condensing the 10 documents into five. The combination of these changes effectively abandoned the rolling programme principle, resulting in only one decision-making conference within the policy cycle.

In parallel with these alterations, the electoral cycle for the NPF was changed. In late 2003 the NEC agreed to postpone the 2004 elections for constituency representatives and to elect all these places in 2005. In addition, following Robin Cook's resignation from the post in 2001, a new quasi-convention developed that the appointed party chair would also be the chair of the NPF.[34] Given the loose structure agreed in 1997 none of these adaptations required rule changes, demonstrating the fragility of the arrangements.

Discontent with the process spilled over onto the conference agenda of one of the party's largest affiliates, UNISON, in May 2003. Here a grassroots motion noting that 'there have developed substantial differences between the beliefs and policies of most members of the Labour Party and affiliated organisations and the actions of government over some key policies', won support from the union's executive. In his speech to the conference the union's General Secretary Dave Prentis backed the movers' calls for a review of the party's policy process. Writing later in *Fabian Review* he was highly critical, citing foundation hospitals, faith schools and top-up fees as policies that had been adopted without the NPF's consent. As he suggested, the leadership continued to 'announce [policy] to the world first, and only consult its "partners" later' (Prentis, 2003, p. 14). He argued that a change of approach was needed. Later, when tensions about higher education funding reached the floor of the House of Commons, rebels cited the failure of the party's policy process as a key reason for parliamentary discontent. Even Tony Blair himself was forced to admit that '[p]olicy first and explanation later is not the way to do things'.[35]

The complaints from UNISON were influential, and a review of the process was rapidly announced. In presentations to the NEC and NPF the party's head of policy Matt Carter (later to be appointed its General Secretary) acknowledged some of the system's weaknesses. This analysis left some of the underlying problems untouched, however. Three working groups were established, to consider public engagement, party engagement and government engagement with Partnership in Power. Issues to be addressed included how the process could better consider contemporary issues, how the number of submissions could be increased, and how those making submissions could better be convinced that they made a difference. The more fundamental problems of how large volumes of submissions could effectively be dealt with on limited resources, and how the mindset of government could be changed, were not included.

The process was further undermined in November 2003 when – following an announcement in Tony Blair's conference speech – the party used an NPF meeting to publicly launch the 'Big Conversation'. This 80-page consultation document (Labour Party, 2003) had not previously been discussed by Forum members, although the JPC had been consulted on its content. The main purpose of the exercise was stated to be the gathering of submissions from the public on the party's policy. (In a promise eerily reminiscent of Kinnock's launch of Labour Listens, Blair had called it 'the biggest policy consultation ever to have taken place in this country'.) Within a few days there had been more than 4,000 responses, and after four months there had been 36,000. However, these added to the already high burden on party policy officers dealing with responses to the NPF documents, of which there had been 4,000 since 2001 (Labour Party, 2004). And as with consultation in the party, the 'Big Conversation' would only be judged a success if followed by a visible change of policy.

At the end of this period the new policy arrangements therefore looked fragile. Responding to the consultation on the process Peter Hain, one of its original proponents and now a cabinet minister, concluded that the system was 'losing credibility amongst members' who did 'not believe it influences major policy decisions' (Hain, 2004, p. 32). Indeed he believed that policy forums were widely seen as 'intended to neuter rather than empower the membership' (p. 24). The party's continued scepticism, and frustration at the lack of 'alternative positions', was illustrated at the 2003 conference. This voted, against the platform's wishes, to double the number of contemporary issues that could in future be debated (see Chapter 8). Combined with the breakdown of the rolling programme, and the leadership's antipathy to amendable documents, this indicated that a drift back towards the old system could be underway. A further resolution, promoted by the CLPD, and due to be debated in 2005, would implement the group's original proposal of giving all CLPs the right to submit amendments to policy documents directly, at the conference. If sufficient support could be built for this, particularly in the unions, it would create a process reminiscent of the old arrangements, but even more difficult for the leadership to control.

The unions themselves have increasingly exploited their strength on the National Policy Forum to extract concessions from government. In July 2004 the final meeting on the 2001 cycle of documents was held, at Warwick University. Some 850 amendments were submitted to three documents.[36] Although many issues were discussed, once again the meeting was dominated by the lengthy agreements which the unions were able to reach. Negotiations on these ended at 4am on Sunday, with a form of words agreed between union representatives and ministers. The 56 agreed points, later dubbed the 'Warwick accord', included protection from dismissal for striking workers, a guaranteed 20 days paid holiday per year, and greater government support for manufacturing. With these concessions unions were prepared to support the policy documents, and many other amendments were dropped. In the weeks after the Forum meeting, ministers, including the prime minister himself, were at pains to state their commitment to implement these proposals. More than any previous occasion this episode indicated the power that the trade unions still have to negotiate collectively, through the NPF. However, it also demonstrates the way in which the arrangements themselves are held in tension. Any failure by the government to honour the 'Warwick accord' or similar agreements in future, could prove enough to persuade the unions to support the CLPD's proposed changes to the policy process, resulting in an effective return to the old confrontational system.

EVALUATION

Like many of the reforms discussed in this book, the changes to Labour's policy-making process were driven by different and competing visions of internal party democracy. The result was a negotiated settlement, where all those concerned got at least some of what they had sought. The party leadership, in particular, did achieve significant reforms designed to strengthen its own position. However, it also had to concede to the demands of others in order to maintain stability and to get its own proposals agreed.

Controversies over the Labour Party's policy-making process are as old as the party itself. The most fundamental tension within Labour's democracy was always that the extra-parliamentary party, through conference and the NEC, notionally controlled policy, whilst the party in parliament had no formal power in this process. Neil Kinnock and Tony Blair sought to address this tension by creating a greater sense of partnership between the leadership and the extra-parliamentary party. This however was a difficult task, and one inevitably riddled with conflict and frustrations. After the fractious relationships that had developed from the 1960s onwards, leaders effectively sought to re-establish and formalise the balance of power that had existed in previous years – whereby they could dominate decision making and relatively easily win the party's consent. In doing so they particularly wanted to avoid clashes caused by the party adopting policy positions hostile to those of Labour governments.

The CLPD, in contrast, was established with the objective of making the party inside parliament more, rather than less, accountable to the party outside. Particularly once the leadership had regained control of drafting policy documents in the early 1980s, this group set out to protect the formal policy powers of the party conference, and to defend activists' rights to set its agenda. A third group, including pragmatists on the soft left, organisationally represented by the LCC in the late 1980s, but also including key figures on the NEC and party staff, presented a new alternative of a more consultative and 'deliberative' policy making. It was hoped that this would draw more members into policy discussions, be less confrontational than the old conference system, and give leaders and members better understanding of each other's perspectives. The soft left believed, as did the CLPD, that the old policy-making system would be improved by giving local parties and affiliates the right to amend the policy documents presented to conference by the NEC. They concluded that this should replace the system of disparate conference resolutions that could easily be ignored. However on this point the hard left, and particularly the CLPD, disagreed. They claimed that such a change would compromise constituencies' and affiliates' rights.

The settlement that emerged drew on all of these visions to some extent. The first reforms, implemented under Neil Kinnock between 1983 and 1988, created joint NEC/shadow cabinet policy structures for the first time. These were used to achieve a major shift in policy, away from some of the positions that were seen to have damaged Labour electorally. But the new arrangements also caused anger amongst activists, and led to questions about the sovereignty of annual conference. The next reforms, agreed in 1990, were thus both a genuine attempt by many to deal with the historic problems of policy making in the party, and also a defensive move on the part of the leadership. The system devised, which drew on proposals made by various organisations in the 1970s and early 1980s, was based on two important principles. First, that the division should be ended between 'top down' policy documents drafted by the NEC, and 'bottom up' conference resolutions presented by activists. Instead, there should be one unified system whereby members had input into the preparation of documents. Second, that there should be greater participation throughout the party in this process, with proper consultation and grassroots representation on the bodies overseeing the system. These proposals drew inspiration from the early reform ideas of both the left and the right, and the model agreed closely mirrored that which had been proposed by the LCC.

Although these proposals were partially implemented, the election defeat of 1992 meant that wholesale reform of the policy process was postponed until the 1997 Partnership in Power reforms. By this time the new leader, Tony Blair, wanted to be bolder in asserting the power of the parliamentary front bench over policy, and reforms were more closely driven by the leadership itself. However, even at this point important concessions had to be made. Resistance from activists, and the need to negotiate agreement with the NEC and the trade unions, resulted in a system to make policy documents amendable being formalised, whilst the ability to submit resolutions to the conference remained. Meanwhile for some engaged in Partnership in Power this was the opportunity to implement the original soft-left vision of 'participative' or 'deliberative' democracy, and to strengthen the arrangements for consultation in the party. Elements from all the protagonists' competing visions were again visible in the system that was finally agreed – and, given the loose nature of the arrangements, these have continued to be fought out behind the scenes ever since.

The relative informality of the new process created various difficulties. For example the system for agreeing 'minority positions' was not settled at the outset, and the subsequent arrangements tended to discourage options being put to conference. The fact that submissions were not published meant that the strength of feeling in the party could not be easily expressed, as had been able to occur under the old conference system. Even when minority positions were agreed by the NPF, there was confusion about who 'owned' them, enabling individual movers to come under pressure to withdraw them at the conference without consultation with fellow Forum members (see Chapter 8). The lack of written rules also meant that there was no fixed process for elections to the National Policy Forum. This allowed elections to be cancelled in 2004, without the need for consent by the party conference.

When assessing the new system it is easy to focus on its weaknesses, which are undoubtedly manifold, and some of which were summarised earlier in the chapter. Most obviously – as discussed further in Chapter 8 – the opportunities for the conference to amend documents have been extremely limited. However, it is also essential to carry out any such assessment within the context of what went before. The 1997 package formalised the status of bodies such as the National Policy Forum which were first established in the early 1990s. These, in turn, represented a significant democratisation of the system established in the early Kinnock years. At this time policy groups wholly appointed by the leader, and established under the auspices of the NEC with no formal status in the rules, were given responsibility for producing documents that conference had no power to amend. As Minkin suggests, this made the leader's office 'the basis of a centralised power structure unique in Labour Party history' (1992, p. 630).

Yet the 'old' Labour system that this replaced, in turn, had many problems of its own. Unamendable policy documents did not start with Kinnock, and had existed throughout the party's history. Whilst prior to 1983 the policy committees controlling these documents were under the direction of the elected NEC, the trade unions in practice controlled 18 of the 27 seats on this body. This had, until the 1970s, generally supported the leadership. Annual conference was formally sovereign but, as discussed in Chapter 8, the often muddled and contradictory system of resolutions could offer leaders opportunities to fudge decisions. Furthermore the unions' control of 90 per cent of conference votes meant leaders could generally bargain with them to win support – and dismiss conference as unrepresentative if this was not forthcoming. Kinnock's efforts followed a period when the political balance in the old system had changed, and it had been used to oppose the leadership. But for much of the party's history it was activists, particularly on the left, who found it unsatisfactory. Whilst the new settlement for policy making may be flawed, a glance at the party's past thus shows that there was no 'golden age' of party policy making that was both harmonious and democratic.

The extent of the changes to the policy process, and yet the intransigence of these problems, demonstrate the natural tensions between a party and its government. The new process had the potential to provide for more negotiation between government and party behind closed doors – indeed some of its original creators felt Blair and his colleagues had not realised the extent to which the new system could hold them to account. It also institutionalised contact between Labour ministers and members, with potential for fostering a greater culture of mutual understanding. However, establishing a dialogue with the party at large (rather than just the members of the NPF) showed itself to be far more resource intensive than the old conference system. The extent to which ministers wanted feedback from the party, in any case, remained ambiguous at best. And in general the system continued to be plagued by a lack of trust on both sides. The leadership's firmest opponents chose not to use it to its full extent, whilst the ability of government to brazen out conflicts with the party had perhaps been underestimated. During the 2001 parliament, after the rebellions in the PLP on foundation hospitals and top-up fees, there appeared to be a genuine realisation by leaders that consultation in the party could be beneficial, and help avoid worse confrontation at later stages of policy making. Given leaders' desire to avoid embarrassing conflicts, and to retain members to perform campaigning duties, there remained attractions for both sides in developing a more effective system.

Assessing how power has shifted within the party as a result of these changes is not a straightforward task. The new system remains fluid and many of the old conflicts continue to be played out. It will not be fully tested until it has survived (if indeed it gets that far) different conditions. On the negative side more difficult political circumstances, such as economic troubles or a fall from power, could put the system under severe strain. On the other a new leadership with a greater determination to consult, and to use the membership as a policy resource, could test its ability to do good. A mature policy process able to manage conflict, and at the same time maintain mutual trust between leaders and members, would be a major prize indeed. This was the original vision of some of those who constructed the first National Policy Forum, but whether it will ever (or could ever) be achieved remains to be seen.

Notes

1. There were many issues that frustrated activists about the 1979 manifesto, but one of the most clear cut was the refusal by party leader James Callaghan to include the party's policy to abolish the House of Lords (Golding, 2003; Seyd, 1987; Shaw, 1996).
2. These struggles are well documented elsewhere. See for example Golding (2003), Kogan and Kogan (1982), Seyd (1987), Shaw (1994).
3. For a fuller account of this period see Minkin (1992).
4. For detailed accounts of the Policy Review see Hughes and Wintour (1990), Shaw (1993), Taylor (1997).
5. Between 1979 and 1987 the office costs allowance available to MPs rose from £4,600 to £21,302 per year. In addition the total 'Short money' available to the opposition rose from £290,000 in 1979 to £440,000 in 1983 (Minkin, 1992).
6. Perhaps the most extreme example was *Labour's Programme 1982*, which formed the basis of the 1983 manifesto. This was 279 pages long and put to the conference on a non-amendable basis. At this time it was the party's right which proposed that documents should be amendable at annual conference, a situation that was very soon to reverse.
7. On this occasion the document was taken section by section over four days and 54 amendments were moved. Of these, 25 were defeated, 13 were 'remitted' to the NEC for consideration and a further 16 were agreed. However, on none of them did the decision of the conference go against the wishes of the NEC (McKenzie, 1963).
8. See for example the pamphlet by the Fabian Society's General Secretary, Dianne Hayter (1977).
9. Members of this commission included Vladimir Derer, Frances Morrell, Pete Willsman, Hilary Benn, Eric Shaw and Patrick Seyd (Burnell, 1980). It also worked in close consultation with Geoff Bish of the party's Research Department.
10. Hain was at that point an ordinary party member. He went on to become an MP in 1991.
11. This resolution, and others after it in 1989, also addressed the issue of trade union vote shares at conference. This was covered by the same NEC consultation document, but is discussed separately in Chapter 8.
12. The February NEC had rejected by 23 votes to five a motion from Ken Livingstone that conference decisions should have precedence in such cases.
13. The commission proposed that policy documents should be amendable at conference, with policy commissions working out options for inclusion, which would be put to conference as 'alternative positions'. Topical issues should still be able to be put forward by resolution, with a 'priorities ballot' to decide which were debated. This document was never adopted formally as LCC policy, but many of its

recommendations were later implemented by the party, as discussed later in the chapter.

14. Composite 2, defeated by 2,245,000 votes to 3,704,000.

15. Tim Peacock, Broxtowe CLP (Labour Party 1989, p. 141).

16. The NEC meeting on 14 September 1992 also considered a proposal from Tony Benn that in the light of defeat the proposals should be abandoned altogether, in favour of the traditional conference arrangements. However this was heavily defeated.

17. The CLPD had claimed that the leadership intended to push through rule changes to limit conference resolutions 'by relying on Party euphoria after victory' (Newsletter, October 1990). Whether or not this was correct, no such opportunity had now presented itself.

18. He was replaced the following year by Robin Cook, who served until 2002.

19. For a full account of the campaign to change Clause IV see Jones (1996), Taylor (1997).

20. Karen Price from Neath CLP (Labour Party, 1996, p. 218). This was the constituency that Peter Hain now represented in parliament.

21. The extent to which Blair himself was aware of how many ideas were recycled is not clear – not having been involved in the earlier discussions, he may well have believed the rhetoric of 'newness'.

22. Composite 52.

23. This process is further discussed in Chapter 8.

24. The JPC initially included two NPF 'observers', but direct NPF involvement was later increased, with one member specifically representing CLP and regional members.

25. It was supported by just 19 per cent of those responding, compared to 43 per cent who believed these members should be elected at regional level (Labour Party, 1997a). For a discussion of the changes to NEC elections see Chapter 7.

26. The names of the commissions matched those of their documents, which are shown in the note to Table 6.2. The only exception was the Economic Policy commission, which produced two documents – on Welfare and the Economy. Commissions had nine members, with the NPF seats divided between the three broad 'pillars' of the Forum (trade unions, constituency and regional members and 'elected members' – PLP, EPLP and local government). This arguably left only one grassroots member on each policy commission, and under pressure the representation of constituencies and regions was doubled to two the following year.

27. There were subsequently minor changes to the NPF's membership. In late 2004 it numbered 183 members in total, with the number of constituency representatives having risen to 55, the number of regional representatives having risen to 22, and addition of one representative of Labour Students and two of Labour peers.

28. Minkin notes how trade union members complained in the 1970s and early 1980s that 'NEC policy subcommittees and study groups rarely had fixed times of regular meeting, papers often went out at a late stage, membership was large but sometimes changed, meeting by meeting, as individuals found they could or could not attend'. (1992, p. 407). Shaw comments that in this period policy development was 'the preserve of a narrow enclosed world of Shadow Cabinet and NEC members, Head Office Staff, trade union leaders and outside advisers' (1993, p. 114). Although the commissions were now more representative, they still suffered from many of the same problems.
29. The PFI was also later the subject of a conference defeat, in 2002. See Chapter 8.
30. Ironically, at the first ever meeting of the NPF in 1993 Tony Blair, then shadow minister for Home Affairs, had presented a document entitled *A New Agenda for Democracy* which committed Labour to 'replacing the House of Lords with an elected second chamber'.
31. Edinburgh Central, quoted in Labour Party (2000), p. 26. The party's honesty in publishing such views must however be noted, and demonstrates that not all consultations stifle unwelcome comments from local parties!
32. If the trade union seats on the NEC are included this figure reaches 23 per cent.
33. See Robin Cook, 'Mr Blair will survive Hutton – but the row over the Iraq invasion will continue', *The Independent*, 23 January 2004.
34. This was the case with Charles Clarke, from 2001–02, and then later Ian McCartney, who was already vice chair of the NPF when appointed party chair in 2003. The exception was the short period when John Reid was party chair from October 2002 – April 2003. For discussion of the new post of party chair, see Chapter 7.
35. 2004 interview in *Fabian Review*, 116(1): p. 7.
36. An earlier meeting, also at Warwick, had dealt with the other two documents, to which there had been 250 amendments submitted with three minority positions agreed.

7

The National Executive Committee

The National Executive Committee (NEC) sits at the heart of Labour's democracy. The highest authority within the party between conferences, it traditionally had day-to-day responsibility for both policy and organisational matters. It is the body to which the party's General Secretary, and therefore all staff, formally report. The dominance of the trade unions on the NEC historically provided a 'loyal base responding to the initiatives of the "politicians", particularly the Parliamentary leadership' (Minkin, 1992, p. 626). However it had no formal link to the PLP apart from the *ex officio* seats given to the leader and deputy leader. Thanks to shifting attitudes in the unions in the 1970s the NEC increasingly became a competing centre of power, backed by activists on the left.[1] It thus began to back policy positions that were rejected by Labour leaders, and ultimately helped secure the CLPD's organisational reforms. This showed the body's potential to frustrate the parliamentary leadership, and created a determination by many, particularly moderates and right-wingers, to achieve reform.

The changes to the NEC's role in overseeing policy making were described in the previous chapter. But reforms to the Executive have been more wide ranging than that. Following many years of debate the composition of the body was changed, first through the way in which constituency representatives were elected, then in terms of its overall structure of membership. Its role and functions were also further altered, largely as a result of the Partnership in Power reforms. All of this has had important consequences for the status of the Executive, and thus for the relationship between the parliamentary and extra-parliamentary parties.

Changing the Method of Election

The first change concerned the election of the NEC's constituency section. By tradition, the NEC was elected by that body it represented – the party conference. As conference was dominated by the trade unions so too was the NEC, and it was not until 1937 that constituency delegates won the right to elect their own representatives.[2] By the 1980s constituency delegates elected seven members, and trade union delegates 12 members, with the party Treasurer and five women members elected by conference as a whole – i.e. giving trade union delegates 90 per cent of the votes. The socialist societies were collectively entitled to one representative and a youth representative was chosen at the party's youth conference.

Following the left's domination in the late 1970s, a loyalist majority was first re-established on the NEC in 1982 (Golding, 2003; Minkin, 1992). As discussed in Chapter 6 this allowed the incoming leader, Neil Kinnock, to gain control of the policy-making process. However, the rebalancing had been achieved primarily through organisation in the trade unions with respect to the trade union and women's seats on the NEC. There remained concerns that those chosen to represent the constituencies were not properly representative of grassroots members' views. From the late 1940s left-wingers (overwhelmingly MPs) had gained ground in these seats, and from the 1950s onwards the constituency block was dominated by the left. This reflected the preferences of constituency delegates to conference, who had normally been mandated by their local General Committees.[3] Despite the efforts by right-wing groups such as Solidarity to organise 'slates' of candidates for the NEC, they had negligible success in the constituency section.[4] The option of widening the franchise to include ordinary members rather than just activists in these elections had been suggested to the 1980 Commission of Enquiry by the right-wing CLV. As in parliamentary selections this could be seen as a genuinely democratising move, but might also be expected to come up with more moderate results. It was thus attractive to the Kinnock leadership. In the later 1980s the LCC, by then committed to OMOV, started to call for this reform.

In 1989, for the first time, the Executive recommended to constituencies that they ballot their members on which seven NEC candidates their conference delegate should vote for. As with balloting in the constituency section of the leadership electoral college, the trade unions were happy to support the proposal, since it would have no direct impact on their own section of the NEC. And the enfranchisement of non-activist members rather than GC delegates apparently had a dramatic effect. At the 1989 conference leading left-winger Ken Livingstone lost his seat and was replaced by John Prescott. Livingstone publicly blamed the switch to OMOV for his defeat. The CLPD, always supportive of the power of activists, was equally concerned by the development. A model resolution circulated by the group at this time argued that OMOV would reduce the local influence of trade unions (since unions had a share of GC votes), be cumbersome and costly, and 'give undue advantage to members who receive publicity in the mass media and local press at the expense of hardworking rank and file trade union and party members'.[5] Notwithstanding these claims the 1989 conference voted to support the principle of OMOV, as part of an omnibus resolution on policy making and party organisation moved by the GMB.[6]

In 1990 the NEC went further, proposing a rule change to conference to make local ballots compulsory.[7] The CLPD remained implacably opposed, suggesting that 'to ensure that "their own people" are elected, the [NEC] majority is relying on those party members who do not attend meetings and therefore rely on the media for information about Labour Party matters'.[8] Nonetheless these arguments did not move the majority of conference delegates, and the change was duly voted into the rules. In the first elections under the new compulsory system right-winger Gerald Kaufman was among those elected. The following year, 1992, left-winger Dennis Skinner lost his seat and shadow cabinet members Tony Blair and Gordon Brown were elected for the first time. In 1993 the left's iconic figure, Tony Benn, lost his seat on the Executive after 35 years' continuous service. His replacement, Harriet Harman, could hardly have been more symbolic of Labour's modernisers.[9]

OMOV thus seemed to be meeting the expectations of both its supporters and its opponents. Leadership loyalists celebrated the fact that six of the seven constituency places were now held by members of the shadow cabinet, whilst the remaining seat had been won by Kinnock after he stepped down as leader. The CLPD lamented that, just as they had predicted, ordinary members were voting for those with high public profiles, and support for left-wing critics was declining. At the 1993 conference the new system was cemented, when a rule change established a national OMOV ballot for the constituency section. This freed CLPs of the administrative duty of running the ballot and, more importantly, ended their casting of block votes for the NEC. It also effectively ended the tradition whereby the NEC was elected at the conference.[10] Instead members' votes would now be counted and totalled nationally in advance of the event. All members were to be sent a booklet of election addresses with their ballot form, and OMOV was also extended for the first time to the CLP votes for the women's section and the Treasurer.[11]

When Tony Blair became leader in 1994 the system had therefore already been reformed along the lines that he himself would have wished. As a proponent of OMOV he had long believed that this would not only provide incentives for ordinary members but, by producing results that were more representative of the membership at large, also favour the point of view of moderates. Elections to date had certainly borne out this thesis. However, immediately after Blair's election the tide seemed to change. In the OMOV ballot in 1994 Dennis Skinner regained his seat on the NEC. In the same election the quota for women, introduced in 1993 and expanded from one seat to two in 1994, produced victory for left-winger Diane Abbott.[12] Even if she had not been elected, the next highest ranking male candidate was Ken Livingstone. Suddenly, and quite possibly in an attempt to counterbalance the leader they had just elected, members were starting to use OMOV ballots to reward the party's traditional left.[13]

Results for the next couple of years were relatively stable, with the only change being Mo Mowlam's displacement of Jack Straw as a result of the further extension of the women's quota. However, the ultimate setback for Blair came in 1997 when Gordon Brown decided to stand down from the Executive. This created a vacancy that Blair's confidante Peter Mandelson hoped to fill. However, following much press speculation during the summer, Mandelson was easily beaten in the ballot by Ken Livingstone. The announcement of this result at the 1997 conference was a symbolic moment, and confirmation that OMOV, which Mandelson had personally celebrated as favouring moderate candidates, did not always have the anticipated effect (Mandelson and Liddle, 1996).

This same conference considered Partnership in Power which, as discussed below, proposed significant changes to both the makeup and functions of the NEC. It is notable that these reforms did not include the extension of OMOV, for example to election of members of the new National Policy Forum. Indeed the pressure if anything was in the other direction. Some of those closest to the leader proposed that Partnership in Power should end the use of OMOV for election of the reformed NEC constituency section, and instead this should revert to election by constituency delegates at conference. This, they believed, would make NEC elections easier to control. However others involved who had strongly supported OMOV at earlier stages believed that it was neither desirable nor politically credible to turn the clock back. Hence reforms were restricted to those described below. Given some of the later results under OMOV, some of those that defended it in 1997 may have come later to regret their decision.

One further reform first proposed in the 1989 consultation, but rejected by respondents, was a move to biennial rather than annual elections for the NEC constituency section. This question was put again to local parties ten years later (Labour Party, 2000). Although the majority of respondents again opposed this reform, the NEC proposed a rule change to the 2001 conference arguing it in part on cost grounds. This having been accepted by conference, the potential embarrassment of NEC election results was at least restricted to a two-yearly occurrence.

CHANGING THE MEMBERSHIP

Proposals to change the structure of NEC membership can be traced back over many decades. This project particularly captured the imagination of the party's right after the left took control of the constituency section in the early 1950s. At the time there were even suggestions from the loyalist leader of the TGWU, Arthur Deakin, that the constituency section should be abolished altogether (Hunter, 1959). Though this was clearly politically infeasible, other structural reforms could more realistically be pursued.

There were two inter-related issues raised by reformers. The first, which some members complained of as early as the 1930s, was that grassroots members found it difficult to be elected to the NEC (Pimlott, 1977). In practice the constituency seats were almost invariably taken by MPs. The second issue was that those MPs elected by the constituencies were overwhelmingly from the left, and thus not representative of the PLP. Soon after this phenomenon had first become established Anthony Crosland (1960) had thus suggested that the PLP should elect its own members to the Executive. In 1972 the Tribune Group pamphlet by left-wingers Frank Allaun, Ian Mikardo and Jim Sillars proposed that the PLP and the rank and file should each be free to elect their own representatives. When the right-wing CLV was founded in 1977 it made the restructuring of the Executive one of its central demands, pointing out not only these problems, but also that other groups seen to be moderate, such as Labour councillors, had no direct representation on the NEC.

These matters reached prominence when the Commission of Enquiry was set up after the 1979 election defeat. Given the left's dominance on the Executive, party leader James Callaghan favoured a restructuring as a means of winning back leadership control. The CLV's submission to the Enquiry proposed creation of a regional group on the NEC, made up of grassroots members with MPs ineligible to stand, and separate sections for the PLP and local government. Similar proposals were made by several trade unions. These proposals were generally seen, however, as a means of seeking factional advantage. The CLPD, seeing a risk to the high-profile left-wingers on the NEC, opposed a bar on MPs standing on the basis that this would deny choice to CLPs. In the event the right did not manage to secure reform, and instead won back a majority on the Executive within the existing structure. The matter then largely disappeared from view until the late 1980s.

By this time the LCC had taken up the cause of structural reform. Its proposals were less obviously driven by factional concerns, and centred on the lack of constituencies' direct voice on the NEC. Since Harold Laski departed from the Executive in 1949 the only constituency member never to have been an MP was David Blunkett (then leader of Sheffield City Council), elected in 1983 (McSmith, 1996). But even he had since entered the Commons. In the background was also the long running dispute about the election of the women's section (discussed in Chapter 5), and suggestions that women's representation should be increased through the introduction of quotas on other sections of the NEC.

In 1988 a conference resolution backed by the LCC noted the unrepresentative nature of the NEC and the dominance in the constituency section of MPs. It asked the Executive to draw up proposals whereby each region could elect its own representative. However it failed to be timetabled for debate. The report of the LCC's 1989 commission on party democracy nonetheless went on to set out a blueprint for change, drawing on many of the earlier proposals. It suggested more lay representation, abolition of the women's section and replacement with quotas, a new PLP section and a bar on MPs standing in other sections. It also proposed a reduction in the size of the trade union section, to give unions and constituencies seven members each (LCC, 1989). At the 1989 conference a nod to these ideas was included within the GMB's omnibus resolution.

However, following consultation the NEC limited itself to proposing the introduction of OMOV and women's quotas, rather than any structural reform. The major changes proposed in *Democracy and Policy Making for the 1990s* related to the new policy-making mechanisms, which alone were an ambitious target. Satisfactory change to the NEC, the document noted, would require complete reorganisation, as simply giving one seat to each region would conflict with the more urgent priority of applying quotas to every section (Labour Party, 1990a). The LCC continued to lobby on the issue and their demands were again debated at the 1995 conference.[14] However, it was not substantially returned to by the NEC until the Partnership in Power reforms.

The future of the NEC was absolutely central to Partnership in Power, seeking as this programme did to avoid the kind of conflicts that had occurred between the PLP and extra-parliamentary party in the 1970s. Seven of the 11 main proposals in the January 1997 consultation paper related directly to the role of the NEC, and the section dealing with its future was by far the longest in the document (Labour Party, 1997). One of the four taskforces was to deal with the NEC and, crucially in this context, its convenor was UNISON's Maggie Jones, who had been a member of the LCC's 1989 commission.

The Partnership in Power package sought to change both the NEC's structure and its function. The latter proposals are discussed below. With respect to structure the proposals closely followed the approach that had been set out by the LCC. The consultation paper used the concept of stakeholders to argue that there were important groups within the party that had traditionally been denied representation on the Executive. These included the PLP, European Parliamentary Labour Party (EPLP), local government, grassroots members and the frontbench. Behind the scenes the taskforce sought to apply a rough logic of thirds, with one third of seats to affiliates, one third to members and one third to elected representatives. The group took evidence on the structure of executives in other overseas parties, in voluntary organisations and in the private sector. From this it concluded that smaller executives were often the most powerful and effective, and that the NEC, at 29, was larger than was desirable.

The taskforce proved unable, however, to negotiate a reduction in the NEC's size. By far the largest group on the Executive was the trade unions, and at the outset the party's General Secretary Tom Sawyer had envisaged a 'radical dilution' of their representation (Anderson and Mann, 1997, p. 324). But the unions proved resistant to any reduction. This in turn made the pattern of thirds unachievable without a growth in the size of the Executive. The biggest gain was to be made by abolishing the five-seat women's section (which in practice the unions controlled) whilst ensuring through quotas that the overall number of women members did not decline. Somewhat ironically, given the rhetoric of better grassroots representation, the constituency section was also to shrink from seven seats to six.[15] Any space thus created was more than filled by the creation of new seats for the PLP and EPLP, government, and local councillors. The old and new memberships of the NEC are shown in Table 7.1.

Table 7.1: Membership structure of NEC before and after Partnership in Power

	Old NEC	New NEC	New NEC quota
Trade unions	12	12	6
CLPs	7	6	3
Women	5	-	-
Socialist societies	1	1	-
Youth	1	1	-
Government	-	3	1
PLP (including EPLP)	-	3	1
EPLP leader	-	1	-
Local government	-	2	1
Black Socialist Society†	(1)	(1)	-
Treasurer	1	1	-
Leader	1	1	-
Deputy leader	1	1	-
Total	29	32	12

† The Black Socialist Society had been promised representation in 1991 conditional on its membership reaching a certain size. The reforms maintained this commitment, but representation had not been achieved by 2004.

One of the biggest controversies contained within these reforms was the proposal that MPs should be barred from standing for all sections apart from those for the PLP and government. This clearly had particular resonance with respect to the constituency seats.[16] On the one hand, it was argued that constituencies had long been denied proper grassroots representation, and that since many members of the constituency section now sat in cabinet they would be unable to give time to properly represent members' interests. On the other, it was argued that breaking the link between the parliamentary 'big hitters' and the grassroots would make these members less responsive to the interests of party members, including in debates around the cabinet table. At the same time their replacement by relatively obscure figures would also weaken the authority of the NEC. Under the new arrangements there would be seats for government members on the Executive, but these would be chosen personally by the party leader. Those pursuing reform were clearly aware of the veracity of both these opposing arguments, but the long standing demand to remove MPs won through. NEC members expressing scepticism, such as Robin Cook and Clare Short, could easily be accused of self interest, while outside the support for the reform had grown. It was now backed not only by the LCC and the right but also by the CLPD. Since the introduction of OMOV for the constituency section had resulted in its domination by the shadow cabinet, the CLPD had reversed its position and now supported the removal of MPs. With such broad support for the most controversial change, the proposals passed the 1997 conference easily.

With MPs barred from standing, it was far from clear who would be able to muster enough support to be elected to the new constituency section. The first such elections were held in 1998. On this occasion left groups in the party ensured they were ready to respond to reform. The CLPD and Labour Reform came together to form a broad left group which they called the Grassroots Alliance, in order to promote a 'slate' of candidates for these elections.[17] Their candidates included Mark Seddon, editor of the left-wing weekly *Tribune*, Pete Willsman, a long serving member of the party's Conference Arrangements Committee and founder member of the CLPD, Cathy Jamieson, a well known Scottish activist (later to become a minister in the Scottish Executive), and Liz Davies, who had achieved notoriety in 1995 by being barred by the NEC from standing as the parliamentary candidate in Leeds North East.[18] The potential election of Davies and Seddon, in particular, was seen by the leadership and loyalists on the NEC and at head office as a threat. A competing slate of candidates more acceptable to the leadership was hurriedly put together under the banner 'Members First'. Its six members included actor and gay rights activist Michael Cashman, and Diana Jeuda, a member of the NEC since 1986 in the now abolished women's section. With covert help from head office staff and funding from the AEEU, leaflets urging support for this group were mailed to constituencies and advertisements were taken out in the *Guardian* and *New Statesman*. However, the shoestring operation of the Grassroots Alliance, based on the CLPD's mailing lists and a £100 contribution from each of the candidates, proved more successful. Grassroots Alliance candidates were helped by endorsements in a *Guardian* editorial and articles, including one by Labour's former deputy leader Roy Hattersley.[19] The result of the election, held in the full glare of publicity over the summer of 1998, proved a major embarrassment to the leadership. Mark Seddon topped the poll and the Grassroots Alliance took four of the six seats, with Willsman, Jamieson and Davies also elected. The only two of the 'Members First' group to be elected were Cashman and Jeuda, both of whom had well-established national profiles.[20] As in the recent past, OMOV had performed well for the leadership's critics.

In subsequent years there were many arguments about the conduct of elections for the NEC constituency section. To avoid a rash of stories during the quiet summer news period, the elections were moved to earlier in the year. As their timing had been decoupled from the annual conference and did not appear in the party's rules the elections became a somewhat moveable feast, making grassroots organisation difficult.[21] There were also controversies about issues such as the availability of membership lists to candidates and alleged involvement by party staff. For example, in 2002 *Tribune* claimed to have obtained an email sent by an officer in the General Secretary's office seeking nominations for particular candidates.[22] The extent to which these factors affected the outcome cannot be gauged, but successful Grassroots Alliance candidates were reduced to three in 1999 and two in 2000, rising again to a steady three in 2001, 2002 and 2004. The sum total of the reforms had thus been to reduce the number and prestige of left-wing members on the NEC, but not to eliminate them altogether.

One final change to membership rules, made by the 2003 conference after several years of debate, was extending the bar on MPs standing for election to also cover members of the House of Lords.

Many members were angered by the bid of retiring General Secretary Tom Sawyer, now Lord Sawyer, to stand for the NEC in 1999. Sawyer had served as a trade union representative on the Executive from 1982–94, before being appointed to the staff. His high profile helped secure his re-election in 1999, unseating Pete Willsman. But it was widely argued that this contradicted the spirit of the proposals, that he himself had championed, to end parliamentary influence in the constituency section. From that point on, the CLPD sought to achieve rule changes at conference to bar peers from these elections. The proposal was consistently blocked by the NEC with the support of the trade unions, but after Sawyer's departure from the Executive in 2001 attitudes softened. The NEC eventually conceded the principle in 2003, leaving peers as one group with no guaranteed representation on the NEC. Although this was a victory for the CLPD it also added another group of high-profile members to those already barred from representing the constituencies, potentially weakening further their collective clout.

CHANGING THE AGENDA

The ultimate aim of the Partnership in Power reforms was to change the nature of the relationship between the Labour frontbench and the NEC, to prevent the re-emergence of the competing centres of power that had characterised previous periods in office. In part this was achieved through the changes to membership which brought in more members that understood the pressures of executive office, some of them directly appointed by the leader. The changes to the constituency section, in addition, removed the opportunity for PLP critics to use the NEC to gain a platform through the extra-parliamentary party, as figures such as Tony Benn and Eric Heffer had done in the past.[23]

Questions remained, however, about the role that the NEC should have when the party was in office, and this formed much of the debate in Partnership in Power. One of the key objectives of Tony Blair and Tom Sawyer in negotiating the changes was to make clear that the NEC was subordinate to the government when it came to policy decisions. As the consultation document put it, the NEC 'should be adequately informed and their *views taken into account* on key policy discussions and decisions. These rights should be matched by the responsibilities, clearly understood, to help sustain a Labour Government' (Labour Party, 1997, p. 12: emphasis added). Such a role was a far cry from that which the NEC had sought in the 1970s, and that the CLPD had come close to cementing in the party's rules in 1980, through giving it sole control of the manifesto. However it did match the role that the Executive had more traditionally taken. Now, it was argued, the NEC needed to be 'quite clear about ... its own distinctive role and responsibilities and those of the Government' (Labour Party, 1997, p. 19).

The Partnership in Power document had of course been drafted by taskforces dominated by members of the NEC and approved by the NEC itself – so the compliance of the Executive with this world view was already clear. Indeed the important precursor to the NEC's reduction in formal powers was the change in political balance amongst its members, with most wanting to promote a harmonious relationship between the party and its leader. This shift had, as we have seen, occurred years earlier under Kinnock and had since been maintained. As a result the NEC had already given up much of its *de facto* power over policy making (as discussed in Chapter 6) and concentrated increasingly on its organisational roles. The extent to which it could be marginalised was demonstrated, for example, by Blair's failure to discuss his proposed change to Clause IV with the Executive before he put this to conference in 1994.

The proposals in Partnership in Power left some of the NEC's traditional policy roles, such as its involvement in agreeing the manifesto, unchanged.[24] However, they introduced a series of more low level reforms that have profoundly changed the status and powers of the Executive. The most important of these was the establishment of a new committee system, with day-to-day policy responsibility given to the Joint Policy Committee (JPC), where government representatives appointed by the leader would hold equal numbers of seats to NEC members. Organisational matters, such as decisions about selection procedures or disciplinary cases, would continue to be handled by the Organisation Committee. However, crucially, all of these committees were now to be given full delegated powers so that their decisions need no longer be ratified by the full Executive. In addition, the creation of the new committees was to be accompanied by a reduction in the number of NEC meetings, moving from a monthly to a bimonthly cycle.

Thus in practice much of the responsibility previously resting with the NEC itself was shifted to its subcommittees. This has a number of implications. One relates to transparency. Whilst membership of the NEC is known and published in the party's annual report, subcommittees are less visible. Unlike the NEC the cycle of committee meetings is not widely known, making both lobbying and reporting of these meetings more difficult. The second major change relates to representation. Aside from the very significant fact that NEC members are equalled by leadership appointees on the Joint Policy Committee, many NEC members can be excluded completely from important decisions. Thus whilst awkward members cannot be prevented from winning election to the NEC itself they may not find themselves appointed to its key committees. Though this was always potentially the case (see for example Golding, 2003), such committees did not previously have final decision-making power.

In practice the number of decisions delegated by the Executive to its committees has risen over time, although some key decisions have been retained by the NEC itself. For example, the decisions to exclude Ken Livingstone from membership of the party and then, in December 2003, to readmit him, were taken by the full NEC. However, the almost equally controversial decision in 2003 to expel George Galloway MP from membership of the party over his comments about the Iraq war was taken under the delegated powers of the Organisation Committee, rather than by the full NEC.

On policy matters, as described in Chapter 6, it is the Joint Policy Committee that has taken responsibility for overseeing the National Policy Forum, policy commissions and policy documents. Its meetings have often been short, with overworked ministers not particularly focussed on the process, leaving significant leeway to party and ministerial staff. Its decisions do not require ratification by the NEC, and this body's consideration of policy matters has become increasingly restricted. In recent years it has continued to regularly question the party leader and, for example around the Iraq war, has passed a small number of policy motions. But generally such motions, even when tabled by NEC members, are now forwarded to policy commissions for consideration. Indeed in 2002 there was a change to NEC Standing Orders to formalise this as standard practice. Curiously at annual conference it is the NEC that retains power to decide whether or not resolutions should be supported, whilst the JPC has this role with respect to amendments discussed at the National Policy Forum. Although the number of conference resolutions is now small, this is an important residual power. In 2003 the usually loyal NEC came close to endorsing a resolution hostile to government policy on foundation hospitals.[25]

A final blow to the authority of the NEC was felt in 2001, when the position of 'Party Chair' was created within the cabinet. This arrangement, mirroring that of the Conservative Party, created ambiguity about the role of the elected NEC chair, traditionally also chair of the party.[26] The change was thus highly controversial inside the party. The NEC chair (then Maggie Jones) retained responsibility for chairing the Executive and annual conference and built a constructive working relationship with the newly appointed minister, Charles Clarke. However, in practice the status of the NEC chair has declined, and the role of liasing between the party and the government now rests firmly with the prime minister's appointee.

EVALUATION

The changes to the status of the National Executive Committee are perhaps the clearest example within this period of the extended leadership control that many associate with Labour's modernisation. Most other changes to the wider democracy of the party, discussed elsewhere in this book, were subject to significant negotiation with activist groups and other forces which resulted in ambiguities about the winners and losers. With respect to the NEC, in contrast, it was the undiluted demands of the party's right which came to be implemented, and this has resulted in a stark shift in formal power relations. This was hastened by the complicity of members of the NEC in the institution's own relative demise, and the obscurity of these reforms from the perspective of the wider party. When the party entered power after 18 years of opposition, NEC members were almost as keen as leaders to cement a new partnership arrangement that would prevent internal divisions undermining the government. The result was directly the obverse of the 'strengthened role' and 'higher profile' for the Executive that Partnership in Power had formally promised (Labour Party, 1997a, p. 8, 9). In practice this simply cemented the role that the NEC had traditionally held of supporting the parliamentary leadership, which some had suggested made it 'no more than a minor offshoot of the Downing Street command post' (Aitken, 1966, pp. 22-3).

These changes prompt two kinds of questions: first, over whether they were justified and second, over whether they could in future be reversed. In many ways the NEC is now more representative, and the old structure was likely to accentuate conflict. The election by MPs, MEPs and councillors of their own representatives gives the Executive a broader base and wider accountability. Only the trade union section (ironically the place where changes in the 1970s resulted in the leadership losing control) is unreformed. The key change was the one to the constituency section. This is both more representative as a result of the exclusion of MPs, but also significantly weaker. The CLPD, in reversing its position to back this reform, committed a clear tactical error. The domination of the constituency seats by shadow cabinet members appears in retrospect to have been a strictly temporary phenomenon. By the time the Partnership in Power reforms were enacted OMOV was already delivering leadership critics, and it has continued to do so. By mid term cabinet members would either have had to 'play to' the party in order to retain their NEC seats, or would have been replaced by more critical MPs from the backbenches. Yet, following reform, no rebel MP today could use the NEC to achieve a power base in the party in the way that Nye Bevan did in the 1950s. There may have been strong arguments for seeking to avoid such conflictual arrangements, and to establish a stronger culture of partnership. But with a PLP section of only three members, and the leader appointing the only representatives of government, the arrangements implemented in 1997 helped to stifle leadership critics and removed a major check on leadership power.

To a large extent the new arrangements simply confirmed the power structure that had already grown up voluntarily. The crucial change in frontbench–NEC relations was not structural but cultural, and dated to the change in political balance amongst NEC members in the 1980s. The regaining of a loyalist majority on the NEC saw it become a willing partner its own political decline. This returned it to the role it had performed in the 1950s and 1960s when it 'took little part in policy discussions, concentrating its efforts on mobilizing support within the Party for whatever was decided by the Cabinet' (Shaw, 1996, p. 59). This role has now become more institutionalised as a result of at least semi-formal constitutional change. As a result the party's General Secretary, and therefore staff and financial resources, report on a *de facto* basis to the leader rather than to the NEC. This rebalancing began under Kinnock but strengthened under Blair.[27]

The shift back to leadership control raises the question of how the arrangements would perform if the mood or political balance amongst NEC members changed. Although the rules have been amended much remains within the discretion of the NEC, so some reassertion of power would be possible if this were what NEC members wanted. This would be most likely to happen if there were another shift in the unions of the kind which destabilised relationships in the 1970s – though representation of leadership critics could also potentially increase in the PLP and local government (as well as constituency) sections.

The earlier reform to the constituency section illustrates a separate point, on the unforeseen consequences of OMOV. Though initially expected to ensure election of more moderate candidates, OMOV in fact brought wider legitimacy to the success of candidates with a similar political complexion to those previously elected by activists. The potential dangers posed by these members was neutralised by the bar on MPs. However, the results also created nervousness about OMOV amongst some of its previously most vocal supporters. Once agreed it was not felt politically possible to move away from the principle for these elections. It had become embedded by the time the settled result of the system was seen. But the experiences on the NEC did help change perceptions of OMOV amongst both left and right in the party with consequences, for example, affecting selection of candidates for public office, as discussed in Chapter 4.

Notes

1. Party leader Jim Callaghan is said to have described NEC meetings in the late 1970s as being 'like purgatory' (Golding, 2003, p. 121).
2. This followed a campaign by the Constituency Parties Movement – see Pimlott (1977).
3. Aitken suggests that the election of the constituency section at the conference was an annual ritual where 'the constituency delegates lustily cheered their own audacity in electing a solid block of Bevanite candidates which was frequently their only consolation in an otherwise arid week' (1966, p. 20).
4. Thus for example in 1985 the members of this section were all left-wing MPs: David Blunkett, Eric Heffer, Michael Meacher, Jo Richardson, Dennis Skinner, Audrey Wise and Tony Benn.
5. CLPD newsletter, April 1989.
6. Composite 3, which also contained proposals on changing the structure of the NEC, as discussed below, and policy making, as discussed in Chapter 6.
7. This followed the consultation leading to *Democracy and Policy Making for the 1990s* (see Chapter 2). Responses from CLPs had been split on the issue of OMOV for the NEC.

8. CLPD newsletter, October 1990.
9. Note that although Harman's election was an indirect result of the introduction of the women's quota on the NEC (discussed in Chapter 5) in that one man was certain to lose his seat, she won significantly more votes than Benn – 548,000 to his 269,000.
10. Although results, at least initially, continued to be announced there. And new members continued to take their seats on the NEC only after the annual conference.
11. This change also included votes for the Conference Arrangements Committee and National Constitutional Committee on the same ballot. However, responsibility for electing these bodies later reverted to conference.
12. For discussion of the quota system see Chapter 5.
13. See Chapter 11 for more discussion of this phenomenon.
14. Composite 63 was backed by previous LCC executive member Peter Hain, by then an MP, who insisted that the NEC must not be a 'no go area for reform' (Labour Party, 1995, p. 259).
15. The balance of seats between the CLPs and other sections had long been disputed, although most groups had proposed that CLP (or regional) representation be increased, rather than reduced. At the 2004 conference a grassroots proposal to increase the size of the constituency section from six to eight seats was narrowly defeated, and this issue may return to the conference agenda in future years.
16. MPs were also regularly elected in other sections of the NEC. In 1950 they made up 18 of 27 NEC members (McKenzie, 1963). In the 1970s John Golding MP and Tom Bradley MP, for example, were elected to represent the unions, whilst John Evans MP represented the socialist societies until 1994. Members of the women's section were also almost invariably MPs.
17. The Grassroots Alliance continued to organise in future elections, and in other forums such as the National Policy Forum, later drawing in further groups such as Labour Left Briefing.
18. See Chapter 4 for a brief account of the Liz Davies case.
19. 'Broad Church Vote for Labour Diversity', *The Guardian*, 10 August 1998; Roy Hattersley, 'Why I Might Vote for Liz', *The Guardian*, 20 August 1998.
20. Diana Jeuda had been a soft-left member of the NEC and was, alongside Grassroots Alliance members, endorsed in Roy Hattersley's article as being independent minded. Her election, which also drew on loyalty from members accustomed to voting for her over the last 12 years, could thus hardly be considered a victory for loyalist 'fixers'.
21. Turnout in these elections became a concern. Although official figures were not released, Ann Black for example topped the poll in the 2004 election with only 20,587 votes. At this time there were around 190,000

fully paid up members eligible to vote. Turnout was said to be around 22 per cent.

22. 'Control freakery continues, leaks show', *Tribune*, 27 September 2002. Note that allegations of staff involvement in internal elections, which were also made often with respect to the NPF, were not an entirely new phenomenon. Kogan and Kogan (1982, pp. 143-4) report complaints about staff ringing members in attempts to influence parliamentary selection contests in the early 1980s.

23. The reforms of course did create three seats elected directly by the PLP. By convention one of these seats came to be occupied by an EPLP representative, whilst since 1999 one seat has been held by independent minded backbencher Helen Jackson and the other by veteran left-winger Dennis Skinner. However, these members are now accountable to the PLP, largely behind closed doors, rather than to the wider party.

24. Under Clause V of the party's constitution the NEC and 'Parliamentary Committee of the PLP' were responsible for deciding which items from the party's policy programme would go in the manifesto. The 'Parliamentary Committee' was previously the shadow cabinet, but following Labour's election to government had taken on a new form, including elected backbench members. This sparked a revision of Clause V at the 2004 conference and the relevant meeting now has a far wider membership, which is likely to further diminish the NEC's role.

25. At the special conference meeting to decide attitudes to composites the Executive had voted by 16 votes to 15 to support the government's position, with several trade union representatives voting against. *The Times* (2 October 2003) claimed that Tony Blair, whose vote had been needed to secure victory, was heard coming away from the meeting complaining that 'this is getting like the f***ing 1970s'.

26. In practice the chair of the NEC is elected by 'Buggin's turn', being the longest serving member who has not yet been chair. By coincidence in 2004 Ian McCartney became chair of the party in both senses, having been appointed the previous year and also taking on the elected role.

27. Its extent was illustrated by the departure of General Secretary David Triesman, which was simply reported to the NEC in November 2003 after he had been effectively sacked by the party leader. See *Daily Telegraph* interview, 'Strummed out by Blair', 10 January 2004. Larry Whitty had also effectively been removed by Blair in 1994 (see Sopel, 1995, p. 259-61) but this had to be negotiated more cautiously with the NEC. However, it must be noted that in the party's early years the division between the leader and General Secretary was fuzzy at best. Its first two Secretaries – Ramsay MacDonald and Arthur Henderson – were senior MPs, and Henderson served as both PLP leader and chief whip at the same time as holding the party's senior post (McKenzie, 1963).

8

Annual Conference

The Labour Party conference has, since the party's foundation, formally been its authoritative decision-making body. Famously described by Clement Attlee as the 'Parliament of the movement' (1937, p. 93), the party's 1918 constitution stated that it was the annual conference which would decide 'what specific proposals of legislative, financial or administrative reform' would 'receive the general support of the Party, and be promoted ... by the National Executive and the Parliamentary Labour Party'. The curiosity of a parliamentary party ostensibly controlled by an extra-parliamentary body has long exercised political scientists and politicians alike. However most have concluded, through at least most of the party's history, that the party leadership had significant freedom to make its own policy decisions.

Since the very outset, the authority of the Labour Party conference was disputed. As early as 1907 Keir Hardie, the first Chairman of the PLP, threatened resignation rather than be held to conference policy on female suffrage (McLean, 1975). Generations of Labour leaders, when faced with unwelcome conference decisions, chose to ignore them with varying degrees of subtlety. Hugh Gaitskell, faced with the decision by conference in 1960 to back unilateral disarmament, chose 'open defiance of the authority of the Conference' (Minkin, 1980, p. 280), and set about work in the party to get the decision reversed the following year. Later, during the Wilson governments of the 1960s, 'the authority of the Conference sunk to a new low as the Government carried out a range of policies diametrically opposed to Conference decisions. Defeats for Government policy at Conference became as repetitive as they were ineffectual' (Minkin, 1980, p. 290). These episodes, of course, fuelled demands from activists for greater accountability by the parliamentary party, as well as the desire by leaders to find more rational ways of developing policy.

Although conference authority may in formal terms have always been dubious, Minkin's study showed that annual conferences have nonetheless been pivotal both to the party's internal dynamics and to how it was perceived externally. Meeting by the seaside for one week each autumn, representatives of local parties and affiliated organisations negotiated, debated and voted upon statements presented by the NEC and numerous resolutions based on the words that they themselves had submitted. In practice, the dominance of the trade unions – holding to up to 90 per cent of conference votes – provided significant scope for the parliamentary leadership to negotiate positions behind closed doors and avoid much, if not all, public confrontation. Hence Richard Crossman's description in 1963 of the real dynamics of 'old' Labour's decision making as 'the concession in principle of sovereign powers to the delegates at the Annual Conference, and the removal in practice of most of this sovereignty through the trade union block vote on the one hand, and the complete independence of the Parliamentary Labour Party on the other' (Crossman, 1963, p. 42).

Until the early 1990s the organisation of Labour's annual conference had barely changed. Since then, however, in a series of reforms which had been long debated, its dynamics have altered fundamentally. This chapter traces the reforms to the composition of the conference, beginning with a shift in the balance of vote shares from the unions to the constituencies, and the implementation of quotas for women, which transformed both its public face and its culture. Further changes followed under the Partnership in Power package, which radically altered the format and agenda of the event. These reforms together raise interesting questions, not only about how and why they happened, but also about their lasting effects. They included major revision both of the party's federal structure and the dynamic between the parliamentary and extra-parliamentary parties. Looking back, many inside and outside the party have tended to assume that the ultimate result was a strengthening of leadership control. However, considering the entirety of changes that have taken place, and the historical context, this chapter suggests that such a conclusion is, at best, debatable.

LOOSENING THE UNIONS' GRIP

One of the longest running arguments over organisational reform in the party's history has concerned the division of votes at annual conference. The first time local Labour parties were given formal representation at the conference was in 1918. At this event trade unions held 2,471,000 votes and other affiliates 48,000, to the 115,000 (4.4 per cent) held by the local parties (Minkin, 1992).[1] In later years the share of votes held by the constituencies fluctuated, but was always a minority. By the mid 1980s it had settled at approximately 10 per cent.[2] The number of votes held by each trade union depended on the number of members it chose to affiliate to the party, whilst local parties were considered by convenience to each have at least 1,000 members.[3] Block votes were then cast in multiples of one thousand, by both affiliates and CLPs.

Trade union block votes were long controversial in the party, particularly on the left. The degree of control exercised by trade union leaders gave the party leadership significant scope to negotiate, and traditionally much latitude on non-industrial issues (Drucker, 1989; Harrison, 1960; Minkin, 1992; Reid, 2000). Constituencies provided most of the resolutions submitted to conference, as each organisation, however large, could submit only one. Thus in 1968 constituencies submitted 386 resolutions, whilst unions sub1mitted 29 and other affiliates four (Minkin, 1980). They also provided most of the speakers – at the same conference Minkin tells us that speakers from the floor included 87 from CLPs, 30 from trade unions, one from a socialist society and 25 parliamentarians and parliamentary candidates. Yet despite the constituencies' influence in setting the agenda, it was the trade unions that decided which proposals were supported. Putting it bluntly, through much of the party's history, '[a]ctivists could send as many critical resolutions to Conference as they liked since the general secretaries of the major unions ensured they had no impact' (Fielding, 2003, p. 123). So obvious was this dichotomy that by the height of union loyalty in the 1950s Minkin suggested that '"the block vote" began to mean more than any procedural definition; it was virtually defined as a political formation. Some called it then "the Rightwing block vote"; others simply called it "the block vote", meaning the Right Wing' (1992, p. 310).

Those on the left of the party had thus long supported a reform of the trade union role at conference. In the 1930s the Constituency Parties Movement aimed to dilute the power of the block vote (Pimlott, 1977; Tanner, 2000). In the 1950s Nye Bevan, in his quest to be elected party Treasurer, fought aggressively to expose the way in which votes cast by union leaders often did not represent their members' views. The shift by the TGWU which saw them join with activists in defeating the platform on nuclear disarmament in 1960 marked the beginning of change. As trade union votes began to support the left on a regular basis it was moderates and right-wingers that saw injustice in the system and began to support reform. Nonetheless, some on the left kept up the demand for a rebalancing of conference vote shares away from the unions and towards the constituencies.

By the 1980s there were a number of factors adding to pressure for reform. As Minkin (1992) notes, a series of union mergers to create bigger and more general unions had made the block vote significantly more apparent. By 1980 the TGWU wielded 1,250,000 votes alone, compared to the total of 689,000 held collectively by the CLPs. The four biggest unions together controlled five times as many votes as the constituencies.[4] The questionable democracy of this situation was visible not only to party members but to the party's opponents, and critics in the press. Whether union votes were used to defeat the leadership or defeat the demands of activists, questions of legitimacy arose. Such criticism was potentially damaging not only to the party but also to the unions, and to the authority of the conference itself. These concerns arose in an environment where the unions were under widespread attack, both inside and outside the party (as discussed in Chapter 2). After the 1979 defeat, proposals to the Commission of Enquiry from many CLPs, and even the unions themselves, suggested reform of the conference block vote.[5] The LCC's submission suggested that constituencies and affiliates should each hold half the conference votes.

In 1981 Alex Kitson of the TGWU, then chair of the NEC, took up the cause in his conference speech. He proposed that constituencies should have a vote share at conference that broadly reflected their financial contribution to the party. At that time this was around 19 per cent, so such a reform would have approximately doubled the constituencies' share of the vote.[6] There were, however, obstacles to this reform, and no immediate action was taken. It raised concerns about the impact of giving more votes to constituency activists, not only on conference policy, but also on elections to the NEC. As discussed in Chapter 5, the five women's seats on the NEC were a key battleground between the left and right in the latter's attempt to regain control of the Executive in the early 1980s. As these seats were elected by conference as a whole, a rebalancing from trade unions to constituencies could prolong the left's control. Thus, although there was significant support in the unions for reform, a nervousness about the politics of activists also created resistance to change.

By the early 1980s the CLPD was actively campaigning for a reduction in trade union vote shares, and circulating model resolutions on the subject on a regular basis. The LCC was also urging support. A resolution to this effect at the 1983 conference was remitted to the NEC for consideration, after assurances that there was a desire to act and achieve a 'speedy resolution' (Labour Party, 1983, p. 107). Following this Alex Kitson himself urged the NEC to act, claiming that other union colleagues also wished to see reform. As a result a consultation paper was circulated by the NEC, with decisions promised at the 1986 conference. The paper sugg-ested reforms along the lines of the original Kitson proposals (Labour Party, 1984a). The response from local parties was strongly in favour of a rebalancing, with the CLPD view being that this should give constituencies up to 40 per cent of the vote. However, the trade unions had by now reverted to their more traditional role of support for the leader. Whilst some senior trade unionists were convinced of the arguments for change, and increasingly supported it publicly, there was security for both the leader and the unions in leaving matters as they were.

The CLPD continued to press for change in 1984 and 1985, but when the matter was returned to at the 1986 conference it had not been adequately resolved. The NEC proposed that 'in the light of the very serious disagreements, the proposition be not put that the matter be considered further' (NEC, 1986, p. 17). Rather than prop-ose the promised rule change the NEC therefore set up a further working group which, it was suggested, would report in 1988.

Although by 1988 Bill Morris, then Deputy General Secretary of the TGWU, had referred to the reform of the block vote as 'an idea whose time has come', change was still not forthcoming (quoted in Minkin, 1992, p. 364). At the 1988 conference the NEC proposed yet another consultation. By this time constituency activists, fuelled by the demands of the CLPD and LCC, and the unions' reversion to type, were becoming increasingly exasperated. Their frustration at the NEC's inaction was expressed by the seconder of the model CLPD resolution, who asked 'how much longer do they want for god's sake?'.[7] The resolution instructed the NEC to bring forward rule changes to the next year's conference. The Executive resisted and asked the movers to remit. However, when they refused, sufficient trade union delegates gave the resolution their support that it passed, against the NEC's wishes, by a show of hands.

Despite this clear instruction, the NEC continued to resist change. Whilst reform had the backing of major unions such as the TGWU and GMB, those more sympathetic to the right, such as the AEU and EETPU, were opposed. The leadership, meanwhile, remained nervous. Firm proposals were not brought to the 1989 conference and instead there was further consultation. This linked the issue of vote shares to the broader questions of reforming the policy process, which had also been raised at the 1988 conference (see Chapter 6). A consultation paper issued in September 1989 explored these issues and promised action in 1990 (Labour Party, 1989a). In response the LCC, on whose proposals the resolution on the broader policy process had been based, called for the settlement to include an increase in the constituency share of the vote to 30 per cent (LCC, 1989). At the 1989 conference it was clear that the matter would not rest much longer. Neil Kinnock managed to secure trade union support to defeat a resolution complaining about inaction, but this was achieved only with firm promises that proposals would follow the next year. Meanwhile a survey of party members found that 72 per cent thought the block vote at conference 'brought the party into disrepute' (Seyd and Whiteley, 1992).

Agreement was thus finally reached as part of the overhaul of policy procedures due to be implemented after the general election.[8] *Democracy and Policy Making for the 1990s*, which also proposed the National Policy Forum and reform of voting for the NEC, set out the proposals to the 1990 conference. The document finally conceded that the trade unions' control of 90 per cent of conference votes was 'not defensible and needs to be changed' (Labour Party, 1990a, p. 8). In its place a new settlement was proposed giving the CLPs 30 per cent of the vote, as they had in the leadership electoral college. In future, it suggested, other groups such as the PLP and EPLP might be given voting rights at conference, to mirror the electoral college more closely still.[9] Initially, however, it proposed only to change the roughly 90:10 arrangement to one of 70:30. Conference agreed that this reform would take effect after the general election. It was the least controversial element of the reform package, and passed the conference with barely a mention.

The change to the rules was duly made at the 1992 conference, and came into effect in 1993. However, the environment was not to be the victorious one the leadership had hoped for. Instead this was a time of reflection on defeat, and the role of the unions was a significant focus in these debates. Polls suggested that the relationship with the unions had damaged Labour electorally, and modernisers had begun attempts to loosen or even break the trade union link. As discussed in Chapter 3, this was central to the debates about changing selection procedures to embrace OMOV. At the same time, some 'modernisers' proposed that conference might be reformed to exclude the trade unions altogether. The position of the traditional left thus changed to one of defending the party–union link. The CLPD urged (as indeed it had previously) that there must be limits to how far the union vote was reduced, and that the change agreed must not be a first step to divorce.

Given the controversy at the time, the issue of the trade union role at conference became part of the agenda for the NEC's review group on the union link. This group, established after the 1992 election, devised the reforms of local parliamentary selections and the leadership electoral college.[10] Yet although agreement had already been reached in 1990, there were also those who wanted to use the opportunity to go further in reforming the conference block vote. These included Tony Blair, who joined the group in October 1992. Blair and others wanted to see a further reduction in the unions' role and, where trade union votes did apply, that these should be cast by individual delegates rather than as blocks.[11] These issues were controversial within the group, where trade unions were defending their role on many fronts. Having conceded a major change in 1990, and with this due to come into effect at the 1993 conference, little further agreement was possible. Instead of proposing immediate reductions in trade union votes the group's report to the 1993 conference thus reaffirmed the 70:30 split, noting that there were 'strong arguments for maintaining [this] balance for at least a few years' (Labour Party, 1993, p. 12). However the report also proposed that a further shift towards the constituencies to achieve a 50:50 balance should occur over time if there were substantial increases in party membership. This fitted with Blair's vision of turning Labour into a mass membership party with members empowered as individuals. It was agreed that the trigger for the first such rebalance should be an increase from the current 260,000 members to over 300,000 members. The group also 'strongly' recommended that trade unions should be able to split their conference votes on a one delegate one vote basis (Labour Party, 1993, p. 13).[12] These proposals were agreed by the 1993 conference.

When Tony Blair took over the party leadership in 1994 he sought to pursue these matters with a new urgency. The 1993 change had gone smoothly, and attracted media attention to the reduction in the trade union role. Thus whereas Kinnock had been cautious, Blair was keen to go further, and the review group's recommendations allowed him to do so. In June 1995 he announced that membership had reached 300,000 – an achievement that few had expected so soon, indeed if at all.[13] This set off the mechanism that had been agreed less than two years before. With some discontent expressed, a rule change was thus passed at the 1995 conference moving straight to a 50:50 arrangement, with near unanimous support from the unions. The arrangement came into effect in 1996.

After decades of discussion, and particularly intense debate since the early 1980s, a radical shift in trade union votes from around 90 per cent to 50 per cent was thus implemented within three years. This was a major symbolic reform, but also marked the start of profound changes in the dynamic of the party conference. Whilst in the past the votes of constituencies had been relatively peripheral, they were now central to conference decisions. The 1993 conference – the first where constituency votes reached 30 per cent – saw constituency delegates lobbied seriously for the first time. The close decision on OMOV taken at this conference (see Chapter 3) may not have happened were it not for the greater role for constituency delegates, and winning them over became a key objective for campaigners on both sides.

Constituency delegates became more important still after the shift to a 50:50 balance. The concept of conference 'management' has thus taken on new meaning as a result of these reforms. Whilst the task of the leadership was previously to win over trade union leaders, influencing constituency delegates has now become equally important. This was particularly true under the old compositing system, but continued even after the agenda had been changed. New briefing meetings for delegates, before and at conference, are used to explain the key issues and seek support for leadership positions. On important votes something similar akin to the 'whipping' operation at Westminster has also developed, with delegates taken to meet ministers and subjected to pressure to vote with a particular line. This can raise questions of propriety, but also demonstrates the importance now attached to constituency delegates, giving them an access to senior figures far beyond that existing in the past. The unpredictability of managing such a disparate group ultimately helped feed the further reforms to the conference, described below. As Paul Webb suggested in 1994 'the departure of the unions from the policy-making arena of the party could ... destabilise the internal balance of power in unpredictable ways' (1994, p. 4). It was partly a desire to re-establish this stability that drove the subsequent changes under Partnership in Power.

WOMEN'S QUOTAS AND THEIR EFFECTS

If annual conference was traditionally dominated by the trade unions it was also, and by no coincidence, traditionally dominated by men. In the 1970s it was estimated that 89 per cent of conference delegates were male.[14] By the early 1980s this situation had changed only marginally. Minkin (1992) found that 82 per cent of delegates to the 1983 conference were men, with women particularly poorly represented amongst trade union delegations. Just 45 of 602 union representatives (7 per cent) were female, compared to 171 (27 per cent) of the 624 delegates representing local parties.

The system of quotas for women introduced from 1990 (described in Chapter 5) rapidly changed this situation. Rules passed by the 1991 conference required trade unions to include women in their delegations in at least as high a proportion as existed amongst their membership. At the same time, constituencies were required to send a woman delegate at least every other year. These new rules changed the face of the conference. Some large unions (for example the health workers, COHSE, and shop workers, USDAW) were required to send delegations that were majority female – although others such as the transport workers could remain largely male. In the constituencies the quota established a floor below which women's representation could not fall, whilst setting no similar minimum for men. Probability would thus now put women in the majority amongst this group. These changes, implemented in 1992, were very visible to those at the conference. They were equally apparent to those watching on television, and thus played an important role in changing the party's image. But they also changed the atmosphere and, arguably, the style of the conference. Clare Short suggested in 1996 that the introduction of quotas meant conference debates were 'serious and considered, and less confrontational, and that is good for all of us' (Labour Party, 1996, p. 56). Women's voices, quite literally, came to be heard far more frequently. Whilst in 1983, 29 per cent of speakers at the conference were women, in 2004 this proportion reached 47 per cent.

Women's greater participation also had some unintended consequences, particularly for constituency representation. In the policy's early years constituencies regularly raised complaints that they could not find a woman prepared to act as delegate. However, the NEC was unsympathetic to such claims and required strict adherence to the rule. Whilst in the past some CLPs sent the same delegate to conference year-on-year this was no longer possible (at least where this delegate was a man).[15] The changes thus significantly reduced the potential for conference to act as an annual meeting place for the same constituency activists. Instead, a higher proportion of delegates were now always new to conference and its procedures. Hence at the same time that the voting power of constituency delegates was increased, the ability of activist factions to control these votes was also diminished. This is something of which the CLPD has become keenly aware. In recent years it has supported proposals to increase the number of delegates per constituency, in order to regain continuity of representation. At the 2004 conference it backed a rule change which would have allowed each CLP at least two delegates – one man and one woman. However this was defeated. If such a change were introduced, it could have important consequences for the collective power of the CLPs.

The impact of quotas in terms of policy outcomes is of course difficult to measure in any reliable way. The arrival of more novice delegates, combined with greater 'management' of those delegates, would imply a more compliant attitude by constituency representatives to leadership demands. This certainly appears to be borne out by recent events, where these delegates have been less likely to participate in platform defeats than their trade union counterparts, as discussed below. Similarly the impact of greater women's representation in terms of specific outcomes is generally difficult to judge; however, on occasions this is likely to have been significant. One such example was the close and highly symbolic vote on OMOV in 1993. The bundling of this decision with the proposal to introduce all-women shortlists – itself controversial – may not have succeeded if it were not for the new women's quotas amongst constituency delegates and, crucially, on trade union delegations.

PARTNERSHIP IN POWER AND THE CHANGING AGENDA

None of these changes directly affected the form of business that conference was asked to discuss, or the way in which debates were held. The implementation of such changes did not occur until the Partnership in Power package was agreed in 1997. Until then a significant portion of the topics for debate were determined by the resolutions submitted by local parties and affiliates. A document listing the resolutions that had been submitted was circulated throughout the party in the summer. Each organisation then had the opportunity to submit an amendment to one of the published resolutions. The fruits of these two rounds of consultation formed the basis of much of what was debated.

The means of turning the submissions from hundreds of local parties and dozens of affiliates into a manageable set of topics for debate was never particularly satisfactory. Resolutions and amendments were grouped according to subject, and those organisations that had submitted texts were invited to a meeting at the start of the conference to produce 'composite' resolutions. These had to be based on words actually appearing in the earlier submissions, and were often both lengthy and broad in their scope. Once they were agreed the NEC, at a special meeting at conference, took a view on which composite resolutions it felt able to support. The composites were rapidly printed, and placed on delegates' seats for the first day of debate. The Conference Arrangements Committee (CAC) then had responsibility for setting the daily agenda, and only resolutions on those topics that had generated the greatest interest were assured a place in the timetable. In 1986, for example, there were 531 resolutions, which were boiled down to 66 composites, of which 50 were debated.

There were many difficulties inherent in this system. One was simply timing, with frantic activity by party staff at the start of conference to circulate composite resolutions that delegates had little time to read and on which they were unable to properly consult their respective organisations. Another concerned the text of the composites themselves, which was drawn together quickly and could be unwieldy and even incoherent, whilst omitting many of the words that had been carefully crafted and submitted. Further, resolutions covered a random collection of subjects with some issues raised by many CLPs at once or over many consecutive years (particularly where groups such as the CLPD had circulated model resolutions) whilst other issues were rarely raised at all.

This uneven process did hand significant control of the agenda to local parties and affiliates and could, if the trade unions were willing, lead to embarrassing defeats for the leadership. However, from the leadership's perspective it also had its advantages. The omnibus nature of composite resolutions meant that the NEC could reject a resolution ostensibly on the basis of one issue, whilst avoiding difficult questions about the rest of its content. Inclusion of several issues within one composite could also allow trade union delegations to interpret their mandates creatively, often to the benefit of the leadership. Constituency delegates were in a similar position, particularly given their inability to consult their local parties on how to interpret their mandate, and they could easily be subjected to pressure. Meanwhile the 'compositing' process was itself open to games of various kinds. One favourite tactic deployed by party staff was to use the meeting to polarise opinion around two composites on an issue, one of which the NEC could happily support and the other which was clearly so extreme that few delegates would vote for it. The most dangerous form of resolution was one that contained important proposals that the big trade unions would support, but also lines that the leadership did not accept. However there always remained (particularly before 1993) the option of dismissing a defeat as 'unrepresentative' since it had been determined by trade union votes. Finally, since composites were patchy and left many areas uncovered, the NEC could justify presenting conference with comprehensive policy statements to agree. These in practice often made up much of the conference agenda.[16] Yet, as discussed in Chapter 6, delegates were presented with them at the start of the week and, even if they did not chime with activists' views, had no power to amend them.

Chapter 6 gives a detailed account of the changes to the policy formation process from the early 1980s onwards. Central to this was the argument about the amendability of NEC policy statements, and opportunity for wider consultation on these in the party. Tentative agreement was reached on this point in 1990, and the National Policy Forum (NPF) was established to oversee the production of documents in 1993. However there was no firm action on amendability by conference until the Partnership in Power reforms of 1997.

The consultation document circulated in advance of this package gave significant attention to the party conference. It expressed concern about both the image and the ethos of the event, stating that public rows could be damaging and provide a focus for the leadership's opponents. Conference was not only a democratic body, it was suggested, but also a 'showcase' for the party (Labour Party, 1997, p. 13). Whilst it had an important decision-making role, its other functions such as providing a platform for government ministers and facilitating political education, broader policy discussion and campaigning work, should therefore also be recognised.

As discussed in Chapter 6, the new arrangements under Partnership in Power ended the vast majority of submissions direct to conference from local parties and affiliates. Instead the main focus for the party was to be policy documents, which would be agreed by the NPF and circulated in draft inside and outside the party. When documents were finalised the NPF could agree 'alternative positions' on which conference – still officially the sovereign policy-making body – would be able to vote. In return for the power to amend these documents, resolutions direct to conference were to be confined to 'contemporary issues' not otherwise covered by the policy programme. As discussed in Chapter 6 this concession had been essential to winning trade union support for the Partnership in Power package, but the details had been left rather vague. Local parties and affiliates could each submit one such resolution, and the Conference Arrangements Committee would decide whether these met the strict criteria set. Those which did would be composited in the usual way. The stringency of the criteria would limit the number of topics allowed for consideration. But in addition it was left to the CAC to decide how many topics would be debated.[17] A 'priorities ballot' would then be held at the conference to determine which were the most popular topics. Some of those close to the leadership who had only reluctantly conceded to this mechanism hoped that the CAC would timetable no more than one or two contemporary topics for debate. In the event, however, the number settled on four or five, which was enough to ensure that each of the big unions could get its favoured topic onto the agenda.

With so many fewer resolutions to discuss, there was scope for significant change to the conference timetable. The Partnership in Power plans included adding 'question and answer' sessions with ministers, 'small group' discussions, and sessions on campaigning (Labour Party, 1997a). Such proposals had been urged in earlier years by the CLV and LCC, and had been piloted in other arenas in the party. For example a series of Political Education Conferences had been held from 1995, with members invited to discuss policy with a view to building campaigning skills. These conferences had been well attended and popular. In 1994 the first National Women's Training Conference had been held, and was also considered a success. At these events the emphasis was primarily on top-down education about policy, rather than bottom-up democratic control, although the opportunity for dialogue could lead to some informal influence. The National Policy Forum, which first met in 1993, also followed a workshop format though with the purpose of influencing documents through deliberation, and where possible by consensus.

From 1998 the agenda of conference was thus changed, to accommodate the new policy process and bring it closer into line with the culture of these other events. Debates primarily related to policy documents, which were discussed not only in plenary sessions but also in smaller workshops. Here delegates could engage directly with ministers and comment on documents in a private setting away from the eyes of the media. In the conference hall more time would be given to ministerial speeches, and occasional question and answer sessions with ministers on current issues.

Despite the emphasis on the new power to decide between 'alternative positions', the nature of the policy cycle included little scope for conference to influence the detail of policy documents. Under the new 'rolling programme' documents in their first year were only consultative and could not be amended. In practice there were thus only two years in each four to five year policy cycle when conference would be faced with 'alternative positions'. This situation was exacerbated by the fact that the first set of documents to complete the cycle, in 1999, included no such alternative positions. Although there was relatively more choice on offer in 2000, this remained limited. Then the policy cycle was redesigned after the 2001 election (see Chapter 6), leaving all final decisions to the 2004 conference. Thus in only two years during Labour's first two terms in office did conference delegates have any direct ability to amend policy documents, as shown in Table 8.1.

The lack of control by conference over policy documents (even given the 'safety valve' of contemporary resolutions) caused frustrations, which sometimes spilled over onto the conference floor. For example at the 1999 conference there were attempts to 'refer back' sections of the Economy document relating to the private finance initiative. Delegates argued that they had been promised amendable documents and this was a valid way of rejecting part of the text.[18] The chair's response was that since this was a document in its first year of consultation, amendment was not appropriate. In rebellious mood, conference then voted against the entire document. However, in a highly unusual move, the vote was re-run the following day and the document was accepted.

Table 8.1: Policy role of annual conference 1997–2004

Year	Issues for conference to agree
1997	Composites, in the traditional way Partnership in Power proposals
1998	First year documents, first wave (not amendable)
1999	First year documents, second wave (not amendable) Second year documents, first wave (no alternative positions)
2000	Second year documents, second wave (seven alternative positions)
2001	Documents on implementation of manifesto (not amendable)
2002	First year documents, first wave (not amendable)
2003	First year documents, second wave (not amendable) Second year documents, first wave (not amendable)
2004	Final documents, first and second wave (four alternative positions[19])

The change in the profile of conference delegates almost certainly made these protests more muted than they might otherwise have been. And the changed nature of conference in turn fed further change to the profile of delegates. Whilst in the past experienced activists were keen to attend conference to participate in negotiations about composites and then debates on an activist-driven agenda, places were increasingly taken by those members happy to play a more passive role. Indeed concerns were expressed by groups such as CLPD that many constituencies were choosing not to send delegates to conference at all. Of the 641 constituencies where Labour organised, only 527 sent delegates to the annual conference in 2002 and 500 in 2004. However, not all CLPs had sent delegates to conference in the past. Writing in 1980 Dianne Hayter had suggested that around a third of constituencies failed to do so (Hayter, 1980).

21ST CENTURY CONFERENCE

Changes to both the agenda and delegate base of annual conference have made it a calmer and more leadership focussed event. Nonetheless, recent years have shown that it still retains some of its rebellious spirit. The failure of the new policy-making process to offer conference real control over policy documents has resulted in tensions being aired in other ways – through 'contemporary resolutions' and rule changes – and has demonstrated the party's continuing ability to use conference to embarrass its leadership.

At the 2000 conference the platform was defeated for the first time since Tony Blair became leader, over a contemporary resolution on pensions. This issue had been substantially dealt with in the Welfare policy document, which had been agreed by conference the year before. However, in negotiating the words in this document (as discussed in Chapter 6) ministers had promised that there would be a review of pension policy and particularly of the link between the state pension and earnings. With this promise they had won trade union support for the document. When the review failed to live up to expectations trade union delegates had unsuccessfully tried to raise the issue at the NPF in 2000 in respect of the Economy document. The ruling out of these proposals on the basis that the matter had already been dealt with simply aggravated the unions. Consequently UNISON and the GMB submitted contemporary resolutions advocating that rises in the state pension be linked to earnings. Although the NEC argued that these should also be ruled out of order the Conference Arrangements Committee (chaired by a UNISON official) disagreed. The topic thus became one of four contemporary issues timetabled for debate. Despite last-minute negotiations and concessions the movers of the resolution refused to remit it and the platform was defeated by 60 per cent of votes to 40 per cent. Ministers were keen to emphasise that only 36 per cent of constituency delegates, compared to 84 per cent of affiliates, had supported the resolution, and made clear their intention to ignore the defeat.

In this same year conference debated the first 'alternative positions'. Of the seven, two – on House of Lords reform and votes at 16 – were defeated. Two – on rail safety and penalties for directors of polluting companies – were supported by delegates against the wishes of the platform, although these defeats attracted little media attention in contrast to the pensions debate. The two least controversial positions – on extending Sure Start and the New Deal for Schools – were accepted by the platform. The remaining one, on education funding, was remitted by the mover for further consideration by the relevant policy commission. This raised awkward questions, exacerbated by the fact that the procedures for dealing with alternative positions had never been written into the party's rules. Once such a position had been adopted by the National Policy Forum it should arguably have become the 'property' of the Forum as a whole, rather than the original mover. However, in the absence of other precedent the old system that had applied to conference resolutions was adopted. This paved the way for pressure to be applied to movers of minority positions in future, not only at the Policy Forum meeting when they first made their proposal, but right up to the vote at annual conference.

Further defeats over contemporary issues followed in 2002, on the Private Finance Initiative, and in 2003 on 'foundation' hospitals. In each case these were issues in which the major unions took a strong interest and that they had been instrumental in putting on the agenda. The Private Finance Initiative had been the subject of negotiations at the National Policy Forum, with unions unable to achieve satisfactory concessions. Proposals for foundation hospitals, in contrast, had never been discussed under the party's policy process but had been announced unilaterally by ministers. In both cases the fact that these matters ended in confrontation at the conference demonstrated a failure of the new policy process to manage disagreement between the party's stakeholders. Where the leadership sought to impose its view the unions were prepared to push matters to public conflict. This angered leaders, who in each case stated immediately that they would not be bound by conference decisions. On both issues the majority of constituency delegates – now subjected to ministerial charm offensives and lectures about the perils of leadership defeat – voted with the platform. After the health defeat in 2003 briefings from leadership sources said that Tony Blair was 'incandescent' and that the trade unions were 'playing with fire' by imposing a decision opposed by the platform and constituency delegates. However, Chief Whip Hilary Armstrong was said to have conceded that there should have been more consultation in the party.[20] As discussed in Chapter 6 the issue went on to cause large rebellions in Labour's parliamentary ranks, which only acted to reinforce this conclusion.

In 2004, when conference was again faced with 'alternative positions', some of the same patterns were apparent. One position proposed rail renationalisation, and had been tabled by the transport union TSSA. This was passed, but there were calls for a (recorded) card vote, which showed that 99.5 per cent of unions had supported the proposal, compared to only 28 per cent of constituency delegates. In time-honoured fashion, ministers could thus present this as an 'unrepresentative' result. The second proposal passed was on council housing, where constituency support was more apparent. Notably, this was not pressed to a card vote. An alternative position on the House of Lords (seeking to make it 'as democratic as possible') was accepted by the platform, whilst a proposal (once again) to reduce the voting age to 16 was remitted.

The contemporary issues process gave the unions the opportunity to get key concerns onto the new style conference agenda, but created frustrations for constituencies. Although they continued to provide most of the resolutions submitted, the ballot at conference to decide which topics would be debated was effectively controlled by the unions. Union leaders could consult each other before conference began about what issues they intended to support in the ballot, and by exchanging block votes were almost guaranteed success. Although constituencies held half the votes in the ballot, lack of co-ordination between hundreds of delegates, with numerous issues on offer, resulted in their votes being split. Thus in 2000, for example, 'education and employment issues', on which resolutions had been submitted by the AEEU and two CLPs, were chosen above 'health issues', where resolutions had been received from eight CLPs.

To avoid these problems, the CLPD proposed from early on that there should be two separate ballots, one for affiliates and one for constituencies, so that the highest priority issues for each group were guaranteed debate. This was initially resisted by the unions, but the situation whereby they alone effectively decided the contemporary issues came to be seen as ever more iniquitous. The matter reached the conference agenda in 2000, in a CLPD model rule change submitted by 13 CLPs.[21] This proposed that at least the first four contemporary issues chosen by constituencies, and the first four chosen by affiliates, would be selected for debate. This left the unions' rights unaffected, but would expand the space for contemporary issues on the agenda. It was thus opposed by the NEC, which successfully argued that the proposal should be remitted. In return it was promised that a compromise would be sought, and the Conference Arrangements Committee was asked to experiment with some kind of weighted voting. In 2002 the CAC therefore proposed that any topic winning more than 50 per cent support from amongst constituency delegates would be timetabled for debate. Through this route composites on the threat of war in Iraq, supported by 85 per cent of CLPs, got onto the agenda, along with another composite on Israel and the Palestinians. The success of this move was used to fend off calls for formal rule changes.

In 2003, however, the proposal returned. Despite continued pressure to change the rules the NEC again sought to run the system devised the previous year. But whilst the four issues winning the ballot were those that had been raised by the four biggest unions, the most contentious issue amongst CLPs – again the war in Iraq – won only 39 per cent of their votes. Constituency delegates had been strongly encouraged by party staff and ministers to vote for one of the 12 other topics on offer. This short-term success in fending off a potential platform defeat however just stoked support by delegates for a rule change. The same CLPD model proposal had once again been put on the agenda by four CLPs, and was this time pushed to a vote. The NEC urged that a more flexible approach should be found, and offered to reduce the 50 per cent threshold to get constituency concerns onto the agenda. The rule change, claimed NEC speaker Mike Griffiths, would 'destroy Partnership in Power'. However, it was narrowly pushed through in a 55 to 45 per cent vote. Ironically these constituency rights were won on the votes of the newly rebellious unions, who supported the change by 67 per cent to 33 per cent, whilst only 42 per cent of constituency delegates voted in its support.[22]

EVALUATION

The period since the late 1980s has seen a complete transformation of the Labour Party conference. From an overwhelmingly male body made up of seasoned constituency activists, regularly outvoted by loyalist trade unions, conference has become a less aggressive, more representative and generally more supportive 'showcase' for the party leadership. This has been both an intended and an unintended consequence of reform. Changes to the composition of the conference made it less predictable, and potentially less controllable by leaders. At the same time, reform of the agenda generally had the opposite effect, although it is possible to overstate the degree of central control that resulted.

The initial reforms that transformed conference were driven not by the leadership, but by the left. Although now associated with Blairite 'modernisers', the reduction in trade union votes had been a long held objective of the left and came to be accepted by Kinnock in 1990 only after an extended battle by groups such as the CLPD and LCC. There were fears amongst leaders that such reforms would destabilise the conference and move it leftwards. This danger had long been recognised. As early as 1930 Sidney Webb had noted that 'the constituency parties were frequently unrepresentative groups of nonentities dominated by fanatics and cranks, and extremists, and that if the vote of the Trade Unions were eliminated it would be impracticable to continue to vest the control of policy in Labour Party Conference' (quoted in McKenzie, 1982, p. 194). The shift away from trade union control was thus made reluctantly by Kinnock – although it was later embraced by Blair. But it was forced on the leadership by two factors, in addition to the pressure brought to bear by the constituencies. First, the mood of hostility in the 1980s towards the trade unions and their relationship with Labour made renegotiating this relationship central to modernising the party's image. Second, the unions themselves recognised that they had more power than they could use, and that this was damaging both their own legitimacy and that of the conference as a whole. It was they who ultimately forced reform on a reluctant party leader.

The effect of the reform has not been what some of its early opponents might have feared. Far from a shift to the left, there has been a high level of acquiescence by constituency delegates to leadership proposals, and indeed in latter years it was the trade unions which sought to inflict platform defeats. Constituencies and unions having equal powers after 1995, both now also had equal responsibility for maintaining party stability – but also equal freedom to act less responsibly if provoked. Consequently the behaviour of both blocks of delegates has changed. Meanwhile leaders have prioritised winning support from CLP delegates, and tended to dismiss defeats that do not gain majority constituency support. As in the electoral college (discussed in Chapters 3 and 4) this brings the stability of the party's traditional federal structure into doubt.

The shift in the balance of votes has led to a redefinition of conference 'management'. Discussions with trade unions continue in the traditional way behind the scenes, but new mechanisms to win support from constituency delegates have now developed. The complaint from the Constituency Parties Movement in 1935 that 'stage management of Conference' made attendance by constituency delegates 'an expensive futility' might still ring true with many today (Pimlott, 1977, p. 121). However, the circumstances are now very different. The attention given to CLP delegates, including access to ministers and senior party staff, was not available to these early constituency representatives. This attention may in many ways be unwelcome, but it is an indication of the far greater power (at least in terms of voting strength) that has been won by delegates from local parties.

In these circumstances, the only means of responding to the dilemma posed above by Sidney Webb was to reduce the conference's formal powers. Constituency delegates would thus have more power, but over less. This route was pursued, through reform of the conference agenda, in part as a result of the change in vote shares. The new policy arrangements promised documents that included alternative positions on which conference could vote (another long-held demand of the left), in return for a reduction in the power to submit resolutions. This concession was resisted by the leadership, and the failure of the process to deliver it in practice, coupled with its inability to resolve some major policy issues, has been followed by old-style clashes and defeats. Unlike often in the past it has been the trade unions, frustrated when they cannot negotiate mutually acceptable compromises with the leadership, that have taken the lead on these occasions.

Partnership in Power severely limited the agenda-setting ability of both constituencies and affiliates, and their facility for 'voice'. Whilst policy documents – unlike before – are circulated in advance, there is now no opportunity for CLPs to see and comment upon each other's proposals. This was one function that the resolution booklet had fulfilled. Nonetheless the remaining opportunities at the conference, particularly through submitting contemporary resolutions, have been widely exploited and indeed were extended in 2003. This mechanism had also been accepted only reluctantly by the leadership in 1997 and its extension was fiercely opposed. The ability to debate up to eight highly contentious issues potentially gives conference equal media impact to that it had in the past, when many resolutions were on more humdrum issues. And the ability remains for conference delegates to reform the agenda further through rule changes, if they are sufficiently provoked by the leadership. The success of initiatives such as the 'Warwick accord' of 2004 between leadership and unions over policy (see Chapter 6) can thus be seen as essential to the stability of the existing arrangements. If such agreements are breached, the potential remains for unions to support campaigners on the left who want to return greater control to the conference over its own agenda. The control that the leadership holds is therefore conditional on the consent of the conference itself to these arrangements.

Although the conference may have been tamed in some respects, it thus remains a body that most Labour leaders would prefer not to have as an adversary. It continues to be an important site of negotiation between the leadership and the party, and leaders will try and avoid confrontation with constituency delegates in particular. In order to prevent public conflict and embarrassment the leadership would still usually rather negotiate than face a conference defeat. Given the long history of such defeats the stakes for challengers are also high, as each one that is shrugged off threatens to diminish the standing of the conference further. Even after all the reform that has taken place, the central controversy of Labour's democracy – the myth of conference sovereignty over policy – remains officially intact. The desire to protecting this myth is important in containing disputes between leaders and party.[23] Yet finally, it is the potential media impact of conference defeats, and their ability to set the public agenda, that remain amongst the party's greatest weapons.[24] The greater legitimacy of Labour's reformed conference structure has thus potentially enhanced its real influence, even if its formal powers are at the same time on the decline.

Notes

1. Throughout the party's life the socialist societies have also held a small share of conference votes in the affiliates section. Throughout the chapter I therefore refer to the balance between affiliates (i.e. overwhelmingly trade unions) and constituencies.
2. Minkin (1992, pp. 64-5) notes that prior to this the constituency vote share had peaked at 25 per cent in 1946, following a rapid rise in

individual membership. The potential increase in influence of the left that might result caused concern to leaders, and contributed to a change in affiliation rules which saw a 53 per cent rise in affiliated trade union members in 1947.

3. Neither of these arrangements necessarily reflected true membership accurately. Trade unions were not required to affiliate on the basis of the numbers of their members paying the political levy, and could choose to affiliate at a higher or lower level (see Minkin 1992, pp. 286-90). By the 1980s many constituencies had significantly fewer than 1,000 members, as the figures in Chapter 9 demonstrate.

4. The Engineers held 928,000 votes, the GMWU 650,000 and NUPE 600,000.

5. See Minkin (1992, pp. 366-8) for a summary of some of these.

6. Note that the affiliation fee for individual party members was significantly higher than that for trade union affiliated members. The two forms of affiliation fee were identical until 1980, after which they were allowed to diverge. By 1986 constituencies were paying £5.50 to the central party for each member, whilst other affiliated organisations were paying just 75p (Minkin, 1992).

7. Tony Wright from Castle Point CLP. Note that unlike many of the other characters in this story, this individual did not go on to have a parliamentary career. He was neither the Tony Wright who became MP for Cannock Chase or the Tony Wright to became MP for Great Yarmouth.

8. For a full discussion of these changes see Chapter 6.

9. These further proposals were never implemented. Whilst the failure of conference to formally recognise the PLP by giving it votes had long been noted, arguments against included the danger that conference would become an arena for clashes between MPs and leaders best confined to the privacy of PLP meetings.

10. See Chapters 2 and 3.

11. This proposal had previously been made by the left. For example an independent commission including key CLPD members (Burnell, 1980), and Eric Heffer in 1980 (Golding, 2003).

12. In reality this latter arrangement has rarely, if ever, been used. As the culture of the trade unions is one of collective adherence to majority decisions, delegations continue to discuss and agree their positions on issues at conference and then vote as a block.

13. As shown in Chapter 9 the party's membership had generally been comfortably below 300,000 since 1981, though there were exceptions. It dropped back below this figure in 2001.

14. Hills (1981). In contrast Hills estimated that 38 per cent of delegates at Conservative conferences were women. The Conservatives had long operated a women's quota for conference delegates (Maguire, 1998).

15. In an extreme case in 1990, for example, one (male) delegate boasted in his conference speech that he had represented his constituency every year since 1945.

16. In 1945 the party conference spent three days debating 'Let us Face the Future' and in 1949 spent two days on 'Labour Believes in Britain'. In 1953 the conference spent an extraordinary four days on the document 'Challenge to Britain' but – in a unique experiment – this was presented on an amendable basis (McKenzie, 1963).

17. For the criteria see Chapter 6. In 2000, for example, over 150 contemporary resolutions were submitted on 35 subjects. However, only eight subjects were ruled in order by the Conference Arrangements Committee and four went on to be debated.

18. 'Reference back' was a mechanism traditionally used at conference by those seeking to oppose part of a document without voting against the whole document. Such moves were frequent and generally, but by no means always, failed.

19. There were actually five alternative positions agreed by the National Policy Forum, but in an unexpected move one of these – which sought to remove a reference to foundation hospitals as a good example of local democracy – was later accepted by ministers.

20. *The Times*, 2 October 2003.

21. Partnership in Power gave constituencies and affiliates the option to submit a rule change in place of a contemporary resolution. CLPD have increasingly sought to exploit this opportunity.

22. In 2004, when the new rule was first applied, the constituencies managed to neuter their own power. Strongly encouraged to do so by party staff, many constituency delegates voted for those topics known to be favoured by the unions – which were already certain to be debated. The only additional topic supported by the CLPs was, again, Iraq.

23. However, many of the same dynamics are visible in the relationship between Conservative Party leaders and their conference, which formally shares none of the Labour conference's powers. It nonetheless enjoys *de facto* power, as leaders seek to avoid confrontations with its delegates and are attentive to its mood (Kelly, 1989).

24. An interesting example was the defeat on foundation hospitals in 2003 which the main opponents David Hinchliffe MP and Frank Dobson MP used as a springboard for a House of Commons rebellion and in turn to encourage defeat of the measure in the House of Lords. See 'Unions Reject Reid's Plea on NHS Reform', *The Guardian*, 2 October 2003.

9

Reform Frustrated: The Grassroots

An outsider's view of the Labour Party sees its elected members in parliament and elsewhere, its national conference and, perhaps, its NEC. But most of those who are active in the party engage with it primarily at a local level. Whilst national structures may change it is thus the organisation of local meetings, campaigns, social and other events that has greatest potential impact on most party members.[1]

Whilst those seeking to reform the party had competing visions, it was perhaps in the treatment of membership and local parties that these created the greatest barrier to change. Crucially even amongst the 'modernisers', drawn from the party's right and soft left, there were many disagreements over such matters. On only one objective – that of building a bigger, more welcoming, party – was there real consensus from the early 1980s. Yet this proved to be extremely difficult to achieve. Meanwhile, there was no agreement on the more fundamental issue of what the role of party members' should be, and thus what a 'mass membership' party should actually do. In addition the pure organisational complexity of redesigning the party at the grassroots, and the fondness of many members for existing practices, created formidable barriers to change. As a result, the long period of party 'modernisation' saw no single co-ordinated programme directed at local parties succeed.

Nonetheless, the reforms discussed in earlier chapters had a major impact at the local level – resulting in many of the traditional functions of constituency structures being gradually stripped away, whilst new technologies changed the relationship between members and the national party. But the fundamental questions about the role and purpose of party members, even today, remain unresolved.

THE PURPOSE OF PARTY MEMBERS

Before turning to discussion of events in the Labour Party it is worth briefly reviewing what political scientists have said about the different reasons why individuals seek to join parties, and why parties, in turn, might want to attract members. These issues have been the subject of much academic discussion. Some of the same points made in these forums featured highly in Labour's own debates from the 1980s onwards.

The classic analysis of members' motivations for joining parties suggests that there are three distinct kinds of incentives to do this.[2] First, 'purposive' incentives relate to the party's ideological objectives – members will join if they are sympathetic with the policy direction the party seeks to take and want to help it achieve its goals. Second, 'solidary' incentives are those that members may enjoy as a group, such as the opportunity to meet other like-minded individuals, and engage in social activities with them. Finally, 'material' incentives are those of direct economic benefit to the member, for example gaining paid work through the party.

By the middle of the twentieth century academic analyses were suggesting that the mass political party was in decline.[3] Changes to working patterns and availability of new leisure pursuits led to a weakening of the 'solidary' incentive, in particular. In the Labour Party many members had originally been attracted by local 'Labour clubs', but the advent of television, as well as growing disposable income, made these less important to local social life. This was almost certainly a causal factor in the declining Labour membership that was seen from the early 1950s onwards. If party membership shrank, it seemed likely that those remaining were more driven by the 'purposive' incentive – that is, that they were the more ideologically committed. This would present a potential difficulty for leaders, as these members might resist moderate policy positions with broad electoral appeal. Hence political scientists predicted that leaders would seek to free themselves from members' influence, and might even want to dispense with them altogether (Katz and Mair, 1995; Kirchheimer, 1966; Michels, 1962; Panebianco, 1988).

Whether this occurred, however, depended on the other side of the equation – the reasons that party leaders needed members. One of the most obvious benefits that members brought was their ability to act as a campaign resource – to spread messages for the party and encourage others to support it. However, in the late twentieth century, given the growth of the mass media and leaders' consequent ability to communicate directly with the public, some saw this role as increasingly redundant.

This is far from the only advantage that members can bring to leaders, however. Probably the most complete list of potential benefits has been put together by Susan Scarrow (1996), in a more recent study of political party membership. The factors that she cites include:

- 'labour' benefits – including work on local campaigns;
- 'financial' benefits – through subscriptions and donations;
- 'outreach' and 'linkage' benefits – by keeping the party in touch with others in the community on a day-to-day basis;
- 'innovation' benefits – generating a flow of new policy and campaign ideas;
- 'personnel' benefits – in terms of providing the pool from which future candidates and leaders are drawn;
- finally, and importantly in the developments below, 'legitimacy' benefits – through demonstrating that the party and its leader have a popular following.

As Scarrow noted, leaders have to weigh up all of these benefits before deciding whether they can afford to dispense with party members. The Labour Party (which acted as one of Scarrow's case studies) provides a nice example of how these dilemmas play out.

THE 'MASS MEMBERSHIP' PARTY

Labour's traditional organisation, based on a federal structure in which the affiliated trade unions held most of the formal power, determined its attitude towards membership recruitment. Individual membership was not introduced within the party until 1918, and by the late 1970s the unions still provided most of its income and – though the payment of affiliation fees – around nine tenths of its official members. Thus even in international terms 'of all the mass membership parties, the British Labour Party [was] perhaps the one where membership recruitment [was] taken least seriously' (Ware, 1987, p. 146).[4]

In the 1980s and 1990s party membership took on a new importance, in part as a result of Labour's problems in the recent past. Moderates believed that declining party membership had facilitated 'entryism', enabling hard-left activists to gain control of constituencies and mount assaults on the leadership. The precise pattern of membership decline was not known, as from 1963-79 each local constituency had been required to affiliate a minimum of 1,000 members, which therefore distorted national membership figures. When this façade was taken away, membership in 1980 was revealed to be under 350,000. This fell well short of the individual membership of about a million that the party had claimed in the early 1950s – the last time that more reliable figures were available.[5] Yet already shortly after this many local parties were seen as moribund. This was noted by the committee chaired by Harold Wilson in 1959 which famously compared Labour's organisation to a 'Penny Farthing Machine' (Labour Party, 1959). Some, including 'revisionists' such as Anthony Crosland, were unmoved by such concerns, being sympathetic to the analysis that the mass media made members largely redundant (Tanner, 2000). However, alongside the general decline came the perceived influx of younger, more middle-class and left-wing activists (Seyd, 1987). The combination of these factors led moderates to complain that the party had been 'captured' by the hard left. By the late 1970s many thus came to think that increasing the membership base was a desirable means to dilute the influence of left activists. And, as well as bringing some of the generic benefits identified later by Scarrow, a larger membership could also help free the party from its trade union dominated image.

Whilst some on the right saw factional advantage in membership recruitment, some on the left saw it as a way of strengthening the extra parliamentary party. From its formation the LCC supported a 'mass membership' model, suggesting that the party could learn from other social movements by drawing people into an active, campaigning, organisation which prioritised policy discussion and built strong links in local communities. In 1982 this case was put in a pamphlet co-authored by Charles Clarke – by then working for Neil Kinnock (Clarke and Griffiths, 1982). When Kinnock became leader in 1983 he accepted many of the arguments from both the soft left and the right. Thus membership recruitment began to be a priority for the party leadership in a way that it had never been before.

How to achieve this was a far more difficult matter. One theme that emerged in the later 1980s was the opportunity presented by the large pool of people who were already 'affiliated' to the party by paying the political levy in their trade unions, but who did not have individual party membership.[6] Whilst by 1987 there were under 300,000 party members, there were 5.8 million union levy payers. That year a pamphlet published by the left-wing Tribune Group of MPs proposed a 'levy plus' scheme which would enable these trade unionists to sign up to the party for a reduced rate (Tribune Group, 1987). This was seen as an easy way of achieving membership growth, which would have presentational advantages. To the outside world it would show that Labour was becoming a mass membership party, whilst to the unions it could be presented as strengthening, rather than weakening, the traditional 'link'. The 1988 party conference agreed such a scheme as part of a mass membership drive. This allowed members of affiliated trade unions to join the party for £5 – half the standard rate. Once the scheme was agreed, Kinnock boldly stated his intention of returning individual party membership to over a million.

A more significant reform at this time, however, proved to be that made to the method of administering membership at head office. With funding provided by the GMB, a new National Membership System was established. This enabled people to join and have their membership administered centrally for the first time, rather than doing this through their local parties. Until this time head office had no automatic access to lists of local party members, and this change therefore hugely strengthened the vertical links between the centre and the membership. At the same time it potentially weakened both members' local links with each other, and the autonomy of local parties.[7] The National Membership System enabled head office to sign up members directly, approach existing members for donations, and send them unmediated communications. This was an essential step to later innovations such as national ballots for the NEC and party leader.

The aim to increase membership was ambitious, particularly given that falling party membership was not simply a Labour Party phenomenon, but had become common in political parties throughout the developed world (Norris, 2002; Scarrow, 2000). Reasons such as declining class identifications and changing work and family patterns were, however, matters over which political parties had little, if any, control. It is no surprise then that the impact of Labour's initiatives was limited – as shown in Table 9.1. Party membership steadily declined from 1984-88. Although it did lift after the Kinnock schemes had been introduced it quickly dropped back again. In particular, four years after the scheme for trade union members was established, only 23,000 levy payers were found to have signed up (Brooks, 1993).

The drives to recruit members continued into the 1990s with limited success, alongside moves towards OMOV – which some hoped would create new incentives for membership. After the 1992 election defeat the efforts intensified, with the attraction of more members seen as essential to Labour becoming viewed as a vibrant and renewed electoral force. As argued by Gordon Brown in a further pamphlet on *Making Mass Membership Work* in 1993, a bigger party would be able to speak with more authority, be more representative of Labour supporters and help to keep leaders in touch with local communities (Brown, 1993).

Table 9.1: Individual party membership 1980–2003

Year	No. members	Year	No. members
1980	348,156†	1992	279,530
1981	276,692†	1993	266,270
1982	273,803†	1994	305,189
1983	295,344	1995	365,110
1984	323,292	1996	400,465
1985	313,099	1997	405,238
1986	297,364	1998	387,776
1987	288,829	1999	361,000
1988	265,927	2000	311,000
1989	293,723	2001	272,000
1990	311,152	2002	248,294
1991	261,233	2003	214,952

† In 1981, 1982 and 1983 a minimum number of affiliated members per constituency (256, 128 and 167 respectively) still applied, so figures may be inflated.
Sources: Seyd and Whiteley, 1992; NEC Annual Reports

From the late 1980s onwards the campaign to recruit individual trade unionists also became central to arguments about OMOV. As discussed in Chapter 3, the moves towards enfranchising individual members raised concerns about the removal of collective trade union voices from the final stage of parliamentary selection. Some argued that this loss could be compensated by the involvement of many more trade unionists as individuals through some kind of 'registered supporters' scheme. This subject became a central issue in the discussions on the trade union review group after the 1992 election. The group came close to agreeing a scheme whereby all levy payers could gain some automatic rights to participate in the party as individuals. However the option ultimately chosen, and narrowly adopted at the 1993 conference, was simply a renewal of the 'levy plus' scheme, allowing trade unionists to join at a reduced rate.

Tony Blair was one of those who passionately wanted to see the party made more legitimate by creation of a larger mass membership. Before he was party leader Blair's own constituency of Sedgefield had sought to serve as an example of how a mass membership could be built, and he spoke proudly of its 'roots in every part of the community' (quoted in Smyth, 1996, p. 63). In 1993 Sedgefield was one of 25 constituencies granted permission to pilot new approaches to membership recruitment. Under their scheme supporters could join the party for as little as £1, rather than the standard membership rate of £15. The constituency party would be required to pay £10 per member to head office, making up any shortfall through local fundraising. These initiatives succeeded in trebling the Sedgefield party's membership, to over 2,000, in the three years to 1994. Although some members complained that disproportionate time was now spent on fundraising to cover the costs of these members, the party had significantly widened its base of support (Smyth, 1996). This addressed Tony Blair's explicit strategy of making the local membership not only larger but also more moderate and closer to the perspective of the electorate as a whole.

Once Blair took over as leader in 1994 there were thus determined moves to boost party membership. Huge resources were put into membership recruitment after he was in post, with the budget for this work increased roughly tenfold in a year. Much of this money was spent on marketing through leaflets, newspapers and magazines. Blair also sought to extend more flexible attitudes to membership recruitment, and his constituency tabled resolutions to conference annually to this effect. Deputy leader John Prescott took responsibility for pursuing membership campaigns under slogans such as 'recruit a friend' or 'member get member', and revived Kinnock's claim that a membership of one million was attainable.

Initially Blair's leadership did seem to have a rapid effect in inspiring supporters to join the party. At the 1995 conference it was reported that 100,000 people had joined in the previous year.[8] This achievement enabled Blair to activate a rebalancing between trade unions and individual members that he had pressed on the trade union review group in 1992. As described in Chapter 8, when numbers exceeded 300,000 this triggered an increase in the constituencies' vote share at party conference from 30 to 50 per cent.

After 1995 membership continued to rise, reaching over 400,000 in 1996 and 1997. At this point John Prescott predicted a membership of 500,000 by New Year 1998. However, following the party's election victory the trend rapidly reversed, and by 2002 membership levels were once again below where they had been in the low points of the 1980s.

The extent to which the membership recruitment initiatives met their objectives is thus, at best, open to dispute. The success of the schemes in the mid 1990s, alongside other changes, helped promote the image of a vibrant individual member democracy replacing the traditional union-dominated party. Crucially, it also provided a direct trigger for reducing the unions' role at the annual conference. There were initially high hopes that a new kind of mass membership party could be formed. However, in the end many of those that joined in order to contribute to a Labour victory were less motivated to remain once this had been achieved. One reason may have been that – as discussed below – leaders were not completely sure what to do with these new members once they had arrived.

Over the same period the extent to which the party depended on the trade unions financially also sharply declined. Paul Webb calculates that in 1983 as much as 96 per cent of central party income came from the unions, but that by 1997 the equivalent figure was just 40 per cent (Webb, 2000). This was a dramatic change, but – despite the rhetoric of leaders at the time – did not come about primarily thanks to membership growth. In 1999 large donations accounted for 20 per cent of party income, and 10 per cent came from commercial sponsorship. Both of these sources had been boosted by the party's proximity to power. Equally important, however, the move to the National Membership System had altered the basis of the figures. In the early 1980s income from membership subscriptions was paid to local parties, with only a portion reaching head office. By the mid-1990s all membership income was paid directly to the centre. This change, combined with the effects of membership growth and other income, created the stark contrast which is often quoted.

Meanwhile another key objective of membership recruitment – that of creating a more moderate party, less critical of its leadership – was also of questionable success. Most importantly, obviously, the growth achieved had been wholly lost by the end of the period. But even as membership peaked in the mid 1990s, individual member democracy did not deliver results quite as leaders had anticipated –

as discussed in Chapters 4 and 7. Seyd and Whiteley's (2002) membership surveys found that there was relatively little difference
between the attitudes of those joining Labour after Blair became
leader and the views of more established members.[9] This might
have been different, of course, if membership levels had reached
those that the most ambitious in the party had aimed at. Had every
constituency achieved the same results as Sedgefield, membership
would have reached approximately 1.3 million: over three times the
total achieved at the peak of the party's recruitment success.

CULTURAL CHANGE

The bigger question was not whether Labour should seek to recruit
members – on this there was broad agreement, but rather what
these members' role in the party should be. For some reformers,
from early on, addressing this question was recognised as extremely
important. As Clarke and Griffiths suggested, a successful mass
membership party would need to 'develop an outward-looking,
open and involving approach to politics' (1982, p. 29). The LCC
believed (as discussed in Chapter 6) that the party would benefit
from a culture of deliberative discussion about policy, backed up by
a programme of political education and more active local campaigning. This, it was thought, would offer incentives to members to
be active whilst providing a crucial link between leaders and the
public. Similar ideas had been floated in the party since at least the
1950s (Fielding, 1999).

This ideal was seen as rather different to the prevailing culture in
many local parties. These were traditionally structured around local
branches (often based on local government wards), co-ordinated by
a constituency Executive Committee (EC) and General Committee
(GC) comprising delegates from the branches, women's section(s)
and local affiliated organisations. These structures, each of which
met monthly throughout the year, were relatively formal in their
operation and governed by a rigid set of rules. Although many
members did engage in campaign activity, particularly at election
time, the most active members were also expected to show commitment to the party by attending these meetings, often several times
each month. In 1990 Seyd and Whiteley (1992) found that 30 per
cent of members had attended party meetings 'frequently' and a
further 20 per cent had attended 'occasionally' in the past year.
Extrapolating from their overall figures on party activism they

suggested that 147,000 members devoted at least some time to party matters in the average month, with 30,000 giving 10 hours or more per month. Yet much of this time was spent in meetings with other members rather than engaging with the local electorate.

In some constituencies in the early 1980s new members who attended party meetings might be baffled not only by formality and jargon, but also by vicious arguments between competing factions. There were thus concerns among some senior party figures that membership drives were doomed to fail, as new members would either become absorbed within the prevailing culture or be quickly alienated. Neil Kinnock, General Secretary Larry Whitty, and members of the NEC were supportive of ideas to create a party that met the LCC objectives of being less bureaucratic, more welcoming and outward looking, and better connected to the local community. However, there were arguments about whether this could be achieved through prioritising membership recruitment, or whether it was necessary – or indeed possible – to change the culture of local parties before new members were invited in.

There were also more fundamental arguments about the appropriate roles of local parties and members. Whilst there was general support for increasing the membership base, there were some at senior levels who were sceptical of the continuing value of local party organisation. After all, local parties had helped put many unwelcome issues onto the policy agenda, whilst some thought that the benefits they traditionally brought could be achieved by other means. Whilst the mass media could potentially enable leaders to communicate messages to voters, new polling techniques and the growing use of focus groups could communicate voters' concerns to leaders in a more professional and dispassionate way than local members were able to do. In the late 1980s and early 1990s there were thus serious questions about whether the task was to revive and refocus local parties, or simply to let them decline. Some key figures supported an alternative model, influenced by the US Democrats, where individual members had a relationship primarily with the party at the centre. In this way a direct member democracy could fund, and be co-ordinated by, a powerful central party machine.

Research in the early 1970s had suggested that local campaigning made little difference to election outcomes (Kavanagh, 1970, Pimlott, 1971). But later academic research into this subject started to draw different conclusions. The work of Seyd and Whiteley (1992) and Denver and Hands (1993) was influential in maintaining commitment by many at the top of the party to local constituency organisation.[10] Following the 1992 general election Denver and Hands showed that in seats where the most vigorous local campaigns had been run, the swing to Labour had generally been larger. The party's own analysis meanwhile suggested that whilst the national campaign had been more professional than ever before, local organisation was poor in some areas. Given that the Conservatives had won by only 21 seats, these factors were considered important. The balance of opinion thus tipped towards those supporting the regeneration of local parties, with the added incentive that this could strengthen Labour's electoral chances.

The 'Regeneration Project' was thus launched by the NEC at the 1993 annual conference. Its aim was to encourage local parties to examine their practice and consider reorientating it to better achieve their own and the national party's goals. These were likely to include winning seats by mounting effective campaigns, recruiting more members, being more welcoming to those members who did join, initiating more fundraising and social events, and generally focussing on activity outside of meetings. However the approach to local reform continued to be riven by conflicts. On the NEC there were disagreements not only about the relative priorities of regeneration and recruitment, but also over which parties should be regenerated first. Those that were most likely to achieve best practice were the ones which were already relatively functional and needed a little help to improve. But the biggest worry to the NEC were the small number of local parties that were stagnant, dysfunctional, and even corrupt. As well as making life miserable for local members, these had the potential to cause the party public embarrassment. Although significant resources went into regeneration, they were disproportionately spent on these failing constituencies, which were unlikely in the foreseeable future to reach model status. Other parties were given guidance and asked to draw up local development plans to decide their objectives, but had relatively little central support.

One obstacle to reform of local party culture was the perception by activists that leaders were seeking to divert local energies into benign activities in order to free themselves from accountability over policy. The claims by some that local parties should have fewer meetings and instead 'undertake campaigning, education and socialising, which are more interesting and stimulating' (Mandelson and Liddle 1996, p. 215) hinted to members that their traditional role of feeding into policy was under threat. This reflected a genuine conflict amongst senior party figures between those supporting the old LCC view that a more outward-looking party would be better qualified to inform policy and could boost the accountability of leaders, against those who saw the flow of information in a modern mass party as being wholly top down. As discussed in Chapter 6, this plagued internal debates about the new policy process, as well as about local organisation. A political education drive, launched in the early 1990s, was seen by some as a means of drawing members into more productive policy deliberation locally. Others, however, saw such developments as a way of making individual members the passive recipients of decisions made at the top. Meanwhile a third group continued to believe that the 'post-activist' party was inevitable, or even desirable (Clifton, 1994).[11]

It is impossible properly to gauge how much the culture in Labour's 600-plus constituency parties altered during this period. A survey in 1995 which built upon Seyd and Whiteley's 1990 results found that many of the same problems still applied. Members were devoting the equivalent of 7,000 person years of voluntary effort to the party annually, which in comparison to the work of the party's 200 paid staff, was a huge level of voluntary effort. One fifth of the total – the annual equivalent of 1,400 person years – was still spent in internal party meetings (Pitt-Watson, 2000). Questions to new members also found that whilst they joined the party in order to express support, once they were signed up local parties were often unclear how best to use them.

In any change that did take place the contribution of planned regeneration initiatives was almost certainly dwarfed by other factors. By the mid 1990s the decisions delegated to local parties had significantly diminished and the role of the GC, in particular, had been transformed. In the mid 1980s the GC had been responsible for selecting the parliamentary candidate, choosing who the constituency would support in leadership contests, mandating conference delegates on how to vote in NEC elections, and devising resolutions and amendments that set much of the annual conference agenda. Ten years later the first three of these responsibilities had passed to individual members and the third was about to almost completely disappear. The scope of collective decisions that rested with constituency parties had thus fundamentally changed, requiring them to either focus on other activities or wither away. At the same time the programme of women's quotas introduced in 1990 had brought many previously inactive or marginalised members into office locally, transforming the activist base. Irrespective of whether women naturally favoured a more inclusive and less confront-ational style (as some had argued), the presence of this number of new activists amounted to a significant renewal in itself.

The objective of refocusing local party activity remained prom-inent during the Partnership in Power discussions of 1996-97. One of the four taskforces, chaired by Diana Jeuda (who had also been the lead NEC member on the Regeneration Project), concentrated on 'building a healthy party' at the grassroots. The consultation document reiterated that '[s]trong, representative and active local parties have an enormous amount to contribute to the success of a Labour Government in providing ideas and feedback on the Government's work, taking Labour's message out into the local community and undertaking the vital work of maintaining a strong election machine'. It suggested that without this 'the success of a Labour Government [would] be threatened' (Labour Party 1997, p. 29). The belief in the potential value of local members to Labour electorally, and more importantly the threat that a troublesome grassroots could pose to Labour in power, had by now been widely accepted. Furthermore there was a clear perception that insufficient reform had taken place, and the NEC declared itself 'committed to continuing the change in culture throughout the party' (Labour Party 1997a, p. 13). However, the target of this cultural change remained unresolved. As political scientists had long noted, the price for member engagement was traditionally for leaders to give members real influence – though as Scarrow (1996) proposed, this offered potential benefits to both sides. Some in the party recognised this, and the 'healthy party' model included the notion, proposed by the LCC in 1996, that local members would act as 'party ambassadors' in their local communities, explaining and defending the actions of the Labour government (LCC, 1996, p. 1). The means to achieving this crucial cultural change, however, remained elusive.

STRUCTURAL CHANGE

In trying to achieve change in the party on the ground the obvious approach was to shake up local structures and, as with reform to other aspects of the party's organisation, pursue cultural and behavioural change by amending party rules. The structure of branches, ECs, GCs and women's sections had remained largely unchanged since 1918.[12] Under this formalised system of local representative democracy delegates elected to the EC and GC were responsible for taking decisions on a constituency-wide basis, and in turn elected delegates to represent the local party at annual conference. These arrangements also mirrored the federal model that applied nationally, structuring the local relationship between the party and its affiliated organisations. Delegates to constituency-wide organisations represented not only the geographical branches, but also women's sections and local branches of affiliated trade unions and socialist societies.

It had been argued since at least the 1960s that these structures were no longer appropriate.[13] Following the crisis of the 1970s and early 1980s the arguments for change became more numerous, and support for them more widespread amongst moderates and right-wingers. The system rewarded the most assiduous attendees at meetings and those who put most energy into organising through local structures, and yet the activists who had gained control of many local parties were believed to be unrepresentative of the wider party membership. The less politically driven, those with work or family responsibilities that limited their ability to attend meetings, and those who simply did not value this form of activism, were disadvantaged in decision making. For many of those promoting the individual member model through OMOV, it seemed natural that the structure of local parties should reflect this same principle.

With the focus on more immediate priorities such as parliamentary and leadership selections, and the policy process, the national party did not turn its attention to the structure of local parties until the late 1980s. The issue was then raised as part of the NEC's general review of party organisation that was reported to the 1990 conference in *Democracy and Policy Making for the 1990s*. The commission established by the LCC in response to this consultation was amongst those proposing radical change. It supported the moves that had already taken place to enfranchise individual members – for example, in NEC elections and local parliamentary selections – and argued that this principle should be applied more widely. In this new environment local GCs were viewed as 'an unnecessary tier of bureaucracy' that 'could easily be abolished' (LCC, 1989, p. 4). Instead it was suggested that the local unit of organisation should be the branch, as this was open to all members living in the area.

These were, however, extremely contentious proposals. The LCC itself was divided both on the extent to which direct democracy could replace previous representative bodies, and also, crucially, on the implications for the trade union link. The abolition of the GC would largely end these links at the local level, as branch Labour parties made no allowance for trade union representation. These controversies caused internal divisions in the LCC and its AGM failed to endorse the commission's proposals. When the party's own consultation ended, *Democracy and Policy Making for the 1990s* largely omitted discussion of local organisation, though it did conclude that 'proposals which largely relate to the superstructure of party policy-making would be incomplete, and to some extent ineffective, without serious consideration of the inadequacy of the way in which CLPs, branches and local government level party organisations are currently structured' (Labour Party, 1990a, p. 9).[14] A review of these questions was promised, with decisions to be taken after the impending general election. But following the 1992 defeat no such proposals were brought forward.

The Regeneration Project that followed the 1992 election – as discussed above – aimed at changing local party culture rather than structures. There were proposals at the time that this should be used as a vehicle for structural reform, but the rule changes made in association with the project allowed local experimentation where parties sought it, rather than imposing any specific model. Indeed the obstacles to more fundamental reform were extensive, as demonstrated by the earlier differences within the LCC. At a time when trade unions felt that their relationship with the party was under threat, and negotiations were tense over the introduction of OMOV, a weakening of local trade union links would not have been accepted. Indeed the fact that GCs would still draw up parliamentary shortlists (though the final selection was in future to be by the membership as a whole) was an essential part of securing the narrow victory for the OMOV package in 1993. Aside from opposition from the unions, activists would almost certainly have been unenthusiastic about dismantling local structures. The agreement on OMOV thus further reduced the formal role of local federal and representative structures, but left them intact.

The next opportunity for structural reform came with Partnership in Power. At this point too, however, there were higher priorities amongst reformers at senior levels of the party. This time the battles with more traditional elements, particularly the trade unions, came over the structure of the NEC and the policy-making role of annual conference. The 'healthy party' section of the consultation document ultimately confined itself to proposing non-prescriptive cultural change. Local structures did continue to be discussed, however, and the focus remained on dismantling the local GCs. This was now firmly backed by the LCC, which had changed its political complexion and was now less sympathetic to the left. Its second commission on party democracy concluded that 'constituency parties [were] overburdened with formal structures' (Flint, 1996, p. 82) and that the party's traditional federal structure 'should be abandoned' (LCC, 1996, p. 9). Instead only individual party members should have voting rights, and all local positions – including constituency officers and conference delegates – should be elected by OMOV. A leaked memo from the party's regional director in the north west, David Evans, proposed a similar model, suggesting that 'representative democracy should as far as possible be abolished in the Party', which, it was suggested, would 'empower modernising forces within the Party and marginalise "Old Labour"'. Blair himself was known to be sympathetic to such an approach.

Much of the suspicion over Partnership in Power amongst activists focussed on these rumoured local changes, and responses from local parties showed hostility to any such proposals. The trade unions, already making other concessions, were also inclined to defend the status quo. The rule changes that resulted therefore confined themselves to allowing more experimentation. This time CLPs were allowed to pilot moving away from GCs and towards all member meetings or other locally tailored solutions. One such example was the Enfield Southgate CLP where management of the constituency was taken over by the Executive Committee. This facilitated meetings on a bi-monthly basis to which all members were invited, and the GC and branch meetings were abolished. Such exemplars were quoted widely by those proposing more radical reform. However they were not without their difficulties, and Enfield Southgate itself later partially reversed its reforms.

As the party entered government in 1997 some of the difficulties with abandoning formal structures became apparent. Although local parties remained somewhat bureaucratic, and there was a perception that attendees at meetings remained unrepresentative of the wider membership, these structures were virtually all the government had in terms of local 'ambassadors'. A major overspend on the 1997 election campaign left the party very short of resources following its victory. This severely limited the central party's contact with individual members. Using them as ambassadors would require regular circulation of information about what the government was doing. But the party's financial difficulties were such that it produced only one all-member mailing per year in 1997 and 1998. The best it could manage was a low-budget newsletter which was sent on a monthly basis to branches and constituencies, and was thus only accessible to activists. Regional offices co-ordinated local policy forums on an all-member basis, but resource constraints also meant that their coverage was limited and discussion increasingly became concentrated in more traditional forums. Meanwhile, the national party continued to place demands on local parties which required regular functioning meetings. Requests for nominations to the NEC and new National Policy Forum, for example, and for comments on draft policy documents, often required a quick response. In addition some key tasks – such as shortlisting in party selections and electing conference delegates – had been left with GCs. All-member meetings were potentially more vulnerable to 'packing' by particular factions, and in rural areas would tend to disadvantage those living furthest from the venue. Furthermore, where members were not explicitly elected as members of a constituency-wide body there was also a greater danger that they would simply fail to turn up. Such decline could reduce the pool of volunteers to help at election time, and given the party's dependence on a relatively small group who continued to work locally, was a cause for concern. Thus although some at the centre remained basically opposed to the existence of delegate structures, it became increasingly clear that these could fulfil various functions which would otherwise be difficult to complete.

Reform of local parties has never fully left the organisational agenda, and documents continued to appear regularly after 1997 seeking views on how local organisation could become less bureaucratic and more welcoming. The Partnership in Power reforms were followed by the '21st Century Party' initiative which was launched by the NEC at the 1999 annual conference (Labour Party, 1999). This initially took an aggressive tone, suggesting that the local structures of the party were inadequate for modern needs and inviting views before rule changes at the 2000 conference. However, no such proposals were put. This was explained partly by continued resistance from the trade unions, but also by the reaction from local parties, which rejected prescriptive change and many of whom supported preserving existing structures (Labour Party, 2000). With little appetite for upsetting the party's remaining active members, the NEC's approach instead has continued to be one of encouraging local innovation. Acceptance has grown that there is likely to be no 'one size fits all' solution which can accommodate large and small local memberships, urban and rural constituencies, and seats with or without Labour MPs. Instead more recent documents have provided examples, leaving it to individual constituencies to decide whether to copy from one another (Labour Party, 2000; 2003). There are increasing numbers of these experiments, with local parties choosing to merge branches, hold meetings at less frequent intervals, open GC meetings to all members or even to merge constituencies into city-wide structures.

At the end of the period the indications are that local Labour parties are structuring themselves in increasingly diverse ways. However, this has not resulted from a nationally agreed and co-ordinated package of reform, but has flowed from the many other reforms implemented over the last 15–20 years. In terms of their powers, local delegate structures have been emasculated by changes to selection procedures and new methods of policy making, with responsibilities passing instead to individual party members. This shrinking agenda has led many local parties to restructure. The obstacles that prevented rapid change after 1997 have increasingly diminished, as new technologies now allow contact with individual members at negligible unit cost. The party website (including a secure member area) provides updates on campaigns, internal elections and policy initiatives, and members with access to the technology can register for weekly email updates from head office.

Although this enables the central party machine to 'reach out', it allows for only minimal two-way communications and does little to enhance 'horizontal' deliberation amongst members. Head office briefings do not attempt to express the breadth of opinion even amongst the party's most senior figures. This was demonstrated for example in early 2004 when the PLP was engaged in a fierce debate over university funding. Email bulletins told members that there was 'no plan B on tuition fees', claiming that 'Labour's higher education plans represent a stark choice between progressive politics with Labour and the regressive attitudes of the Tories.'[15] This in no way reflected the diversity of views which Labour MPs were expressing daily in the media. Such communications thus do not open out debates, but instead further demonstrate the extent to which the party leader controls the party machine. The NEC, ostensibly in control, would undoubtedly have had difficulty agreeing to such a collective line.

Some MPs have similarly established regular email contact with local members, but practice varies as to how much this allows a genuine exchange of views. Thus one of the most important functions of local party structures remains creating accountability between party members and those elected to public office on their behalf. This is not a function that those proposing more informal arrangements have tended to emphasise. However, it is one which local members hold dear, and are likely to continue to battle to protect.

EVALUATION

In the mid 1990s arch 'modernisers' Peter Mandelson and Roger Liddle complained that in the 1950s and 1960s the Labour Party 'was kept together by a combination of monthly meetings of delegates drawn from the branch members and affiliated trade unions and of evening socials and activities' (1996, p. 213). It was the inadequacies of these arrangements which, they said, had left the party as an 'empty shell' in the 1970s that could be occupied by the hard left. The implication in their criticism of past practice was that the party's local organisation was now qualitatively different, and that 'new' Labour would be insulated from such problems. The desired insulation may indeed have come, as a result of the stripping away of local parties' collective powers. But even now local Labour parties continue to be much as Mandelson and Liddle described: held together by cycles of meetings, many of them monthly and many organised on a delegate basis. These structures have been a regular target of modernisers, and the 'meetings culture' of local parties has long been criticised more widely. Yet decades after these criticisms were first made, and although local experiments are common, many old practices still remain intact. Thus whilst the federal and representative traditions have been weakened, they continue to exist at local level in many areas.

The vision of the 'modernisers' was to create a bigger and more representative party, and for a short time after Tony Blair became leader this change really did seem to be occurring. However, it quickly became clear that the membership increase was a temporary one, and the party now has significantly fewer individual members than it did in 1983. In this respect political scientists' predictions about party membership decline may simply have been shown to be correct. However, there were always those in the party who believed that this trend could be resisted if a more resources were put into local parties, and genuine dialogue between leaders and members could be established. This created a huge practical and cultural challenge, and was never fully put into effect. Whether it was always a hopelessly idealistic vision, or whether a real opportunity was missed, is impossible reliably to judge.

Given the extent of other reforms in the party during the 1980s and 1990s the lack of reform targeted at local parties may appear surprising. Four explanations for this inertia can be found. The first is simply lack of priority and resources given to this element of the party's organisation. As in so many things, local parties have been the poor relations when it comes to organisational change. This brings problems for them in terms of lack of support, but also benefits in terms of relative freedom over their own affairs. Both leaders and activists have prioritised big, high profile changes – such as the format of conference or selection of parliamentary candidates – rather than the less visible day-to-day organisation of the party on the ground. The big changes nonetheless did deal with some of the worst problems of local parties as perceived by moderates and right-wingers. The trade unions meanwhile have consistently clung on to local delegate structures (for which, thanks to OMOV, they have increasingly little use), whilst gradually giving ground on reforms that were more important to leaders.

Second, reform of the grassroots has suffered from a lack of agreement over objectives by those seeking change. Reform packages were always an uneasy compromise between those believing that the age of the mass activist party had come and gone, and those wishing to revive it. There was general agreement over the desirability of expanding the party's membership, if this could be achieved. For some this was a political strategy to shift the party onto more moderate ground (a kind of reverse 'entryism' to rival that of the left in the 1970s) based on a belief that the party's members were more left-wing than its supporters. However, campaigns to widen membership were extremely resource intensive, and with the exception of a few years in the mid 1990s managed no more than to offset the flow of members leaving the party.

The third factor was a growing realisation by party leaders that not only do members potentially matter, but also that local party organisation is necessary in order to co-ordinate their work. The earlier belief in the 'post activist' party, facilitated by a mass media and ever more sophisticated polling techniques, mirrored predictions by academics of the arrival of the 'catch all', 'electoral-professional' or 'cartel' party (Kirchheimer, 1966; Panebianco, 1988; Katz and Mair, 1995). The inevitability of this transition was accepted – and indeed welcomed – by some reformers. However, as Scarrow (1996) indicated, partly based on developments in the Labour Party itself, party leaders also remain potentially dependent on many of the benefits that members bring. From the late 1980s onwards leaders increasingly sought to attract and retain members. Yet once the need for members is accepted the requirement for local parties, with appropriate decision-making structures, follows. As well as providing co-ordination of campaign activity such structures help bind members to the local party, boosting the 'solidaristic' incentive and creating a sense of both obligation and motivation. Though sometimes dull and bureaucratic, organisation of this kind has thus shown itself to serve essential functions. The range of tasks asked of local parties (some of them, such as participation in policy discussions, with the express purpose of motivating members to remain active) required organisations which were both responsive and representative. This in turn required some kind of regular meetings and, arguably, delegate structures.

Local activists' resistance to change has proved to be the final constraint. Initially this may have acted as an additional spur to reformers to dismantle local structures – it could be seen as the operation of vested activist interests, against the wider interests of 'ordinary' members. However, as it became clearer that activists – stripped of some of their previous more troublesome powers – were both useful and relatively rare, the momentum for radical reform declined. With the problems of ultra-left 'entryism' far behind, a growing regard for activists led to an acceptance of some of their concerns about the kind of indiscriminate reform that was originally proposed. The need to maintain motivation amongst members in constituencies that are geographically, politically and culturally extremely varied resulted in a retreat from centrally derived solutions. Local parties may have been stripped of many of their previous collective powers, and in more recent years seen their membership decline. But they retain a surprising, and indeed growing, degree of autonomy over their own organisation.

Notes

1. In their 1990 survey of party members Seyd and Whiteley (1992) found that 44 per cent of members had been in contact with their local branch or constituency party 'frequently' and 29 per cent 'occasionally'. These figures had, however, declined significantly by 1999 (Seyd and Whiteley, 2002).

2. For a more detailed discussion see, for example, Scarrow (1996), Ware (1996). The classification system was originally proposed by Clark and Wilson (1961).

3. For example Epstein (1967), Kirchheimer (1966).

4. Indeed Duverger (1954) classified Labour as a 'semi mass' party rather than a mass party, for this reason.

5. In 1952 and 1953 membership exceeded a million, and by 1956 had declined to 845,000. However, the party then introduced a minimum local affiliation of 800 members per constituency (later increased to 1,000), and thereafter figures became highly unreliable (Seyd and Whiteley, 1992).

6. In fact Seyd and Whiteley (1992) report that the first scheme seeking to recruit trade union levy-payers into membership was in 1924.

7. Although it must be noted that the system was beset with problems for many years, during which time local parties continued to be able to administer membership.

8. However, not all of these members had joined so recently. The new funds for the membership department had enabled them to clear the backlog of applications which had dogged the National Membership System. Staff estimated that some 30,000 applications predating Blair's election as leader were included in this total.

9. Thus, for example, the 1997 survey showed that 41 per cent of party members who joined before 1994 agreed that 'the central question of British politics is the class struggle between labour and capital', but 33 per cent of newer members agreed. Amongst 'old' members 76 per cent believed the government should spend less on defence, and this view was shared by 69 per cent of members joining after 1994.

10. See also Whiteley and Seyd (1992).

11. Later the party's former Head of Policy alleged that 'While no Labour politician would publicly subscribe to such views they represent[ed] the implicit consensus in government' (Taylor, 2000, p. 56).

12. For a discussion of changes to the local women's organisation see Chapter 5.

13. For example McKitterick (1960), Bing (1971a), Pimlott (1971) and Hayter (1977) all suggested ending the structure of GCs and opening constituency meetings up to all local members. Similar proposals were made to the 1980 Commission of Enquiry, for example by the APEX union. Ben Pimlott suggested that 'A structure built for the peculiar needs of an extraordinary moment in Labour Party history ha[d] been allowed to survive in all its archaic quaintness'(1971, p. 12).
14. For a discussion of the wide-ranging proposals in the package for policy making and the NEC see Chapters 6, 7 and 8.
15. Email bulletin, 15 January 2004.

10

Change and the Illusion of Change

We have seen that in the period since the early 1980s the Labour Party underwent many fundamental changes to its organisation. The roles of the National Executive Committee and annual conference, both traditionally at the heart of Labour's democracy, altered significantly, and a new system for agreeing policy was established. The way in which the party selected candidates for public office, and the party leader, were the subject of extended debate and some highly contentious reforms. Although local constituency parties in themselves were not the subject of major restructuring, other changes had a considerable impact on both their culture and their formal functions. Finally, a system of quotas led to a transformation of women's representation at every level of the party.

Earlier chapters have explained why and how each of these changes happened, and what some of their effects have been. The task that remains for these final chapters is to draw out some more general lessons. This organises itself fairly neatly into the need to answer two main questions. The first, tackled in this chapter, is what the story in the book tells us about the nature of the reform process in the Labour Party, and what lessons we can draw about political parties in general. The second question, which will be addressed in Chapter 11, is how the fundamentals of Labour's organisation have changed as a result of these reforms, and how power in the party may have shifted as a result.

Many answers have been proffered elsewhere to such questions, ranging from the claims and counter claims of Labour activists, or the assessments of interested journalists, to the detailed analyses presented by the scholars of political parties. One purpose in drawing the material in this book together is to offer each of these audiences a body of evidence against which their existing assumptions can be tested. These closing chapters begin such an analysis, by considering the extent to which these previous claims are substantiated by the evidence about Labour's organisational reform.

THE PROCESS OF CHANGE

Taking the broad collection of reforms in the party over this period, it is first useful to ask what it was that triggered such widespread change at this particular time, from what sources those pursuing reform drew their ideas, and how the specific proposals implemented came to be agreed. In particular, how fair is it to assume, as many have done, that reform was driven by leadership initiative?

Motivation

Panebianco (1988, p. 242) has suggested that factors driving party change can be classified as *exogenous* and *endogenous*. Exogenous factors are those deriving from the environment in which the party operates. Endogenous factors are, in contrast, drawn from within the party itself and the desires of its members for reform.

Exogenous factors may cause endogenous movements for change and, as Panebianco notes, one of the most powerful such factors is electoral defeat. It is no accident that Labour's most intense period of organisational reform – from 1979 to 1997 – coincided with its longest ever period in opposition, during which time the party suffered a record four consecutive general election defeats. This is significant for two principal reasons. Most importantly because defeat focussed increasing attention in the party on what internal changes would help Labour to regain power. But also because the party's long period of opposition left little else that leaders could control aside from the party itself. Whilst the burdens of office made internal party matters somewhat peripheral, the years of opposition turned them into an increasing focus.

The combination of these two features created an internal environment in which leaders and members were thus increasingly eager to prioritise party change. Both groups were aware of the need to improve Labour's electoral chances, and were driven by a desire to remove the Conservatives from office. With each defeat the number of key players who were prepared to make sacrifices in order to see this happen increased, and this in turn resulted in an ever greater determination to display unity and loyalty to the leader. In this way the ability of Neil Kinnock, John Smith and Tony

Blair to gain support for the reforms they advocated was gradually increased. This finally culminated in the implementation of many outstanding reforms after the devastating last defeat of 1992 – notably John Smith's achievements on OMOV and the agreement of the Partnership in Power package under Tony Blair.

This analysis, however, tells no more than half the story. Labour had suffered election defeats in the past, but its internal structures had proved extremely resistant to change. Even during the long period of opposition from 1951 to 1964 there was little organisational reform. There was thus something very different about the period after 1979.

The key to this was the conflict that engulfed the party in the 1970s, reaching crisis point after the Callaghan government fell from power. From the 1960s onwards party activists and figures in the trade unions had expressed increasing disillusionment with the direction of Labour in government. This anger grew, but was contained when the party was in office and during the brief period of opposition from 1970 to 1974. Increasingly activists concluded that changes to the party's organisation were necessary to establish a new relationship between members and leaders, and these demands were voiced through groups such as the CLPD and LCC. The 1979 defeat offered the opportunity for these changes to be implemented. It was thus activists, rather than leaders, who initially used electoral defeat to move the party away from its 'old Labour' traditions. The success of those on the left in destabilising the old arrangements then acted as an important catalyst for further organisational reform, and helped make this a priority for leaders in a way that it had never been before. The first signs of 'new' Labour in an organisational sense may thus be traced not to the actions of Tony Blair, or even Neil Kinnock, but to the adoption of the CLPD's initial demands: mandatory reselection of MPs, agreed in 1979, and the leadership electoral college, agreed in 1981. Mandatory reselection, in particular, helped drive both the moves to OMOV and to ensure that women were represented on parliamentary shortlists.

The shifting political environment of the 1960s and 1970s which had made these reforms possible was, however, equally important – and in particular the changing patterns of behaviour by the trade unions, which had previously played a stabilising role in the party. Starting from the defeats of Hugh Gaitskell in 1959 (behind the scenes on Clause IV) and 1960 (on the conference floor over nuclear disarmament) major unions increasingly showed that they were no longer always prepared act as the leadership's 'Praetorian Guard' (Minkin, 1992). Disagreements between the unions and Labour governments played out in increasingly fractious relationships within the party machine, with support for the left in the unions growing. This resulted in a majority on the NEC from the early 1970s that was often at odds with the party leader, alongside rising numbers of defeats for the leadership at annual conference. By the late 1970s key unions were supporting the organisational claims of activists in the CLPD, and the unions themselves benefited from reform by winning the largest share of the vote in the new leadership electoral college.

All of this was a far cry from the unions' traditional role, and fed mounting criticism by their opponents outside the party. During this same period the powers of the unions in the economy had become a major issue of political debate, and the cause of mounting public concern. This was seen as a key contributor to the party's 1979 defeat, and the depths of its electoral troubles in the 1980s. The trade unions' role thus also attracted increasing criticisms from within Labour's ranks. Particularly after the SDP breakaway in 1981 – itself linked to the decision on the electoral college – moderates in the party came to see their formerly loyal allies as part of the problem. By the time Kinnock was elected leader in 1983 organisational reform to change the relationship with the trade unions, as well as to respond to the gains of the CLPD, had become a priority for senior figures in the party.

In Panebianco's terms, therefore, there were both exogenous and endogenous drivers of reform. For all in the party the exogenous factor of repeated election defeats was essential. The endogenous factors of activist-led reforms and the changed behaviour of the trade unions inside the party were also essential.[1] But the relationships between exogenous and endogenous are complex, particularly in Labour's case. Defeat in 1979 precipitated the reforms sought by activists, which in turn helped persuade leaders of the need for further change. The behaviour of the unions helped shape the exogenous political environment, at the same time as it affected debates within the party. All of these factors must be understood together to see why Labour started on the road to reform.

Inspiration

The particular objectives of different groups in seeking reform are discussed in the next section. But first it is worth noting where those pursuing change looked for their *inspiration*. A number of patterns emerge from the accounts given in earlier chapters, and four important sources can be identified.

First, and critically given their association with 'new' Labour, many of the reforms that were implemented from the late 1980s onwards had been on the agenda of groups within the party for a very long time. In some cases, such as the reform of the NEC, or OMOV for local selections, the ideas can be traced at least to the 1960s. In others, such as changing the balance of vote shares at annual conference, debates even dated to the 1930s. Protagonists on all sides drew on long traditions and used the opportunities presented in this period to attain aims that had failed to be realised in the past.

Second all groups, but particularly the soft left, sought inspiration from political parties overseas. This is seen strongly with respect to women's quotas, and also in the early attempts to reform policy making. The networks of the Socialist International were important to individual protagonists such as Larry Whitty and Clare Short, and organisations such as the LCC, who sought to import new ideas from other centre-left parties.

Third, inspiration was also drawn from the other parties in the UK with whom Labour had to compete electorally. Immediately after 1981 it faced a major threat from the SDP which, starting with a blank slate, was able to present itself as a centre-left party free of some of Labour's more outdated organisational traditions. For example the new party had dispensed with the trade union block vote and instead organised on the principle of OMOV. This was a major challenge given Labour's traditional appearance. For some of the 'modernisers' the Conservatives also provided inspiration, given their less bureaucratic structures and greater flexibility for the leader in policy formation. They too, in using their position in government to champion economic reform and to slash the powers of the trade unions, could seek to undermine central aspects of Labour's organisational tradition.

Finally, however, the trade unions themselves offered Labour examples of modernisation and internal reform. Trade union representatives in the party, from the NEC downwards – as well as two consecutive General Secretaries (Larry Whitty and Tom Sawyer) recruited directly from the unions – brought evidence of successful reforms. For example membership ballots (in many cases, ironically, imposed by the Thatcher governments) had expanded member involvement and boosted leadership legitimacy, whilst mechanisms to give women a more prominent role had been adopted in order to broaden some unions' membership appeal. The interwoven nature of the party–union relationship meant that many of these examples were readily imported.

Negotiation

A key conclusion drawn from the accounts in earlier chapters is that 'new' Labour was not designed, it was negotiated. This negotiation began long before Tony Blair took over as leader, with much conducted under Neil Kinnock, and key reforms agreed under John Smith. In some cases, such as the decision over OMOV, negotiation took many years. Kinnock first proposed this to the conference in 1984, but it was not finally agreed until 1993. Whilst Blair may have been influential in debates such as this one, he inherited a party where many important reforms had already taken place.

The key point, however, is that most of the proposals implemented did not initially come from the leadership at all, but from party activists of both the left and the right. Those on the right (themselves largely sympathetic to the aims of the parliamentary leadership, and primarily organised from parliament) had, for example, long campaigned for OMOV in local selections and for a widening of the membership of the NEC. These proposals were eventually taken up by the leadership. But many others that went on to be adopted originated with left-wing activists and had the backing of the CLPD. Obviously this applied to mandatory selection and the electoral college, which proved so important in triggering later changes in internal selection processes. But there are other examples of reforms that originated from the left: such as reducing the trade unions' vote share at the annual conference, guaranteeing women seats on parliamentary shortlists and making policy documents amendable by the wider party. This dynamic is overlooked by even some of the party's most seasoned observers. For example, Panitch and Leys (1997, p. 225) report that Neil Kinnock 'got the unions to agree' to a reduction in their share of annual conference votes. In fact quite the reverse was true. Although the leadership could often block unwelcome reforms by mobilising the union vote at annual conference, it resisted this measure and was eventually defeated – by the unions themselves. Similarly the leadership faced a growing rebellion on the issue of amendable policy documents, which forced concessions to be made in 1990. Nor did the leadership always win its own proposals – as, for example, over John Smith's objective of ending trade union involvement in the electoral college, or Tony Blair's desire to end conference resolutions or restructure local parties. Indeed, some of the wilder proposals favoured by 'modernisers' – such as breaking the trade union link, or replacing traditional policy making with membership plebiscites – were never implemented at all.

Much in the story of Labour's internal reform therefore supports Panebianco's assertion that 'the power relation between a leader and his followers must be conceived as a relation of unequal exchange in which the leader gets more than the followers, but must nonetheless give something in return' (1988, p. 22). The extent of negotiation, and the delay caused to major changes such as OMOV in parliamentary selections, illustrate the constraints on the Labour leader's power. Even in the late 1990s, when this power was at its peak, Tony Blair had to make concessions to get his reforms agreed. It is a truism to say that changes to the party's decision-making process had to be negotiated through that same process – but this placed obvious limits on how much the power of influential groups could be explicitly reduced. Unlike in policy making, where the parliamentary leadership often ignores the views of the annual conference, conference decisions are final when it comes to the party's rules.

The trade unions, in particular, acted as a repeated obstacle to changes in their own role – as demonstrated, for example, by the OMOV debate and later the protection of union seats on the NEC. They were often more willing to collude with the leader in agreeing changes that would affect the constituencies – though even then the unions tended to support reform only when most constituencies also did so. The unions remained the most important power block in negotiating reform, even after their share of votes at the party conference reduced to 50 per cent, thanks to their greater ability than the constituencies to organise collectively. Thus during the Partnership in Power reforms it was they who secured 'contemporary resolutions' at the annual conference. Later, they even voted to support an increase in the number of these resolutions from the constituencies, when constituency delegates themselves failed to vote for this reform.

Henry Drucker, in describing the importance of Labour's 'ethos', cited four elements in particular. One of these was the party's dependence on formal, written rules. At the time that he wrote, the rulebook still equated to Labour's 'own self contained quasi-legal system', that specified how the party should be run (Drucker, 1979, p. 17). It is this document that is under the sole ultimate control of the party conference.

One of the recurrent themes in this book has been the extent to which new organisational arrangements lie outside the formal written rules. Whilst many reforms (such as the changes to the leadership electoral college or the introduction of quotas) were detailed minutely in rule changes, many others, particularly in the later stages, were not. This is most notable in the policy process, starting with the important changes under Kinnock that created joint structures with the shadow cabinet for the first time. Although the 1990 reforms to this system, and later Partnership in Power, formalised the arrangements to a large extent, much of the detail of the policy-making process continues to exist outside the rules. The makeup of policy commissions, the system for submitting amend-ments to documents and agreeing minority positions, the timing of National Policy Forum meetings, and even its elections, are all under the discretion of the NEC. Similarly the number of contem-porary resolutions to be debated was not fixed, at least until the rebellion at the 2003 conference. A question on this last point at an NEC meeting in 1999 led party General Secretary Margaret McDonagh to insist that 'it's a rule, but it isn't written down'.[2]

Given Drucker's characterisation of Labour's traditions, this is a stark change. It also has implications for the party's future organis-ation. It is in part the control of the rulebook by the party confer-ence that forced the leadership to negotiate in the past. If important features exist outside the rules, this gives leaders significantly more discretion. Additionally, the new limit on resolutions has made it harder for local parties to get proposed changes onto the agenda. Given the importance of activist pressure in bringing about many features of 'new' Labour, this should give some cause for concern.

INSTRUMENTALISM AND ITS LIMITS

In fact, the main objection is generally found to be less against the method of voting than against the results of the voting.

Clement Atlee (1937, p. 102)

So reform generally resulted from negotiation between competing groups within the party, each with different perceptions of the

desired outcome. But what was it that led groups to support particular reform proposals in the first place? An examination of earlier
chapters shows that both groups and individuals often had
instrumental motives for pursuing organisational change. That is,
whilst reform was argued on the basis of principle, and how it
would improve the party's democracy, those involved tended to
pursue reforms that were likely to benefit themselves or their
group. Thus Tony Benn confessed in his diary in 1979, whilst
vigorously campaigning for activists and unions to be included in
the new leadership electoral college, that 'I don't think I have a
chance of being elected [as leader of the party] by the PLP' (Benn,
1990, p. 568). And Tony Blair, whose relationship with the unions
was far from warm, sought with equal vigour to end the unions'
role in the electoral college and replace it with the OMOV
principle.[3]

However, in most cases where instrumentalism applied it was not
about career ambition or personal gain. To suggest that actors were
driven by instrumental motives is not to adopt a political scientist's
'rational choice' approach.[4] Reformers generally had broader objectives, related to the kind of party that they wanted to create, and the
kind of values and culture that they believed would flourish if a
given form of democracy was established.

Instrumentalism

The different instrumental motives of participants in the Labour
Party's reform have already been discussed briefly in Chapter 2.
Broadly the party's left, particularly through the campaigning of the
CLPD, sought to empower activists at the expense of the parliamentary leadership. It was amongst the active members in the
constituencies, and to a lesser extent in the trade unions, that the
left's support was believed to be concentrated. The CLPD's vision
was thus to create an 'activist' party where those most committed
attendees of party meetings were rewarded with a greater share of
decision-making power. The right wing, in contrast, which was
relatively weaker in the constituencies but well represented in the
PLP, did not share this vision. This group preferred to leave power
with the PLP and loyal trade union leaders or, if there was to be
'democratisation', to empower less active local members who they
believed held more moderate views. By the mid 1980s the 'soft left',
represented organisationally by the LCC, had also become supportive of the OMOV principle. However the 'plebiscitary' party

model, developed by some 'modernisers' such as Blair and Mandelson, whereby OMOV would become the party's central organising
principle, was initially rejected by the LCC. This, it was believed,
would grant leaders too much agenda-setting power. Instead until
the mid 1990s the LCC promoted the middle way of a 'participatory' party. Such a model would institutionalise dialogue between
leaders and members, and thus potentially result in outcomes that
reflected a balance of views (LCC, 1989). Although each of these
models was argued largely on the basis of principle, doubtless on
the whole firmly believed, they can also each be seen to favour the
interests of their proponents. The fact that they were likely to
benefit one faction over another was often relatively explicit in
groups' campaigns.

Given the loyalist ethos of the right, it is not surprising that the
leadership often shared its perspective on organisational reform. It
is generally assumed that leaders will aim to use reform to
maximise their control over party organisation. This is reflected in
Robert Michels' classic 'iron law of oligarchy' (1962), which claims
that over time increasing power will tend to accumulate in leaders'
hands. Even writers who are critical of Michels' analysis tend to
believe that leaders will seek to evade constraints in order to 'obtain
as much freedom of movement as possible' (Panebianco, 1988, p.
15).

In several respects this analysis is found lacking when considering the evidence on Labour's organisational reforms. Even in so
far as there was a single 'leadership perspective' shared by Kinnock,
Smith and Blair, this was not synonymous with the desire to simply
accrue greater power.[5] In fact given the leader's primary responsibility for projecting the party externally, and seeking to maximise
electoral support, their central instrumental objective was to
improve the party's electoral popularity. Certainly one route to
achieving this might be, as Panebianco suggests, to increase their
own freedom, in order to adopt policy positions perceived to have
wide electoral appeal. Thus, as suggested in Chapter 2, in *substantive* terms the leadership wanted internal processes that would
strengthen themselves or other moderates. On this they shared a
common ground with the party's right. But the core instrumental
objective of leaders also had two other important components. First,
to increase the party's electability it was also thought necessary to
change its image. Leaders thus sought to pursue *symbolic* change, in
order to convince voters that the party had broken with its past. The

reforms necessary to achieve this did not always correspond with those pursued by the traditional right. Second, the leadership needed to retain some degree of membership support, not only in order to negotiate the reforms themselves, but also because a large and active membership was seen as an electoral asset. These last two objectives were not necessarily consistent with maximising leadership control. The three distinct components of the leadership's instrumentalism could thus often, in practice, find themselves in conflict.

The most obvious illustration of this conflict for leaders is seen with respect to the trade unions' role. The reduction in union vote shares at the annual conference, for example, was desirable to the leadership for symbolic reasons. But at the same time it had potential costs in terms of the ability to control the conference, given the unions' ability to act as loyal leadership supporters – which under Kinnock had largely been re-established. In balancing symbolic and substantive motives the leadership long prioritised the latter and thus resisted reform, as discussed in Chapter 8. But later, under increasing pressure from members, the media and the trade unions themselves, the leader finally agreed to embrace change. He thereby found instrumental common cause with the left, rather than the right.[6] Similarly, the leadership came to see improved representation of women as symbolically important, although this too had been an objective pursued primarily by the left. In both of these cases the long campaigns organised by activists had struck a chord with the media and the wider public, and this eventually convinced the leadership of the need for change. The same can be said of the campaign by the party's right to achieve OMOV for candidate selection (described in Chapter 3). But this came to be seen by the leadership as advantageous for both symbolic and substantive reasons. It then continued to be pursued at some cost in the late 1980s and early 1990s for largely symbolic reasons, even after the substantive motivations for change (that is, the need to circumvent activists) had largely disappeared.

The most blatant examples of instrumentalism are seen where reforms turned out to have unexpected consequences. In these cases groups would sometimes completely reverse their positions as they saw their interests change. This was most obvious with respect to the attitude towards balloting, both amongst party members and in the trade unions. As earlier chapters have shown, member ballots did not always yield the results that had been expected. Originally thought to favour the leadership, from 1994 onwards (most notably in elections to the NEC) these ballots started to deliver success for the left. Thus by 1999 it was perceived as unlikely that OMOV would result in selection of Tony Blair's favourites as Welsh party leader and candidate for London mayor. Electoral colleges were used for these elections (a defensible decision based on precedent, as argued in Chapter 4). However the requirement for unions to ballot – which for Blair had been an essential element of the leadership electoral college agreed in 1993 – did not apply.[7] In both cases the AEEU, which in 1993 had been amongst the most vociferous supporters of balloting, chose not to do so and loyally cast a block vote for the leader's favoured candidate. Meanwhile by this time the left of the party was insisting – also in a reversal of its previous position – on the principles of OMOV. This demonstrated pure instrumentalism on both sides, by precisely those actors that had previously expressed the firmest support for a particular model of internal party democracy. Another example of this phenomenon was the reversal of the CLPD's position on constituencies' rights to elect MPs to the NEC (described in Chapter 7). The organisation's defence of MPs holding seats in the constituency section (when left-wing MPs were being elected) later turned to opposition once OMOV had been introduced and appeared to be favouring leadership loyalists.

These examples help further to illustrate how leadership power in debates on party organisational change is constrained. Given conflicting objectives, proposals which will not enhance (and may even restrict) a leader's freedom of manoeuvre may come to be adopted. Thus the constituency vote at annual conference was increased in 1993, although this threatened to make the conference less predictable. Similarly leaders conceded in 1990 that the conference should be allowed to amend policy statements, in order to deflect opposition about the Policy Review.

Later episodes showed how it was not necessarily possible for leaders to reverse reforms which they found to be problematic. For example although the use of the electoral college in Wales or London was unlikely to be well received by the party or the press, the leadership chose to go ahead, as the 'correct' outcome was valued over the inevitable bad publicity that would result. That is, the substantive result was initially valued above the symbolic cost. But in the end negative news stories and anger by activists both contributed to poor election results in Wales and London. Consequently the leadership was forced to pledge that balloting would be compulsory in future contests. The reversal of the OMOV principle had proved politically impossible in practice.

The combination of conflicting leadership objectives, pressures from inside and outside the party, and the occasional unintended consequences of reform, make it impossible in practice for a rigid 'iron law' to apply. As Susan Scarrow has quipped, the need by leaders to maintain the support of members means 'it is not implausible to posit that the iron law of oligarchy could bend, or at least begin to rust from within' (1996, p. 151). In Labour's case we see clearly that rather than continually accruing power, the best the leader has been able to do is seek short-term advantage within certain constraints. Where longer-term goals are then found to have been compromised, the leader's ability to reverse reforms that others find advantageous has proved to be extremely restricted.

The limits to instrumentalism

It is also important however to note how instrumentalism, whilst it may be a powerful factor in reform, is far from absolute. Party members are more than just rational actors seeking factional advantage or personal preferment – many are also driven by an innate sense of justice and democratic values. In some cases (notably the representation of women through quotas in the party) activists were prepared to support reforms which might actually compromise their own power. It must also be remembered that the ambition of winning elections is not one which is confined to party leaders. This was the objective of most (if not all) party members, and increasing numbers were willing to compromise other goals in order to see Labour win. This included supporting reforms which might disadvantage themselves or their groups personally.

An interesting example of principle overriding factional benefit can be seen with respect to the left and the issue of vote shares. Left groups remained committed to the goal of increasing constituencies' share of annual conference votes even when, in the 1970s, the trade union block was helping secure victory for their objectives. The LCC in particular supported this change from its earliest days, on the principle that it would give voice to the constituencies and create a more pluralistic party. Later the constituency delegates proved, unexpectedly, to be more sympathetic to leadership positions than did the trade union block. A combination of principle, image motives and unintended consequences resulted in a reform where there was no clear factional winner.

Returning to the shifting perspectives in the 1980s and early 1990s in response to repeated defeats, the key block was undoubtedly the soft left. This group altered its position after each consecutive election defeat, giving it a pivotal role in deciding which reforms went on to be adopted. Having initially been aligned with the CLPD, the soft left increasingly distanced itself and found common cause with the right. As electoral and image imperatives became ever more important to members of this group, new alliances formed which created majority support for some important changes. The fusion of left and right demands which came to be implemented – OMOV, reform of NEC membership and new deliberative forums for policy making (backed up by final decisions at annual conference), alongside the reduction in union vote shares and greater representation for women – thus largely reflected the changing agenda of the LCC.

THE ILLUSION OF CHANGE

> Tony Blair's victory marked a turning point for the party. Because of the introduction of one member one vote, he was the first Labour leader who owed his position not to a group of trade union general secretaries or a handful of activists, but to the party at large.
>
> Stephen Byers, *The Guardian*, 19 July 2004

As we have seen, the need to create a new image for Labour was central in driving organisational reform. Indeed, it can be argued, the symbolism of change was sometimes more important than its substance. The leadership sought to propagate the image of a party that was less trade union, male and left dominated than previously perceived, and which instead was representative, moderate and democratic. The creation of 'new' Labour thus required an explicit emphasis on breaking with past traditions, rather than on continuity. To maximise this effect, two complementary stratagems were used, particularly in the later stages, by party 'modernisers'.

The myth of 'old' Labour

The first tactic was to paint a misleading picture of the past, in order to highlight contrasts. This was not difficult, given the exaggerated and increasingly inaccurate claims made by the party's electoral opponents. As Shaw suggests with respect to Labour's policy positions, 'the past was recreated to serve the present's strategic needs' (1996, p. 217). Precisely the same can be said of organisational change.

The quotation above, from Stephen Byers, one of Labour's keenest modernisers, nicely illustrates this point. Such statements – doubtless sincerely believed by those that make them – have helped to create a myth of 'new' Labour. In this case, those who have read Chapter 3 will know that trade unions and party activists had no role at all in picking the party leader prior to 1981, as this duty rested with the PLP. Even after adoption of the electoral college in 1981, balloting amongst constituency parties was relatively common (and indeed was compulsory in the 1992 contest), and many unions also balloted.

Yet perpetuation of this form of myth about the party's past organisation is relatively common. It often involves drawing contrasts with the period of 1979-83, rather than with the party's longer history. This is perhaps unsurprising, given that these were the formative years for many party modernisers. Yet this was only a brief and wholly exceptional episode in the party's past. Similarly for modernisers the image of 'old' Labour is often one where the trade unions oppose the leadership from the left. Many activists on the left also assert that in the 'old days' members had more control. Both sides forget that for most of the party's history trade union leaders actually provided the party leadership with a firm buttress against activists, whilst the constituencies complained about their own lack of power.

The myth of 'new' Labour

The second tactic used by party leaders was to create an appearance of 'big bang' reform when in fact, as we have seen, change was generally piecemeal and gradual and always resulted from negotiation. This helped to attract media attention, and thus to communicate an image of party renewal to the wider public. Yet many reforms had been under discussion since long before the term 'new Labour' was first aired and most were in fact already complete by this point.

The debate surrounding the OMOV package of 1993 offers an interesting early example of the tactics of the 'modernisers'. At this time key figures such as Tony Blair and Peter Mandelson were not centrally responsible for reform, but were active in briefing the press about its significance. In part due to their own ambitions to go further, reform was 'spun' as being the first step in loosening the party's ties with the unions. This enraged union leaders and many activists, and ensured that the decision at the 1993 conference was tense and highly symbolic. Yet the reality of the reforms, as desc-ribed in Chapter 3, was relatively modest. As Donald Sassoon suggested at the time, '[i]t is not clear what the purpose of these reforms is except to give the impression that something is being reformed' (1993, p. 31). But, in fact, the impression that something was being reformed was extremely important. In this case it was more important to the leadership than reform itself, since there was little factional advantage in expelling loyal trade unions from local parliamentary selections, or reducing their role at the annual conference. A reform that was highly symbolic but not actually that significant (or beneficial to leaders) in substantive terms offered both the press and the leadership what they wanted. The 'victory' for John Smith masked the fact that he had already backed down on the more important reform of removing the unions' powers over election of the party leader.

The success of this approach was to be repeated on many occas-ions, with respect to both policy and organisational change, once Blair became leader. The staging of symbolic battles with the party that the leader could win became an established campaign technique. This was referred to by one interviewee for this book as the application of the 'Mandelson doctrine', which held that with-out high-profile internal battles the public simply would not notice reform. Mandelson provided media support to Neil Kinnock and then later to Tony Blair. Philip Gould is quite open about having used this technique when he was a communications adviser to Blair, suggesting that 'people would shift to Labour only if they were sure that it had changed, and only bold, demonstrable change would convince them of that. Dissent in these circumstances did not reduce our electoral appeal, but heightened it. It was evidence of change' (1998, p. 97). This approach therefore meant that a certain amount of opposition within the party should be encouraged. As Gould advised Blair in the planning of the membership ballot on the draft manifesto in 1996, 'without conflict ... people are simply not convinced' (Gould, 1998, p. 263).

With respect to the implementation of organisational reform, this strategy can be seen to have been highly successful. Reforms were generally well received by the press and were presented as a game with winners and losers, where each successive reform had accumulated further power in the leader's hands.[8] Journalists rarely reported the extent to which negotiation with members or trade unions had been required, and the modernisers were keen to detract from this impression. Yet although gaining power may always have been one of the leadership's objectives, the need to negotiate meant that it was not necessarily the reality. Hence Larry Whitty's observation that the Partnership in Power proposals owed much to his earlier attempts to create a more consultative and deliberative policy process, with the crucial difference that the 1997 version had been 'somewhat overspun' as 'centralising' (Labour Party, 1997b, p. 23).

The story 'spun' by the leadership, and in turn reported by the media, has proved extremely influential in determining how others have perceived reform. This was exacerbated by the fact that activists on the left often did not celebrate the reforms that they had won, instead treating them with suspicion once they had been embraced by party leaders. Even academics (who often use the press as a major source) have tended to assume that reforms were always instigated by the leadership for its own benefit. But as Peter Medding has pointed out, '[t]otal victory for one group ... is, alone, not conclusive evidence that it has imposed its will on the others as, for example, if such a decision represented the majority view and is reached after long and exhaustive discussion' (1970, p. 13). This exactly describes the situation that often applied during Labour's reforms. As discussed above, majorities for reform were built slowly, and often required compromise on leaders' part. Yet the result of 'spin' was that this truth was consistently obscured. Importantly, it was not just the public, or students and academics, who gained an inaccurate picture of what had occurred. This also applied to party members themselves. Consequently most concluded that their rights were being restricted, even if this was not objectively the case. The myth of 'new' Labour was thus propagated partly at the cost of a breakdown of trust between leaders and members. If this resulted in members feeling disempowered and demotivated it has various potential costs for leaders, as discussed further in Chapter 11.

These conclusions about organisational change echo those reached by previous scholars about other aspects of 'new' Labour. Steven Fielding, who has noted the continuity and change in the creation of 'new Labour', comments on Blair's 'disingenuous tactic' of 'continu[ing] reforms initiated during the 1980s, for the benefit of Conservative-supporting *Sun* and *Daily Mail* readers' whilst '[giving] the impression that his leadership marked a decisive break with the Kinnock years'. As a result, Fielding suggests, 'a substantial number of Labour members believed appearance *did* reflect reality: to their minds, New Labour was the antithesis of their party's history' (2000, p. 369).

Turning to the 'modernisers', it is unclear to what extent they themselves believed that the organisational reforms had a decisive impact. This is particularly difficult to judge, given their tendency to exaggerate the results for public consumption. As early as 1990, before any of the most significant changes described in this book had been implemented, Peter Mandelson claimed that 'We have now effectively completed the building of the new model party.'[9] Yet years later, even after all the reforms had taken place, Blair as leader continued to distance himself from the party and to stage regular conflicts with it. This may have represented the repeated use of the 'Mandelson doctrine', but if he believed that Labour had indeed changed in his image, such behaviour would be somewhat irrational. The evidence therefore suggests that Blair himself was, at the very least, sceptical about the impact of change. As recently as October 2003 the press was briefed that the leader and his allies 'accept[ed] that internal party reform is the great unfinished business of new Labour'.[10]

Notes

1. Of course given the nature of the party's relationship with the trade unions, their behaviour can be seen as both an exogenous and an endogenous factor.
2. She was responding to an enquiry from the CWU's representative about exactly what rule specified that only four of these resolutions would be debated (Davies, 2001).
3. Such instrumentalism was not restricted to those who remained in the party, but also to those who left it for the SDP. David Owen firmly supported OMOV and sought to introduce it within the new party when it was formed. Central to his reasons for choosing this method rather than election by the parliamentary party was that 'I didn't think Roy [Jenkins] would be the ideal leader of the party. I wanted therefore to have a leadership election system whereby he would not become leader automatically, as given the make-up of the MPs who were likely

to create the new party, he otherwise would' (quoted in Crewe and King, 1995a, p, 87).

4. The classic text on rational choice is Downs (1957). For an attempt to apply this framework to Labour's organisational reforms see Quinn (2004).

5. Leaders obviously did not wholly share one single perspective. Kinnock was historically drawn from the soft left and gathered a team around him who were instinctively sympathetic to this view. They included General Secretary Larry Whitty, who came close to implementing the participatory model for policy making. In contrast, Tony Blair had a different perspective and arrived with a commitment to introducing policy plebiscites. The change of approach between leaders thus not only depended on circumstances, but also on their own beliefs.

6. It was Kinnock who initially reluctantly accepted this reform. Blair later keenly pursued a further reduction in the trade union vote. This perhaps demonstrates the greater significance he attached to symbolic reform, but also how he (unlike Kinnock) had not (yet) needed to rely on union support to help stabilise the party.

7. As discussed in Chapter 4 there was a precedent for this in Wales, but in London the mechanism was specifically designed in.

8. This helps explain the relative silence from figures such as Blair and Gould about the profound changes brought about by women's quotas. These could not be presented as strengthening leadership power, and had already aroused hostility in papers such as the *Daily Mail*.

9. *The Guardian*, 16 February 1990, quoted in Seyd and Whiteley 2002, p. 6.

10. *The Times*, 2 October 2003.

11

Democracy and Power in 'New' Labour

The previous chapter discussed the process of reform, and what patterns can be seen when we consider the breadth of Labour's organisational changes together. It was suggested that reform has been less centrally controlled than is commonly assumed: that changes were debated over a long period, drew much from the proposals of activist groups and generally involved compromise and negotiation. It was also suggested that the appearance of change was sometimes even more important to 'modernisers' than change itself, since a key motivation was to create a new image for the party that would be more electorally popular. This led them to exaggerate certain aspects of the reform process, which in turn helped to colour the way in which it has been understood.

This final chapter moves away from considering the process, to analyse the *outcome* of the changes introduced. Just as there has been a widespread impression that reform was driven by the party leadership (which the previous chapter questioned), the common perception is that it was the leadership that benefited from it. As discussed throughout the book the leadership's desire was to diminish the power of two main groups in the party: the trade unions and the activists. Reforms with these ends were implemented, albeit in a negotiated way. So what has been the overall impact on the structure of Labour's internal organisation? And who were the main beneficiaries of reform? Central to many of the changes was the drive to empower 'ordinary' less active party members on a one member one vote basis, which has weakened the party's federal and representative traditions. This has been widely interpreted as handing *de facto* power to party leaders. To what extent can this be seen to be the case, based on the extensive evidence in earlier chapters?

These questions are of interest in assessing how the underlying balance of power in the Labour Party has really changed. But they may also suggest more general lessons about the organisation of political parties – particularly since reforms similar to those that

Labour introduced have been seen in many other parties, both in Britain and overseas. It is these questions to which this closing chapter turns.

THE PRINCIPLES OF LABOUR'S DEMOCRACY

The swathe of reforms undertaken by the Labour Party have fundamentally challenged both its federal and representative traditions. As described in Chapter 2, Labour began life as a collective body to represent the trade unions, and only later developed a system of individual membership and local parties. Even after these were established, in 1918, the unions remained numerically dominant at the national level – on the National Executive Committee and at the annual conference – whilst locally, federal principles were adhered to in the structure of General Committees. Although the initial reforms instigated by the CLPD in 1979-81 (most notably the establishment of the leadership electoral college) built on and strengthened the traditions of federalism and representative democracy, the changes from the mid 1980s onwards increasingly challenged the old logic of Labour's organisation.

The power of the trade unions is considered in the following section, where it is suggested that this depends on more than their numerical strength alone. Nonetheless, one of the most striking aspects of Labour's internal reform has been the decline of the unions' *formal* power in the party. This was most notable at the annual conference, where their vote share fell from an overwhelming 90 per cent to 70 per cent in 1993, and then to just under 50 per cent in 1996. The unions in practice now control 13 of the 32 seats on the NEC, down from 18 out of 29 before 1997.[1] On the National Policy Forum, which took over responsibility from the Executive for drafting policy statements, they formally hold just 42 out of 183 seats (23 per cent).[2] Although they won powers in the leadership electoral college in 1981 (which was subsequently copied for other important internal elections), in no main arena of Labour's decision making do the unions now control more than half the votes. In addition, their role in decision making at the local level has been radically reduced, most notably in terms of the selection of parliamentary candidates. The ending in 1993 of trade union involvement in the final selection decision brought their ability to place favoured nominees in safe Labour seats virtually to an end. It was also a symbolically important change for a party whose founding purpose was to see trade unionists elected to parliament.

Table 11.1: Fundamentals of Labour's democracy 1979 and 2004

	Control in 1979	Control in 2004
Electing the leader	Parliamentary Labour Party (PLP).	Electoral college of thirds (PLP, affiliates, constituencies) with compulsory balloting.
Selecting parliamentary candidates	Local general committee (GC).	All member (OMOV) ballot.
National Executive Committee (NEC)†	18 seats out of 29 controlled by trade unions, 7 by CLPs.	Trade unions control 13 seats, CLPs 6, plus new PLP, EPLP, government and local government seats.
Election of NEC constituency seats	By conference delegates, mandated by GCs.	By national OMOV ballot.
Preparation of policy statements	NEC and its subcommittees.	National Policy Forum (NPF) including all parts of the party, overseen by joint frontbench/NEC committee.‡
Votes at annual conference	90% to affiliates (mostly trade unions), 10% to constituencies.	50% to affiliates, 50% to constituencies.

†For detail of the old and new NEC see Table 7.1
‡ For membership of the National Policy Forum see Table 6.1

Thus the old federal tradition has weakened, and in some spheres no longer exists at all. At the same time the representative tradition (itself inherited from the unions), whereby collective decisions were taken by members elected to represent others, has increasingly been undermined. This is particularly the case at local level. In its place came a new principle that all members should be able to participate in decisions. Thus in 1987, even before the trade unions' involvement had been ended, the role of local General Committee (GC) delegates in the final decision in parliamentary selections was handed to the wider membership. Similarly, the power of the GC in other internal elections was gradually reduced. Traditionally it had decided how the constituency's block vote was to be cast in NEC elections, and in 1981 it won the same right in leadership elections. But in the late 1980s the franchise for both of these decisions was widened to include all local members. In 1993 the collective role of constituencies in such elections was ended completely, with the introduction of national OMOV ballots. At this point the role of the trade unions' own representative structures in party decision making was also weakened, with the casting of block votes in party leadership elections disallowed, to be replaced by compulsory balloting. After some wobbles in the 1990s (described in Chapter 4) this principle has now also become firmly established.

Thus a new form of individual member democracy (generally referred to here as OMOV) has now been extended to many of Labour's internal decisions, in place of the old representative principle. The ability to pursue this reform was enhanced substantially by the shift to a National Membership System (discussed in Chapter 9) from 1988 onwards, and then later by new technologies such as email. These changes gradually strengthened vertical communication between the party's central office and individual members, and potentially weakened local links. Rather than being members of autonomous local parties which were affiliated to the national organisation, members are now first and foremost members of a national body which is (to a far lesser extent than previously) organised on a local basis.

The principle of empowering the individual was not a new one. Indeed when Labour's 1918 constitution was debated the party Secretary, Arthur Henderson, made clear that one option was 'a political organisation depending only on individual membership', suggesting that 'if he had to begin afresh that would be the ideal at which he would aim' (Labour Party, 1918, p. 99). However, the federal structure already having been adopted, the 1918 party conference decided to maintain it. Instead the traditional arrangements were simply supplemented by the establishment of local parties. Thus Duverger (1954) classified Labour as having an 'indirect' rather than a 'direct' party structure - although he recognised that it was to some extent 'mixed' or hybrid. The reforms of recent years moved the party decisively in the direction of a more 'direct' structure. Nonetheless they stopped far short of the pure individual member democracy that some had hoped would be the hallmark of 'new' Labour. Whilst OMOV ballots have been introduced for many internal elections, local parties continue to exist and the policy process, in particular, still depends on a federal and representative structure. In short the extra-parliamentary party continues to be a hybrid, which is now of a far greater complexity.

Labour's new structure thus maintains some of the old traditions, but also includes some important new elements. Modern federal arrangements, such as the various electoral colleges, the National Policy Forum and the reformed NEC, give a formal role to the party's elected representatives (such as MPs, devolved assembly members and local councillors), alongside trade unions and grassroots members. Through these arrangements another aspect of Labour's original democracy – the separation between the parliamentary and extra-parliamentary party – has gradually broken down, to be replaced by new 'partnership' arrangements. These are supplemented by the new principle of OMOV for most internal elections. At the same time another principle of democracy – that of equal representation for women – has also been become firmly established.

In the party's new hybrid structure elements drawn from all the competing visions of democracy held by the various proponents of organisational reform now coexist. Thus components of the representative ('activist') model favoured by the CLPD remain, alongside examples of the direct ('plebiscitary') model favoured by some modernisers. There have also been attempts, most notably through the National Policy Forum and local policy discussion, to incorporate the 'deliberative' democracy model championed by the LCC. How stable these arrangements prove to be, however, remains to be seen. The hybrid model is a compromise that necessarily contains tensions and contradictions. In particular the federal arrangements, and the role of the trade unions within them, continue to cause occasional aggravation. Members have questioned the unions' role when they side with leaders (as in the electoral colleges described in Chapter 4), whilst leaders continually challenge the legitimacy of union votes when they bring about defeats at the annual conference (see Chapter 8). Some aspects of the party's democracy thus continue to be unresolved and potentially volatile. But for the moment the major question that remains to be answered is who has benefited from the new arrangements, and how power in the party is now distributed as a result. It is this question that is addressed in the remainder of the chapter.

THE COMPETITORS FOR POWER

In considering the shifts of power that may have taken place within the Labour Party, it is first worth reminding ourselves of the *dramatis personae*. From whom, and to whom, might power have been transferred? This deserves attention, particularly given that the shorthand used to describe different competing groups can sometimes obscure the subtleties of these intra-party relationships.

The most obvious dichotomy is that between the parliamentary and extra-parliamentary parties. Throughout the long debates about the proper role for the annual conference in policy making, it was the freedom of the parliamentary party to act autonomously that provided the focus. Observers such as Ostrogorski (1902) and McKenzie (1963, 1982) expressed concern about the impact of intra-party democracy on the democracy of the state, as this potentially compromised MPs' accountability to the electorate. McKenzie thus concluded that internal party democracy 'strictly interpreted, is incompatible with democratic government' (1982, p. 195). The CLPD, from quite the opposite perspective, also focussed on the relationship of the PLP to the wider party, complaining that 'it is the relative independence of the Parliamentary Labour Party ... which makes it easy for Labour governments to abandon Labour Party policies'.[3] However, it is necessarily simplistic to view the parliamentary and extra-parliamentary parties as the competitors for power. The structure of the extra-parliamentary party is complex, as discussed above. Not only does it include individual members, trade unions, and the (far smaller) socialist societies, but also various structures at local, regional and national levels. Within parliament there is also a substructure, comprising the party leader (and deputy leader), other frontbenchers and their backbench colleagues. The CLPD's problem was primarily with the party leadership. But given that the leader was elected by the PLP, itself dominated by the right of the party, their frustration was directed at the parliamentary party as a whole. Yet once the reforms they proposed had succeeded in creating a leadership elected by the whole party, these relationships began to change.

The result is a complex web of intra-party relations, which has been touched in many ways by reform. This makes it far from simple to assess which actors were the winners and losers.

The trade unions

In 1992 Lewis Minkin suggested that '[p]erceptions of the power relationship in the Labour Movement have always been dominated by polarised alternatives in which either the union leadership or the Parliamentary leadership were credited with supreme and sometimes total power' (p. 395). The dramatic reforms to the unions' role in the party, and the dilution of their representation in most of its internal forums, mean that few would now suggest the party's 'industrial wing' was the dominant partner.

The impact of these changes on the power of the leadership (as already indicated in Chapter 10) is, however, not straightforward. The party's relationship with the trade unions has always been a complex one, with power exercised formally and informally at many different levels. Throughout much of Labour's history, the key union leaders were loyal supporters of the parliamentary leadership, forming a 'Praetorian guard', able to fend off left-wing activists' demands (McKenzie, 1963; Minkin, 1992). At times this relationship broke down – most notably in the 1970s, when the unions chose more actively to use the power that they had always formally held. This led to a questioning of their legitimacy, and was immediately followed by the long period of organisational reform. But the union relationship, when functioning in its more constructive mode, could also bring many advantages to leaders. It enabled them to do deals with a small number of individuals behind closed doors, each controlling a large portion of party votes. During Neil Kinnock's leadership this old stability was regained, with the consequence that the unions became 'both an embarrassment and a necessity' to the leader (Heffernan and Marqusee, 1992, p. 147).[4] The unions' loyalty had traditionally been of use not only in policy making, but also organisational matters (via the NEC) and in parliamentary selections, where their ability to sign up GC delegates could swing results in favour of right-wingers or docile leadership loyalists. The 'problem' of the unions therefore presented a real, and wide ranging, dilemma to leaders. As we have seen, reductions in trade union representation were often implemented primarily in order to modernise the party's image, with leaders sometimes reluctant to proceed, but generally under pressure from the media and opposition parties.

The shift in power from the trade unions represents a profound change in the party's internal democracy. Labour's history meant that it was more than just 'linked' to the unions – their role was central to almost every aspect of its operation. The unions' full formal powers were so overwhelming that they were rarely used, and when they finally clashed with the parliamentary leadership in the 1970s the result was a major constitutional crisis. For the sake of the party it was thus generally essential for trade union leaders to exercise restraint (Minkin, 1992). Ironically, with the unions' formal powers now diminished, this same restraint is less necessary. Arguments between union and party leaders can now become more public and routine. As John Edmonds of the GMB commented in 1999, the reduction of the unions' formal powers made them more 'usable'.[5] In recent years this has been seen to be the case. It is the unions that are now willing to force leadership defeats at the annual conference, with the constituencies proving more responsive to appeals for unity. Whilst they may be diminished in formal strength, the unions can also still operate more effectively as a block (through their internal collective decision making and negotiations between their leaders) than the constituencies. Their leaders remain big figures, backed by impressive resources. They are thus less likely than grassroots members to be intimidated by either the 'technical' or 'psychological' aspects of party leadership power (Michels, 1962). They remain constrained by questions about the legitimacy of their role, but for Labour leaders the unions remain extremely important, either as allies or as opponents.

Party activists

The other key group targeted by 'modernisers' were Labour's activists, who were perceived in the early 1980s as being unrepresentative of party and public opinion, and too easily dominated by the far left. As with the unions, a list of powers lost to this group can be easily constructed, with these primarily resulting from the declining role of the GCs. In internal elections, including parliamentary selections and election of the leader and the NEC, party members at a local level won some of the powers that the unions lost. However, as a result of OMOV, activists were forced to share these powers with less active party members.

In terms of policy making the picture is more complex, however, as local parties won a significant gain from trade unions by increasing their vote share at the annual conference. This is effectively a shift of control *towards* activists, as GCs remain responsible for selecting annual conference delegates, and delegates themselves are drawn from the activist pool. But whilst constituencies gained a greater share of influence at the conference from 1993, after 1997 (in part as a result of this) the structure and powers of the conference itself were changed. In addition, women's quotas reduced the continuity amongst constituency delegates from year to year.

CLPs have now largely lost their rights to submit resolutions and amendments to the conference, and to use these to shape its agenda. In return they won the right to see policy documents in draft, and to discuss and comment upon them, but the system for doing so is opaque. The old resolution process, though with questionable impact on the party's policy in practice, was more transparent, providing an important means of 'horizontal' communication between members in different CLPs. Like a kind of internal party graffiti, resolutions allowed activists from different parts of the country to convey their concerns to each other, and enabled campaign groups such as the CLPD to demonstrate the strength of feeling on issues. This can be likened to the system of 'Early Day Motions' in the House of Commons, whereby MPs sign up to published statements in order to demonstrate a breadth of support. Whilst having no formal impact on the parliamentary agenda, these can stimulate public attention and thus put pressure on government.[6] In the party, statements from CLPs are now instead mediated vertically, through policy commissions in which staff have significant control. Submissions from constituencies are not routinely circulated to National Policy Forum members, and are invisible to the media and other outside observers. This has greatly reduced the ability of local activists to exercise 'voice' (Hirschman, 1970). The barring of MPs and peers from election to the constituency section of the NEC multiplied this effect, with both changes making it far more difficult for campaigns in the party to gain momentum or to potentially embarrass the leadership into action. Activists have thus seen both important gains, and important losses, from reform.

Just as trade unions have been freed to behave less responsibly as a result of their loss of formal powers, constituencies' increase in power has resulted in greater pressure on them to act with restraint. Prior to reform it had been suggested that the tiny share of votes held by CLP delegates 'actually encourage[d] rebelliousness' (Yates, 1960, p. 311). Later Peter Hain, in calling for change on behalf of the LCC, predicted that 'if CLP votes actually mattered, their delegates might act more judiciously'.[7] This prediction has been shown to be correct. Since the change in the balance of vote shares in 1993, no recorded defeat of the leadership at annual conference has yet been backed by a majority of constituency delegates.[8] This has enabled party staff and ministers to continue to dismiss defeats by pointing out the 'unrepresentative' nature of trade union votes. The symbolic importance of maintaining the support of constituency delegates has, however, made them subject to far greater attention and lobbying. The fact that something tantamount to a 'whipping' operation now exists amongst these delegates is a clear indication of their potential power. Whilst constituencies have thus made gains from the trade unions, they have also inherited the responsibility that this brings.

The winners?

If the trade unions and activists are the main candidates that might have lost power, two obvious groups might also have gained. One is the 'ordinary' member and the other – perhaps as a consequence – is the parliamentary leadership. The extent to which this is borne out by the evidence is discussed in more detail in the remainder of the chapter. This also considers how the power of the parliamentary party as a whole may have been changed as a result of reform.

However, before turning to these discussions, it is important to note that one further group has undoubtedly gained influence in the party, though these gains are less often acknowledged. As recently as 1991 women held just five seats on the party's National Executive, all of them in the reserved women's section. Yet since 1996 they have frequently been a majority on the party's ruling body, and amongst delegates to the annual conference. In 2004 women held 52 per cent of seats on the National Policy Forum and, whilst still being only 23 per cent of the PLP, held 31 per cent of frontbench positions. As discussed in Chapter 5, this is a remarkable transformation. Male dominance was such an elemental part of Labour's traditional ethos that it was overlooked by commentators such as Drucker (1979). Yet at the time that he was writing, feminist activists, largely aligned with the party's left, were starting to draw attention to the gender inequities in Labour's organisation.

Within less than two decades of Drucker's study equal representation for women had become well established as central to the
ethos of 'new' Labour. The changes that resulted were crucial to
reshaping the party's image, and also had important impacts on its
decision making, as detailed particularly in Chapters 5, 8 and 9. Yet
they have gone largely unreported by those who concern themselves with power in the party, as they brought no shift between the
usual protagonists – such as leaders and members, or constituencies
and trade unions.[9] They were also not subject to the same 'spin' by
the party's leaders as some other reforms, since both Kinnock and
Blair only accepted them with a certain degree of unease. Nonetheless, their impact on Labour's culture has been profound.

DEMOCRATISATION AS EMASCULATION?

One of the central changes to Labour's internal democracy has been
the shift towards enfranchising 'ordinary' members through one
member one vote procedures. This approach offered an alternative
to some of the problems of the old organisational principles and, as
it represented a widening of the internal franchise on many matters,
could be presented as 'democratisation'. However, concerns have
been expressed both inside and outside the party over this strategy.

Labour is far from unique in making moves towards empowering
individual members. Political scientists have noted a similar trend
in parties in many other western democracies (Mair, 1994; Scarrow,
1996; Scarrow, Webb and Farrell, 2000). Various explanations for
this have been proposed. As discussed in Chapter 9, commentators
initially had suggested that modern party leaders would seek ever
greater autonomy from members and might even want to dispense
with them altogether. However others, notably Scarrow (1996),
pointed out that many of the benefits that members brought to
leaders were too valuable to give up. One important benefit was
members' ability to *legitimise* leaders in the eyes of the public by
demonstrating that they had a popular following. Extending
members' rights to participate in internal party decisions could
further enhance this perception, thus bringing benefits to leaders.
These arguments were played out in the Labour Party, where some
senior figures initially believed that party members might become
unnecessary, but others argued that the party would be strengthened by a larger and more representative membership. Given the
problems that had resulted from hard-left activists winning control

of under-populated local parties, the latter course of action came to be chosen.

There were also other important factors driving the moves to wider participation. As discussed in earlier chapters, political scientists had suggested that party activists were likely to be more extreme in their views than the voting public, and thus if given too much control could damage parties' electoral prospects. This analysis was encapsulated in John May's (1973) law of *curvilinear disparity*, which suggested that party leaders would adopt positions close to the views of passive party supporters, whilst activists' views would (in left-wing parties) be further to the left. The logic was that those with the strongest ideological commitment were most inclined to become involved in party activity, whilst those who rose to the top were the most aware of electoral imperatives. This seemed to imply that inactive members, being similar to those who vote for the party but do not join it, would hold more moderate policy preferences than activists. The instincts and experience of many in the Labour Party in the 1970s and 1980s seemed to suggest that this was the case. By enfranchising less active members, leaders therefore hoped to gain support for more moderate outcomes. Activists on the left, also accepting the analysis, generally opposed such moves for precisely the same reason.

In the early years of its operation, OMOV was celebrated by modernisers for having delivered the expected results – for example in the leadership election of 1983 and in early elections to the NEC. As Peter Mandelson and Roger Liddle suggested in 1996, 'Labour's introduction of one-member-one-vote democracy for all members has unleashed new energy and support for sensible thinking which was hidden ten years ago' (p. 212). The commitment of party leaders to this approach could therefore be seen as self-interested. One member one vote democracy has generally been viewed by political scientists as a cunning means by which leaders can persuade their parties to give them greater power. As Peter Mair suggested, less active members are likely to be 'at once more docile and more likely to endorse the policies (and candidates) proposed by the party leadership' (1994, p.16). Whilst appearing to empower party members such reforms may therefore just be another example of Michels' (1962) 'iron law of oligarchy' at work. In other words, moves to broaden the franchise to include all individual party members amount to a 'democratization as emasculation' strategy (Webb, 1994, p. 120).

The modern Labour Party offers a good opportunity to test these assumptions. As earlier chapters have documented, the moves towards one member one vote democracy took place over roughly 20 years. Although they stopped far short of the full individualisation that some had originally proposed (as, for example, the use of policy plebiscites was very limited), they demonstrate results in a number of party settings. The most consistent were the elections to the constituency section of the NEC, held annually by OMOV from 1990. The use of OMOV in leadership elections and local parliamentary selections also grew during this period. To what extent did these results support the 'curvilinear disparity' thesis, and can they therefore be seen to have given greater *de facto* powers to the party leadership?

Those who have read earlier chapters will already have realised that these propositions are going to receive a sceptical reply. Whilst it is clear that successive leaders did believe that empowering the wider membership would produce more moderate results, the outcome was not always as had been expected. The clearest example is provided by the NEC elections, where from 1989 to 1993 OMOV seemed progressively to weaken the left – an outcome that pleased the leadership and resulted in the system being cemented in the party's rules. However, from 1994 it began to have the reverse effect, with the left starting to regain seats. The high point of the left's recent success was 1998, when Grassroots Alliance candidates took four of the six available places on the newly configured Executive (subsequently dropping to three). This did not equal the Bevanites' achievements in the 1950s, but was far from what leaders had hoped for.

The proponents of OMOV had been encouraged by its earlier uses in leadership elections: for example, the 1981 deputy leadership ballot in left-wing union NUPE which had favoured Denis Healey over Tony Benn. However, with hindsight these elections contained mixed messages. Notably whilst it was the right-winger Roy Hattersley who urged ballots in the leadership elections of 1983, and these had favoured his joint ticket with Neil Kinnock, it was Kinnock – the candidate of the soft left – who came first in every single constituency and trade union ballot for leader. There thus seemed to be limits to how far rightwards even inactive party members were prepared to go.

Tony Blair was one of the keenest advocates of OMOV in the early 1990s and was frustrated by the timidity of the 1993 package, which left trade unions holding a share of votes in the leadership electoral college. Yet (as documented in Chapter 4) later events saw him move away from the OMOV principle. New arrangements for election of leaders in Scotland and Wales and the mayoral candidate in London retained the electoral college arrangement, but without requiring trade union ballots. In these elections Blair came to rely on block votes cast by reliable union leaders. During the Partnership in Power negotiations Blair's allies gave serious consideration to ending OMOV for elections to the constituency section of the NEC, and returning this responsibility to delegates at the annual conference. This was ultimately felt to be politically impossible, but OMOV was ruled out for elections to the new National Policy Forum. Blair's earlier proposals, such as compelling constituencies to use OMOV to elect their conference delegates, or introducing routine ballots of the membership on policy, were quietly abandoned. In later years it was the left of the party – the very group that all-member balloting had been expected to undermine – that became its firmest proponents.[10]

These unexpected results clearly had implications for leadership control in the party, which are further discussed below. But the remainder of this section examines why the predictions of party managers and political scientists alike proved to be inaccurate in Labour's case. It would be an exaggeration to suggest that OMOV ballots have consistently favoured the party's left. However, it seems clear that they did not reliably deliver results that reflected the views of the party leader either.

There are various potential explanations for this phenomenon. One possibility is that the curvilinear disparity hypothesis accurately described the pattern of members' views, but that the results that leaders had hoped for did not occur because inactive members did not use their right to vote. The turnout in some of Labour's internal elections – particularly those for the NEC – was disappointing. In these rather specialist contests it seems likely that activists would be the most motivated to vote. In contrast ballots with high turnouts – such as that for the draft manifesto in 1996 – did favour the leadership. But achieving this proved to be extremely resource intensive, which was one reason why such experiments were not repeated.

Differential turnouts between activist and non activist members therefore offer one potential explanation. But another is that the curvilinearity thesis simply did not hold or (consistent with the change in NEC results) became less valid over time. In short, that 'ordinary' Labour members were not actually more moderate than activists, or that even if they once were, this gradually ceased to be the case. If the discrepancy between the views of members and activists did change over time, there would be a number of possible explanations. One is that many left-wing activists either resigned from the party, or moderated their views. The decline in 'hard left' activity, and the shifting attitudes of many on the soft left, suggest that both of these explanations probably hold some truth. But this cannot explain the growing success for the left under OMOV.

To investigate this issue requires considerable data. Such data has been collected by Patrick Seyd and Paul Whiteley in their surveys of party members in 1990-92 and 1997-99. As cited in Chapter 2, the first of these surveys appeared to show a significant difference between the proportion of active and inactive members classifying themselves as left wing. This fuelled the beliefs of leaders that the curvilinear disparity thesis was true. However, the responses to the later survey showed rather different results.[11] Whilst the proportion of members in 1997 defining themselves as being on the left had remained roughly constant, there was now little difference between the ideological positions of active and inactive members. Thus 54 per cent of 'very active' members considered themselves to be on the left of the party, whilst 53 per cent of members who were 'not at all active' said the same.[12] By 1999 the figures were if anything showing a slight reverse of the expected curvilinear result, with 58 per cent of activists defining themselves as left wing, compared to 59 per cent of inactive members.

What might have led to such a change? One possible explanation is that many left-wing members became less active under Blair's leadership, but did not actually leave the party, whilst those who supported his position became better represented in activist roles. This would appear to be a rational response on the part of members, and seems to be borne out by the evidence from the survey. Thus in 1999 a slightly higher proportion of left-wing members (53 per cent) than centre or right-wing members (41 per cent) said that they had become less active in the party in the last five years (or since they joined, if they were new members). Such results potentially turn the curvilinear disparity thesis on its head, by suggesting that over time activists might even become more moderate than inactive members. If the victory of the 'modernisers' both widened the franchise and drove left-wingers into inactivity, it would have succeeded in empowering the very people whose influence it had sought to undermine.

It thus seems that the relationship between the views of leaders and members is more complex and dynamic than the curvilinear disparity thesis allows. Members will respond to circumstances, and it may on occasion be those on the left that retreat into inactivity. One potential influence in this period was the party's reforms themselves. As noted in Chapter 10, these were widely presented as strengthening leadership power, and they did strip activists of some important responsibilities. Seyd and Whiteley's survey suggests that this was a significant factor in driving left wing members into inactivity.[13] Over time members may therefore have withdrawn their services, whilst using their remaining 'voice' to protest at their perceived lack of influence in the party.

But another significant factor during this period was the change in party leader. OMOV seemed to support the Kinnock leadership more reliably than it supported Blair, with the shift in the NEC elections occurring immediately after he took over in 1994. Kinnock was generally seen by members as a left-winger who was prepared to compromise his principles in order to get the party into government – Seyd and Whiteley's survey in 1990 found that only 31 per cent of members believed that he was on the right. In contrast Blair was seen as being on the right by a majority of members in 1999. This may help explain why Kinnock was more successful at winning members' support. In contrast it seems likely that members sought to use their votes in an attempt to counter-balance the politics of Blair.[14]

Finally, once Labour came close to regaining power, members may have felt more confident about voting to the left. Indeed, in a further reversal of the curvilinear disparity thesis, members in later years may even have perceived their own views as being closer to the public mood than those of their leader. As Matthew Taylor, previously Assistant General Secretary with responsibility for policy, has suggested, 'on some important issues (recent examples include the Private Finance Initiative and Iraq) the views of the party are not only more left-wing but also apparently more in tune with public opinion than those of ministers' (2003, p. 57).

A final factor is that the power of the media – which the CLPD initially feared would damage the left in OMOV ballots – has latterly tended to be put to the opposite effect. As Blair's honeymoon with the media came to an end it started, for example, to champion NEC candidates who were critical of his style. In the contests to select the Welsh leader and London mayoral candidate, Alun Michael and Frank Dobson were portrayed by the media as 'Blairites' that the leader hoped to impose on an unwilling party. The dependence by the leader on media channels to communicate with members in such contests has thus created a new form of vulnerability.

Figure 11.1: May's law of curvilinear disparity and 'new' Labour

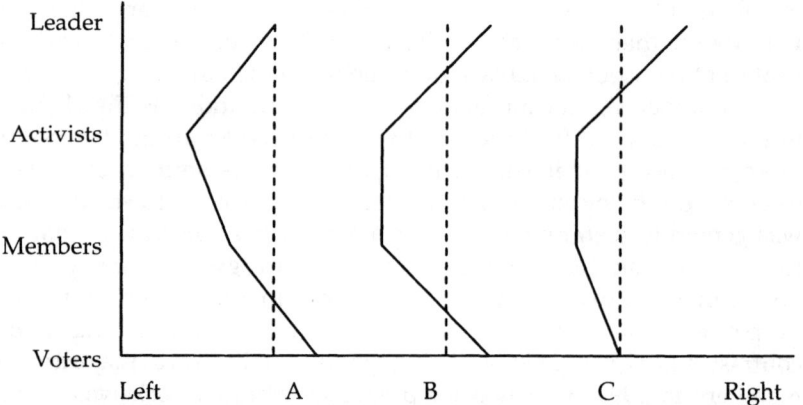

The experience of Labour therefore casts some serious doubts on the argument that empowering ordinary members results in a strengthening of leadership power. Instead it has confronted leaders with a volatile electorate with which it is almost impossible to have a meaningful negotiation. Particularly since the election of Blair as leader the 'law' of curvilinear disparity has looked decidedly shaky.

Summarising this in the terms it is usually put by political scientists, May's law is illustrated in Figure 11.1. The standard picture of this for a party of the left is similar to position A. Here leaders are slightly to the left of voters, but 'sub leaders' (that is, party activists and members) are to the left of both. May did not originally differentiate between activists and inactive members, but the standard assumption (which was adhered to by Labour figures) is that activists are the furthest to the left, as shown in the figure. However, even if this was the case in the past it seems that by the late 1990s the difference between the average activist and the average inactive member was negligible – perhaps as a result of active members becoming inactive and vice versa. If the new leader was now further to the right, and thus in touch with public opinion, but members were to the left, the true picture became more like position B. By this point the incentive for leaders to enfranchise inactive members has disappeared. The alternative interpretation, that the leader latterly was actually to the right of both members and party voters, with the views of these latter groups now more closely aligned, is shown in position C. Within the Labour Party of the late 1990s there does appear to be some evidence for this proposal.[15]

The results in the Labour Party suggest that there are limits to which leaders can push their members whilst maintaining their own stability. If a leader is perceived as being to the right of most party members, the most ideologically committed members may no longer be the most active. In particular, if members become resentful of the leadership (for example because they believe that they have been stripped of influence in the party through internal organisational reforms, or are angered by policy positions that they cannot otherwise control) they may use their new voting rights to voice their frustration. The only option for the leader may therefore be to engage in more meaningful dialogue with the party. If this does not happen, intra-party conflict could ultimately have a negative impact on public opinion, and the party's electoral chances. The 'democratisation as emasculation' strategy therefore appears to be a risky one at best.

CHECKS AND BALANCES IN LABOUR'S CONSTITUTION

So the two central reforms to the party's organisation – the decline in trade union power and the increase in individual member democracy – have both had complex and ambiguous results in terms of leadership power. Tony Blair, in particular, discovered that his original ideal of internal 'direct democracy' could be problematic for leaders, as well as for members. Thus the plebiscitary party model did not go on to be implemented, and member ballots were limited to certain internal elections only. But if Labour's old system of trade union-dominated democracy needed to be changed, and the plebiscitary model has also been found to be problematic, this raises the question of whether some other system exists that would enable party leaders to build a more constructive relationship with party members.

Mediated democracy

Labour's experiments with 'direct', unmediated, democracy simply encountered difficulties that are commonly cited by democratic theorists.[16] In such a system leaders face an amorphous mass of individuals, who are unfamiliar with the detail of issues to be decided, lack the time to study matters more closely, and depend largely on the media for their information.[17] The mass may be empowered, but not to do anything particularly constructive. This does not create strong accountability, and risks falling prey to populism.

In contrast a structured system of representative units, with whom leaders negotiate and bargain, will tend to operate as a more effective check.[18] It is therefore perhaps natural that party leaders sought to dispense with such intermediate units, in order to gain greater flexibility. But this overlooks the benefits to them of a mediated system. Here genuine discussion and negotiation will tend to make those keeping leaders in check both more engaged and more sympathetic to the dilemmas that they face (Cohen, 1997; Fishkin and Luskin, 2000).

In Labour's old democracy it was the trade unions that were almost entirely responsible for this form of mediation. At least formally, the need to negotiate with senior figures in the trade unions placed major constraints on the freedom of party leaders. But it also ensured that those whose consent they needed to secure were 'insiders' who understood the need to operate within economic and political constraints. Deals could also be reached over a number of issues at once, so that all of those involved could derive some benefit. It is these features in the union relationship that Blair himself latterly sought to profit from when designing systems for internal elections. A structure based on intermediate units thus offers potential advantages to both sides. If members are able to co-ordinate responses this does potentially allow them greater power. But it can also facilitate a managed dialogue which need not descend into confrontation.

The 1990 document *Democracy and Policy Making for the 1990s* recognised, far more than its successor *Partnership in Power*, the inevitability of difficult issues arising between the party and its leaders, and that establishment of effective channels for the purposes of mediation could offer benefits to both sides. Following pressure from activists after the perceived problems with the Policy Review, this package sought to change the culture of decision making, and also to create powerful new intermediate structures which would be representative of the whole party (Labour Party, 1990a). These promised to draw a wider range of interests into policy discussions, including grassroots and local government representatives, and members of the PLP, in an attempt to enhance mutual understanding between leaders and members. Policy commissions, as then conceived, would have received submissions from the wider party and had responsibility for drawing up alternative positions for annual conference to vote upon, based on competing strands of opinion in the party. This was an ambitious system, which created nervousness amongst both leaders and members. After the party's defeat in 1992 only certain elements of it went on to be introduced.

The system contained within *Partnership in Power* was agreed later, in an environment where the leadership was under less pressure to compromise (Labour Party, 1997a). It created far weaker bodies than those originally envisaged, and these have proved unable to mediate effectively between the leadership and wider opinion in the party. They have suffered from a lack of transparency and made it difficult for constituency members to get their concerns onto the formal agenda. Whilst some sought to use the new system to introduce a more 'deliberative' model of policy making, its operation lacked some of the essential elements demanded by the proponents of this model. These include genuine commitment from both sides, negotiation based on mutual respect, and real visible results (Cohen, 1997). Although the National Policy Forum has undoubtedly led to a new culture of dialogue, and some gains for the representatives of constituency interests (see Chapter 6), the system remains opaque and riddled with mistrust on both sides. A more effective system would empower members to put their views collectively, but would also depend on some acceptance that leaders, in the end, will decide. Neither side has been prepared to concede to such an arrangement.

The concept of mediation was explicitly rejected by some of those 'modernisers' keenest on the plebiscitary party model. As Philip Gould complained in 1995, 'Labour's structure had become too diffuse, with power shared between the NEC, the PLP, the conference, the unions and the constituency associations.' In a memo entitled 'The Unfinished Revolution', which was leaked to *The Guardian*, he stated that 'Labour must replace competing structures with a single chain of command leading directly to the leader of the party. This is the only way that Labour can become a political organisation capable of matching the Conservatives. It will be more effective, and in a one member, one vote party, more democratic' (quoted in Gould 1998, p. 241, 240). Whilst such a command structure has now been widely accepted as too rigid to foster a good relationship between leaders and members, no effective alternative has yet been found.

Options for intra-party pluralism

Under Labour's old democracy the trade unions were the major power brokers, and at party conference they determined the outcome of votes, on matters largely put on the agenda by constituencies. Although much in this system has changed, the unions continue to represent the most powerful negotiating block within the party. Furthermore the existence of such power brokers has proved necessary to protecting the party from the dangers of unrestrained leadership power. But their involvement maintains some of the original problems from which party reformers had sought to escape. Labour's affiliated unions represent only limited interests (i.e. those of a relatively small proportion of working people) and they can bargain effectively on policy issues that directly concern these members. But they rarely offer a counterbalance on other matters. For example, during the 2001 parliament they played little part in negotiations over two of the most contentious issues for the leadership – higher education funding (the education unions not being affiliated to the party) and House of Lords reform. Now that the formal role of the unions has been diminished, this leaves a space which could potentially be filled by other organisations with broader perspectives. Yet despite leaders winning more freedom on industrial relations matters, party structures have not compensated through providing means of negotiating on the other matters that make up the majority of the policy agenda.

The challenge for Labour thus remains to establish a more pluralistic set of checks and balances in a party where traditionally there was only one power block that could counterbalance the leadership. In other centre-left parties contrasting traditions exist. For example in parties such as the German SPD the federal nature of the state results in powerful geographical blocks and regional leaders (Jeffery, 1999). In contrast the Australian Labor Party has both a federal structure and includes strong left and right factions which have achieved semi-formal status (Lucy, 1993; Swan and Lloyd, 1987). Although these bring some negative effects, they also 'enable the inevitable internal conflicts of the party to be managed in an organised fashion' (Scott, 2000, p. 159). In contrast the British Labour Party's regional organisations are far weaker (with the partial exception of Scotland and Wales), and organised factions have tended to be looked on with suspicion.[19] Whilst groups such as the LCC and CLPD had significant success during the 1970s and 1980s, factional activity in the party has more recently markedly declined.

'New' Labour's complex hybrid structure, which has widened representation on the NEC, and particularly through the NPF, opens sites of negotiation to groups which were largely excluded previously. For example, Labour's federal structure has always included other affiliated organisations, aside from the trade unions. Today these comprise primarily of small socialist societies, most of which are effectively non-factional single issue groups that operate inside the party. These include SERA (the Labour environment campaign), the Socialist Education Association, the Socialist Health Association and the Labour Housing Group. Such organisations (particularly SERA) have had some success in winning concessions at the National Policy Forum through negotiation with ministers. The newly-empowered local government representatives, now with seats on both the NEC and NPF, have been even more successful. For example their support helped secure the 'alternative position' on council house transfers, on which the platform was defeated at the 2004 party conference.

Although neither the socialist societies nor local government representatives have sufficient formal strength on their own to force change upon leaders, they do have a number of other significant assets. Most important amongst these is expertise, which enables them to credibly mount a case against the parliamentary front bench. Even with limited staff and office resources, they can also mobilise support for campaigns within the party amongst more populous groups such as the CLPs. In doing so they can interact with like-minded interest groups outside the party, and use the

media to popularise their demands. This potentially provides significant informal leverage over leadership decisions. Nonetheless these
groups are tiny in comparison to the old strength of the trade
unions. For example SERA has the equivalent of only 1.5 full time
staff, and a budget dependent on its 1,200 members. The Socialist
Education Association has no paid staff at all. And even collectively
the socialist societies hold only three out of the 183 seats on the
National Policy Forum

'Pluralist' democratic theorists have emphasised that formal
power is not necessary in order to achieve influence over policy
(Dahl, 1956, 1961). But without increased representation and resources such groups will never be able to rival the role played by the
party's old power brokers. A strengthening of the formal role of
these kind of groups on the NPF, coupled with a more transparent
system which would allow constituency campaigns to become
established, might have benefits to both leaders and members. But
in practice resource constraints mean that the impact of these
groups will always be limited.

Bringing parliament back in

An alternative to pluralism within the extra-parliamentary party is
for the party in parliament to take a greater role in checking
leadership decisions. In the absence of effective constraints outside,
this may already be happening. Contrary to its old image as a right-
wing caucus loyal to the leader and out of touch with grassroots
opinion, the parliamentary party has since 1997 shown itself
increasingly willing to question leadership judgements and stage
parliamentary rebellions over policy (Cowley, 2002).[20] Old models
that tended to treat the parliamentary and extra-parliamentary
parties as competitors now appear simplistic, and in future more
attention may fall on the democracy inside the PLP.

The parliamentary party is of course exactly the kind of 'insider'
group with which the leadership can bargain behind closed doors,
offering opportunities to reach negotiated agreements. It also has
the advantage that it is part of, rather than a rival to, Britain's
formal system of representative democracy. Labour MPs represent
their constituents as well as their local parties, and leadership
accountability to this group is not subject to the same objections to
intra-party democracy made by theorists such as McKenzie (1963,
1982). In addition the parliamentary party obviously has real power,
possessing a (very public) veto over all the legislation proposed by

a Labour government. Such a power is far greater than that ever enjoyed by constituency parties, or even by the trade unions. It has the potential to place real constraints on Labour's parliamentary leaders.

Although the PLP has traditionally had no formal role in policy making, discontent over government policy since 1997 has found its members ready to contemplate using their powers. After the 2001 general election the PLP's rebelliousness increased further still. On some issues, such as foundation hospitals and university tuition fees, failures to resolve controversial issues through the National Policy Forum spilled over into parliament, with rebels citing the failure of the party's internal processes as one of their motivations. For example Nick Brown, a leading rebel on tuition fees, suggested in the debate on the Higher Education Bill that '[t]he ideas we are discussing today should have been discussed in the Labour Party Policy Forum. We would be in better shape – and so would the proposals – if we had gone through that exercise first to test the ideas ... Instead, the proposals were presented to us first, there was a demand that we should agree with them and we put up a fight to try and amend them.'[21] On this occasion the backbench rebellion reduced the government's majority of 161 to only five votes.

A number of factors appear to have contributed to this greater assertiveness on the part of Labour MPs. One is simply the large size of the government's majority since 1997. More MPs can afford to protest in these circumstances, without threatening an actual government defeat. However, other factors can be traced to Labour's internal organisation, and seem likely to have been affected by its reform. For one thing, the PLP lost control over election of the party leader in 1981, and now has a more independent existence. Even more importantly, Philip Cowley's (2002) research suggests that the adoption of mandatory reselection was influential. Just as the CLPD had originally wanted, mandatory reselection has required PLP members to be more responsive to their local parties. Although few MPs have been deselected, many report coming under regular pressure from local members to vote against the whip.

Attempts to rebalance mandatory reselection by opening local selections to OMOV, meanwhile, are unlikely to have had the intended effect. As discussed above, OMOV results do not appear to consistently support leaders. In comparison to the pre-OMOV system when union votes meant that they (and thus potentially the leadership) could place loyalist candidates into seats, the new decentralised system seems likely to result in the selection of more independent-minded Labour MPs. Indeed the latest intake of Labour MPs, elected in 2001, has been shown to be more prone to rebel than those selected previously. As the authors of this study suggest, '[if] the aim of Labour's selection process was to ensure that only Blairite clones made it to the Commons, then it failed dismally' (Cowley and Stuart, 2004, p. 223). In addition, MPs selected by OMOV can now claim greater legitimacy for their rebellious behaviour, having been backed by all local party members rather than simply a small group of activists on the GC.

Political scientists have found that there is an international trend towards parties giving greater control over candidate selection to their membership, whilst leaderships retain (or increase) power over policy decisions (Katz and Mair, 2002; Scarrow, Webb and Farrell, 2000). This is seen as a trade-off whereby members gain rights, but the rights won are those least likely to compromise leaders. Coupled with a wider franchise for candidate selection, this trend is generally assumed to boost leadership power at the expense of extra-parliamentary parties. However if the Labour case is typical, and OMOV ballots result in support for candidates who are prepared to question leadership decisions, this suggests a possible new dynamic.

The Labour Party's system of candidate selection remains highly decentralised to local constituencies. As discussed in Chapter 4 even the new panel of 'approved candidates' gives little new power to the national party to intervene. Meanwhile a tradition of mandatory reselection (albeit diluted) is now well established, and OMOV has shown itself to be popular and almost impossible to reverse. If this system proves to deliver more independent-minded candidates, responsive to the demands of their local parties as well as their electorates, it will create a real check on leadership power. The result would be a new form of representative democracy within the party, built upon a closer linkage between the PLP and local parties, complementing the wider system of democracy in the country.

It has been suggested (Katz and Mair, 2002) that changes to candidate selection, coupled with greater resources for MPs, will result in the 'ascendancy of the party in public office' over ordinary party members. This is consistent with the developments considered here. Yet results in the Labour Party show that this does not necessarily imply a strengthening of central leadership power. It could instead result in a strengthening of the parliamentary system, with improved links between parliamentarians, local parties and local communities.

Closer analysis of change in the Labour Party suggests that reforms supported by leaders, including those in other parties undergoing similar organisational change, may not be freeing them from the system of accountability within parties, but merely changing that system. If organised activists are disempowered in favour of 'ordinary' members this may result in new democratic rights being used as a blunt instrument to send messages of protest to leaders. If intra-party democracy fails, disputes over policy may come to be resolved in parliament instead, where reform means that MPs are better connected to the wider membership and more confident of their legitimacy. For leaders, unmediated democracy may prove to be problematic and ultimately unstable. A system of genuine debate, deliberation and negotiation within parties over policy goals, coupled with better links between local parties and the public, may prove to be the most advantageous one that party leaders can achieve. Labour's new structures offered the potential to achieve such a system, but this potential, so far, remains unfulfilled.

POWER IN NEW LABOUR

> On balance it is self-evident (above all when the Labour Party is in office) that both initiative and final authority in decision making have in the past been in the hands of the leaders of the parliamentary party.
>
> 　　　　　　　Robert McKenzie on 'old' Labour (1982, p. 199)

> ... Equally shocking, internal democracy has been neutered. Grassroots members have no control. Everything important is decided at the top by the leader and his acolytes.
>
> 　　　　Peter Tatchell on 'new' Labour in *Tribune*, 23 April 2004[22]

So what can we conclude, in summary, about the balance of power in the Labour Party after more than two decades of organisational reform? The party is undoubtedly different – the unions' dominance has ended, the roles of the NEC and conference have altered significantly, and the relationship between the centre and individual members has been transformed. But what, if anything, has fundamentally changed in terms of the freedom and accountability of leaders – the ultimate test of democracy in the party?

It is true that in many ways Labour Party members have been disempowered by the changes since the early 1980s. Crucially the ability of activists to exercise 'voice' has been compromised in various ways, particularly in terms of submissions to the annual conference and through election of major figures to the NEC. But, at the same time, one of 'old' Labour's distinguishing features was the lack of representation for individual members and constituencies in the party's central power structures, and their ability to be routinely outvoted by the trade unions. Even at local level, unions could use their collective strength to secure favoured parliamentary candidates, who were often easily persuaded to follow a leadership line. This balance has now fundamentally changed, and power in 'new' Labour is more widely distributed. Thus leaders cannot afford to completely ignore members' views, and can't rely on negotiating outcomes behind closed doors with loyal trade union leaders, to the exclusion of the wider party. The decline in trade union influence may have freed leaders from one form of constraint, but it has also confronted them with others. One result has been a greater culture of consultation and deliberation within the party. Although this remains inadequate from many members' point of view, it is too crude to suggest that reform simply robbed members of power.

The control that Labour leaders have exercised in recent years results more from cultural change than from any reform of the party's structures. The civil war of the 1970s and early 1980s was followed by a period when more and more Labour activists displayed a desire to see the party returned to government. This allowed the 'moderates' to regain a majority on the NEC, saw the 'soft left' split from the 'hard left', and enabled the leadership and extra-parliamentary party to be largely reunited in their purpose. Consequently unity grew in the years to 1997. After the euphoria of that election victory abated, the inevitable tensions between the leadership and the party re-emerged. However, these have not reached crisis point as they did before. Instead, in an environment of prosperity and economic stability, with Labour continuing to ride high in the polls, there remains more that unites the party than divides it. Should this situation change, the new organisational arrangements would be tested in a way that has as yet been avoided. Though their formal powers have been trimmed, the NEC and conference – both now more representative of the party as a whole – could still inflict significant damage on Labour leaders, should they choose to do so.

In short, a lot has changed in Labour's organisation, but a lot has stayed the same. There was no 'golden age' in which Labour was controlled by its members; the only possible exception was the late 1970s and early 1980s, which were far less than golden in many other ways. As Henry Drucker has suggested, Labour's internal democracy was always its 'central myth' (1979, p. 40). Today, as previously, Labour Party members retain important sanctions, whilst leaders remain largely in control. And, within limits, that is probably the way it has to be. Members may be right to feel aggrieved that reform did not give them more say in the party's affairs, but it is very hard to argue – on balance – that it took their powers away.

Notes

1. This represents a drop from 62 to 41 per cent of seats. Whether the trade unions continue to control the post of Treasurer is a slightly moot point, as this is now elected by a 50:50 vote with the constituencies rather than the old 90:10 arrangement. However, on the basis that trade union deals can easily outmanoeuvre uncoordinated constituency votes (as they have done for contemporary resolutions – see Chapter 8) I have included this seat in their total. In practice the position of Treasurer is rarely contested, but in recent years has always gone to a trade union official.

2. These comprise the 30 seats chosen directly by the unions and the 12 union seats on the NEC. A more generous interpretation would also include the party Treasurer, and some of the 18 seats which are elected regionally, since trade union votes could be decisive in both of these elections. However, even if all of these members are included the unions influence only 61 seats – 35 per cent of the total.

3. CLPD Newsletter, September 1978, quoted in Seyd (1987, p. 85).

4. In 1987, when little reform had yet taken place, it was noted that 'MPs of the right and centre periodically get together to discuss whether or not the links with the unions might be broken or renegotiated to be less embarrassing ... Normally the idea gets dropped because very soon right wing MPs find themselves relying on the loyalty of the union leaderships to stabilise the party against the left' (Wainwright 1987, p. 207).

5. Speech at Labour Reform Conference on 'Parties and Democracy' London. I am grateful to Eric Shaw for providing this quotation.

6. See for example Blackburn and Kennon (2003).

7. *LCC Mailing*, March 1988.
8. It is possible to make this statement only about 'card' votes, where the percentage support amongst CLP delegates is recorded. It may be (as discussed in Chapter 8) that a majority of CLP delegates have voted against the platform in certain unrecorded ('hand') votes. On issues where this appears likely the platform is generally reluctant to concede a card vote.
9. For example Steven Fielding's (2000) chapter on party organisational change in the making of 'new' Labour makes no mention of women's representation. Thomas Quinn's book on the same subject gives this little more than a footnote. Indeed Quinn (2004, p. 175) suggests that 'the twin aims of centralisation and internal legitimation on the basis of OMOV characterised all the major organisational reforms Labour undertook after 1983'. But this was plainly not the case with quotas.
10. If this appears to be ironic it should also be remembered that the left had been dominant at the women's conference until 1988, when it was based on a one delegate one vote system. The trade unions and the leadership then introduced an electoral college system (including trade union block votes) to regain control of the event. This provides a further example of leadership instrumentalism, but in retrospect perhaps also indicated some of the difficulties to come.
11. Seyd and Whiteley themselves concluded that 'The motivation behind most of the organisational reforms which the party had introduced since 1983 ... has been the view that activists were unrepresentative of the wider membership and that therefore members should be empowered at the expense of the activists. However, the evidence gathered from our survey does not support this view' (2002, p. 76).
12. The figures in this section have been largely derived from Seyd and Whiteley's (2002a) original data, which is available from the UK Data Archive at Essex University. It must be noted that the definition 'very active' here relies on participants' own assessment of their activism, whereas the figure from the earlier survey quoted in Chapter 2 was based on an index of activism devised by the researchers. Under scrutiny even the 1989 survey found little difference between those attending party meetings 'frequently' and 'not at all', with 60 per cent and 57 per cent of these groups respectively classifying themselves as being on the left. Seyd and Whiteley included other features, such as campaign activity, in their activism index – yet it was attendees at meetings, not campaigners, who most worried the leadership. Research by Pippa Norris (1995) conducted in 1992 also cast doubt on the ideological differences between active and inactive Labour Party members. The difficulty of far left activists may therefore have actually already ended by the time OMOV was introduced.
13. Looking at why left-wing members became less active, the survey found that 22 per cent cited 'frustration at being unable to influence the

party' or 'changes within the party' as the main reason for their inactivity. Only two per cent of members on the right or centre who had become less active cited these same reasons (Seyd and Whiteley, 2002a).

14. There is evidence from earlier studies that members attempt to use their votes to achieve a balanced outcome, rather than necessarily supporting candidates that reflect their own beliefs. Bochel and Denver (1983) found that that Labour members participating in selection contests were often prepared to vote for candidates whose views were more moderate than their own, in order to maximise electoral benefits.

15. On many issues Seyd and Whiteley (2002) found that members' and activists' views were not very different from those of Labour voters, and in some cases the differences were the reverse of what might have been expected. For example 30 per cent of Labour voters, compared to 23 per cent of Labour members and 27 per cent of activists strongly agreed with the proposition that income and wealth should be redistributed to working people.

16. See, for example, Dahl (1956, 1970), Donovan and Bowler (1998), Fishkin (1997), Haskell (2001).

17. Ironically it was some of these same factors which led party communications specialists such as Philip Gould to make greater use of focus groups, where views are developed through conversation, to test public opinion, rather than relying on the blunter instrument of mass polls.

18. See, for example, Lipset and Trow (1956), Martin (1968).

19. For an account of the traditional hostility against groups judged to be a 'party within a party' see Shaw (1988).

20. In fact as Cowley (2002) points out, the old image of a docile PLP was always a rather inaccurate one.

21. House of Commons Hansard, 27 January 2004, col. 193.

22. Tatchell was explaining why 'new' Labour had finally driven him to resign his party membership and join the Green Party. Although a fairly typical lament by a disillusioned member, Tatchell's conflict with the party's leadership was far from new. In an infamous case he had been selected as parliamentary candidate for Bermondsey in 1981 but was unexpectedly denounced by the then leader, Michael Foot, as an extremist – after which his candidacy was not endorsed by the NEC. See Shaw 1988, pp. 226-8.

Appendix: Timeline of the Reforms

	Context	Selecting candidates and leaders	Women in the party
1979	Labour government loses general election. Commission of Enquiry (CE) set up.	Conference passes principle of mandatory reselection for MPs.	Number of Labour women MPs falls, from 18 to 11.
1980	Michael Foot elected leader. CE reports.	Last leadership election by PLP. Conference supports widening the franchise for leadership elections.	CLPD creates Women's Action Committee.
1981	SDP forms as breakaway party. Electoral college cited as a reason.	Electoral college for the leader agreed. Failed Benn bid for deputy leadership.	
1982	Moderates regain control from left on the NEC.		Demand for 'one woman on a shortlist' remitted at conference.
1983	Labour loses general election. Kinnock elected leader.	First leadership election by electoral college.	Gender gap in voting of 8%.
1984		Kinnock proposes OMOV for parliamentary reselections, but conference narrowly defeats.	NEC and conference reject 'one woman on a shortlist' ('OWOS').
1985		NEC working party established on 'widening the franchise'.	NEC supports OWOS but conference rejects.
1986			Conference approves principle of OWOS.
1987	Labour loses general election.	Conference again rejects OMOV for parliamentary selections. Agrees local electoral college mixing OMOV plus trade union votes.	Gender gap closes. New parliamentary selection package includes OWOS only in seats with no Labour MP.

Making policy	NEC	Annual Conference	Local parties
Submissions to CE propose 'rolling progr-amme' of policy making.	Submissions to CE propose restructuring.	Submissions to CE propose giving more conference votes to CLPs.	Some responses to CE propose dismantling GCs.
No change proposed by CE. CLPD proposal to give NEC control of manif-esto is defeated.	No change proposed by CE.	No change proposed by CE.	No change proposed by CE. Membership found to be below 350,000.
		'Kitson prop-osals' to reduce trade union vote share.	
Tony Benn loses chair of NEC Home Policy Committee.			Membership drops below 275,000.
New joint policy committees with Shadow Cabinet established.		NEC, under left pressure, prom-ises consultation on vote shares.	
		Action promised in 1983 postponed. New consultation.	
Policy Review sets up new joint groups, appointed by leader. Start of 'Labour Listens' campaign.			

	Context	Selecting candidates and leaders	Women in the party
1988			Conference defeats platform to require one woman on *every* parliamentary shortlist.
1989		OMOV ballots made compulsory in member side of leadership electoral college.	Resolution agreed proposing internal party quotas Women's conference reformed.
1990		Local electoral college dropped. Conference agrees OMOV principle for parliamentary selections.	Conference agrees to apply quotas to NEC, conference, NPF, CLPs and branches.
1991			Rule changes to implement internal quotas.
1992	Labour loses general election. John Smith elected leader. Trade Union Review Group established.		37 Labour women MPs elected. Gender gap reopens and may have cost Labour the election.
1993	Trade Union Review Group reports.	Conference agrees OMOV for parliamentary selections and new leadership electoral college with compulsory union ballots.	Conference agrees all-women shortlists (AWS) for half all winnable seats. Women's conference becomes biennial.
1994	John Smith dies. Tony Blair elected leader.	First use of revised electoral college.	Conference defeats attempt to reverse AWS.
1995		Liz Davies blocked by NEC as candidate in Leeds North East.	Blair announces AWS are for one election only.
1996			AWS defeated in industrial tribunal.

Making policy	NEC	Annual Conference	Local parties
LCC resolution calling for rolling programme is remitted.		Conference defeats NEC over demand to rebalance vote shares.	New 'levy plus' system for trade unionists. New National Membership system.
Demands from left to address weaknesses of the Policy Review process.	CLPs recommended to ballot to decide votes for constituency section.		LCC split on abolition of GCs.
Conference agrees establishment of National Policy Forum (NPF) & policy commissions.	Constituency balloting made compulsory.	NEC proposes reduction in affiliates' votes to 70%. Conference agrees.	No change proposed. No rule changes in *Democracy and Policy Making for the 1990s*.
			Local women's quotas come into force.
	Quotas introduced. First ever woman elected in trade union section.	First conference where women's quota applies. Rule change to reduce affiliates' votes to 70%.	
NPF meets for the first time.	Elections to constituency section shift to national OMOV ballot.	First conference based on 70/30 vote shares. In principle decision to shift to 50/50 as membership grows.	Launch of 'Regeneration Project'.
			Membership exceeds 300,000.
Clause IV reformed.		Conference agrees to reduce affiliates' votes to 50%.	
OMOV ballot on draft manifesto.		CLPs have 50% of vote for first time.	Membership exceeds 400,000.

	Context	Selecting candidates and leaders	Women in the party
1997	Labour wins power. Referendums agree Scottish Parliament & Welsh Assembly.	Conference delegates power to NEC to agree devolved and European Parliament selection procedures.	101 Labour women elected to parliament.
1998	Referendum agrees Greater London Authority (GLA) & London mayor.	OMOV very limited for Euro selections. Devolved selections to use closed panels of candidates. Scottish and Welsh leaders chosen by electoral college.	Twinning agreed for Scottish and Welsh elections. Aim to increase Labour women MEPs. Reform to women's organisation.
1999	First elections to Scottish Parliament & Welsh Assembly. First European elections under PR.	Michael defeats Morgan in Wales on minority of member vote. Parliamentary panel agreed.	Labour groups in Scotland and Wales elected with 50%+ women. Twinning agreed for GLA.
2000	First elections to GLA.	Dobson beats Livingstone as mayoral candidate on minority of member vote. Livingstone elected as an independent. Conference re-commits to OMOV.	GLA Labour group in London elected with 44% women.
2001	Labour wins general election.		Number of women Labour MPs falls to 95.
2002		Euro selections conducted using OMOV. Nicky Gavron selected as mayoral candidate.	Legal change to allow parties to use positive action. Labour re-adopts all-women shortlists.
2003	Second elections to Scottish Parliament & Welsh Assembly.	Gavron withdraws. Livingstone readmitted to Labour & becomes mayoral candidate.	
2004	European elections. Second elections to GLA.	Ken Livingstone elected Labour Mayor of London.	

Making policy	NEC	Annual Conference	Local parties
New process under Partnership in Power (PiP) with new NPF & changes to conference.	PiP changes NEC structure including bar on MPs standing in constituency & other sections.	Resolution process to end, except on 'contemporary' issues decided by ballot.	No rule changes in PiP, except to allow local experiments.
New NPF elected and first documents circulated.	First NEC elections under new system. Grassroots Alliance wins four seats.	First conference under new system. No detailed decisions to be taken on documents.	
NPF finalises first round of documents. No 'minority positions'.			'21st Century Party' document suggests rule changes for 2000 conference.
NPF finalises second round of documents. Seven minority positions.		First conference defeats under Blair. CLPD proposal to increase number of contemporary resolutions remitted.	No rule changes forthcoming.
New round of policy consultation begins.	NEC elections become biennial.	Platform defeat on PFI.	Membership drops below 1983 level.
		Concession that contemporary issues with 50% CLP support will be debated.	
All decisions on documents delayed until 2004. NPF elections postponed.	Peers barred from standing in constituency (and other) sections.	NEC defeated on rule change to raise number of contemporary issues.	
Partnership in Power review announced.		Platform defeated on two minority positions.	

Bibliography

Aitken, I. (1966). 'The Structure of the Labour Party', in G. Kaufman (ed.), *The Left*. London: Anthony Blond.

Alderman, K. (2000). 'Stranger than Fiction? The Selection of the Conservative and Labour London Mayoral Candidates', *Parliamentary Affairs*, 53: 737-52.

Alderman, K. and Carter, N. (1993). 'The Labour Leadership and Deputy Leadership Elections of 1992', *Parliamentary Affairs*, 46(1): 49-65.

Alderman, K. and Carter, N. (1994). 'The Labour Party and the Trade Unions: Loosening the Ties?', *Parliamentary Affairs*, 47(3): 321-37.

Alderman, K. and Carter, N. (1995). 'The Labour Leadership and Deputy Leadership Elections of 1994', *Parliamentary Affairs*, 48(3): 438-55.

Allaun, F., Mikardo, I. and Sillars, J. (1972). *Labour: Party or Puppet?* London: Tribune Group of MPs.

Anderson, P. and Mann, N. (1997). *Safety First: The Making of New Labour*. London: Granta.

Attlee, C. (1937). *The Labour Party in Perspective*. London: Victor Gollancz.

Benn, A. W. (1959). 'Modernising the Party', in *Where?*, Fabian Tract 320. London: Fabian Society.

Benn, T. (1990). *Conflicts of Interest: Diaries 1977-80*. London: Hutchinson.

Benn, T. (1994). *The End of an Era: Diaries 1980-90*. London: Arrow.

Bing, I. (1971). *The Labour Party: An Organisational Study*. Fabian Tract 407. London: Fabian Society.

Bing, I. (1971a). 'New Approaches to Democracy', in I. Bing (ed.), *The Labour Party: An Organisational Study*. Fabian Tract 407. London: Fabian Society.

Blackburn, R. and Kennon, A. (2003). *Griffith and Ryle on Parliament: Functions, Practice and Procedure*. London: Sweet and Maxwell.

Bochel, J. and Denver, D. (1983). 'Candidate Selection in the Labour Party: What the Selectors Seek', *British Journal of Political Science*, 13(1): 45-69.

Bradbury, J., Mitchell, J., Bennie, L. and Denver, D. (2000). 'Candidate Selection, Devolution and Modernization: The Selection of Labour Party Candidates for the 1999 Scottish Parliament and Welsh Assembly Elections', *British Elections and Parties Review*, 10: 151-72.

Bradbury, J. and Mitchell, J. (2001). 'Devolution: New Politics for Old?', *Parliamentary Affairs*, 54(2): 257-75.

Bradley, I. (1981). *Breaking the Mould? The Birth and Prospects of the Social Democratic Party*. Oxford: Martin Robertson.

Breitenbach, E. and Mackay, F. (eds.) (2001). *Women and Contemporary Scottish Politics: An Anthology*. Edinburgh: Polygon.

Brivati, B. (1997). *Hugh Gaitskell*. London: Richard Cohen Books.

Brivati, B. and Bale, T. (1997). *New Labour in Power*. London: Routledge, 1997.

Brooks, R. (1993). 'What Future for the Labour Party?', *Fabian Review*, 105(5): 13-14.

Brooks, R. and Eagle, A. (1990). *Quotas Now: Women and the Labour Party*. London: Fabian Society.

Brown, A. (1996). 'Women and Scottish Politics', in J. Lovenduski and P. Norris (eds.), *Women in Politics*. Oxford: Oxford University Press.

Brown, A. (1998). 'Deepening Democracy: Women and the Scottish Parliament', *Regional and Federal Studies*, 8(1): 103-19.

Brown, G. (1993). *Making Mass Membership Work*. London: Gordon Brown MP.

Burnell, J. (ed.) (1980). *Democracy and Accountability in the Labour Party*. Nottingham: Spokesman.

Campbell, A. and Zeichner, D. (2001). 'Partners in Power?', *Fabian Review*, 113(4): 16-19.

Childs, S. (2003). 'The Sex Discrimination (Election Candidates) Act', *Representation*, 39(2): 83-92.

Clark, P. B. and Wilson, J. Q. (1961). 'Incentive Systems: A Theory of Organization', *Administrative Science Quarterly*, 6: 129-66.

Clarke, C., and Griffiths, D. (1982). *Labour and Mass Politics: Rethinking our Strategy*. London: Labour Co-ordinating Committee.

Clifton, D. (1994). 'The Death of the Mass Party', *Renewal*, 2(2): 82-7.

CLPD (1989). *Has Conference a Future?* London: Campaign for Labour Party Democracy.

CLV (1980). *The Future of the Labour Party*. London: Campaign for Labour Victory.

Coates, D. and Lawler, P. (eds.) (2000). *New Labour in Power*. Manchester: Manchester University Press.

Cocks, M. (1989). *Labour and the Benn Factor*. London: Macdonald.

Cohen, J. (1997). 'Deliberation and Democratic Legitimacy', in J. Bohman and W. Rehg (eds.), *Deliberative Democracy*. Cambridge, MA: MIT Press.

Cowley, P. (2002). *Revolts and Rebellions: Parliamentary Voting Under Blair*. London: Politico's.

Cowley, P. and Stuart, M. (2004). 'When Sheep Bark: The Parliamentary Labour Party, 2001-2003', *British Elections and Parties Review*, 14: 211-29.

Crewe, I. and King, A. (1995). 'Loyalists and Defectors: The SDP Breakaway from the Parliamentary Labour Party 1981-2', in P. Jones (ed.), *Party, Parliament and Personality*. London: Routledge.

Crewe, I. and King, A. (1995a). *SDP: The Birth, Life and Death of a Political Party*. Oxford: Oxford University Press.

Crosland, A. (1960). *Can Labour Win?* Fabian Tract 324. London: Fabian Society.

Crossman, R. H. S. (1963). 'Foreword', in W. Bagehot, *The English Constitution*. London: Fontana.

D'Arcy, M. and MacLean, R. (2000). *Nightmare! The Race to Become London's Mayor*. London: Politico's.

Dahl, R. A. (1956). *A Preface to Democratic Theory*. Chicago: University of Chicago Press.

Dahl, R. A. (1961). *Who Governs? Democracy and Power in an American City*. New Haven: Yale University Press.

Dahl, R. A. (1970). *After the Revolution? Authority in a Good Society*. New Haven: Yale University Press.

Dahl, R. A. (1989). *Democracy and its Critics*. New Haven: Yale University Press.

Dalton, R. J. and Wattenburg, M. P. (2000). 'Partisan Change and the Democratic Process', in R. J. Dalton and M. P. Wattenburg (eds.), *Parties without Partisans: Political Change in Advanced Industrial Democracies*. Oxford: Oxford University Press.

Dalton, R. J. and Wattenburg, M. P. (eds.) (2000a). *Parties without Partisans: Political Change in Advanced Industrial Democracies*. Oxford: Oxford University Press.

Davies, L. (2001). *Through the Looking Glass: A Dissenter Inside New Labour*. London: Verso.

Davis, H. (1995). 'All-Women Shortlists in the Labour Party', *Public Law*, Summer: 207-14.

Davis, M. (2003). '"Labourism" and the New Left', in J. Callaghan, S. Fielding and S. Ludlam (eds.), *Interpreting the Labour Party: Approaches to Labour Politics and History*. Manchester: Manchester University Press.

Denver, D. and Hands, G. (1993). 'Measuring the Intensity and Effectiveness of Constituency Campaigning in the 1992 General Election', in D. Denver, P. Norris, D. Broughton and C. Rallings (ed.), *British Elections and Parties Yearbook*. Hemel Hempstead: Harvester Wheatsheaf.

Donovan, T. and Bowler, S. (1998). 'An Overview of Direct Democracy in the American States', in S. Bowler, T. Donovan and C. J. Tolbert, *Citizens as Legislators: Direct Democracy in the United States*. Columbus: Ohio State University Press.

Downs, A. (1957). *An Economic Theory of Democracy*. New York: Harper and Row.

Driver, S. and Martell, L. (1998). *New Labour: Politics after Thatcherism*. Cambridge: Polity.

Drucker, H. M. (1979). *Doctrine and Ethos in the Labour Party*. London: George Allen and Unwin.

Drucker, H. M. (1980). 'The Influence of the Trade Unions on the Ethos of the Labour Party', in B. Pimlott and C. Cook (eds.), *Trade Unions in British Politics*. London: Longman.

Duverger, M. (1954). *Political Parties*. London: Methuen.

Eagle, M. and Lovenduski, J. (1998). *High Time or High Tide for Labour Women?* London: Fabian Society.

Epstein, L. D. (1967). *Political Parties in Western Democracies.* London: Pall Mall.

Fabian Society (1992). *Labour's Choice: The Fabian Debates,* Fabian Pamphlet 553, London.

Fenley, A. (1980). 'Labour and the Trade Unions', in C. Cook and I. Taylor (eds.), *The Labour Party.* New York: Longman.

Fielding, S. (1999). 'The "Penny Farthing" Machine Revisited: Labour Party Members and Participation in the 1950s and 1960s', Paper to annual Political Studies Association conference.

Fielding, S. (2000). 'New Labour and the Past', in D. Tanner, P. Thane and N. Tiratsoo (eds.) *Labour's First Century.* Cambridge: Cambridge University Press.

Fielding, S. (2003). *The Labour Party: Continuity and Change in the Making of New Labour.* Basingstoke: Palgrave.

Finlayson, A. (2003). *Making Sense of New Labour.* London: Lawrence and Wishart.

Fishkin, J. S. (1997). *The Voice of the People.* New Haven: Yale University Press.

Fishkin, J. S. and Luskin, R. C. (2000). 'The Quest for Deliberative Democracy', in M. Saward (ed.), *Democratic Innovation: Deliberation, Representation and Association.* London: Routledge.

Flint, C. (1996). 'Shaping up for Government: The LCC's Commission on Party Democracy', *Renewal,* 4(2): 82-5.

Flynn, P. (1999). *Dragons led by Poodles.* London: Politico's.

Giddens, A. (2002). *Where Now for New Labour?* Cambridge: Polity.

Gill, B. (1999). *Winning Women: Lessons from Scotland and Wales.* London: Fawcett Society.

Golding, J. (2003). *Hammer of the Left.* London: Politico's.

Gould, P. (1998). *The Unfinished Revolution: How the Modernisers Saved the Labour Party.* London: Little, Brown and Company.

Graves, P. M. (1994). *Labour Women: Women in Working Class Politics 1918-1939.* Cambridge: Cambridge University Press.

Hain, P. (1993). 'Neither Mod nor Trad', *Fabian Review,* 105(4): 6-7.

Hain, P. (2004). *The Future Party.* London: Catalyst.

Harrison, M. (1960). *Trade Unions and the Labour Party since 1945.* London: George Allen and Unwin.

Haskell, J. (2001). *Direct Democracy or Representative Government: Dispelling the Populist Myth.* Boulder, Colorado: Westview Press.

Hay, C. (1999). *The Political Economy of New Labour.* Manchester: Manchester University Press.

Hayter, D. (1977). *The Labour Party: Crisis and Prospects,* Fabian Tract 451, London: Fabian Society.

Hayter, D. (1980). 'Within the Party', in D. S. Bell (ed.), *Labour in the Eighties*. London: Croom Helm.

Hayter, D. (2005). *Fightback: Labour's Right in the 1980s*. Manchester: Manchester University Press (to appear).

Heath, A. F., Jowell, R. M. and Curtice, J. K. (2001). *The Rise of New Labour*. Oxford: Oxford University Press.

Heffernan, R. and Marqusee, M. (1992). *Defeat from the Jaws of Victory: Inside Kinnock's Labour Party*. London: Verso.

Hewitt, P. and Mattinson, D. (1989). *Women's Votes: The Key to Winning*. London: Fabian Society.

Hills, J. (1981). 'Britain', in J. Lovenduski and J. Hills (eds.), *The Politics of the Second Electorate: Women and Public Participation*. London: Routledge.

Hirschman, A. O. (1970). *Exit, Voice and Loyalty*. Cambridge, MA: Yale University Press.

Hughes, C. and Wintour, P. (1990). *Labour Rebuilt: The New Model Party*. London: Fourth Estate.

Hunter, L. (1959). *The Road to Brighton Pier*. London: Arthur Barker.

Jeffery, C. (1999). 'Party Politics and Territorial Representation in the Federal Republic of Germany', *West European Politics*, 22(2): 130-66.

Jones, T. (1996). *Remaking the Labour Party*. London: Routledge.

Katz, R. S. and Mair, P. (eds.) (1994). *How Parties Organize: Change and Adaptation in Party Organisations in Western Democracies*. London: Sage.

Katz, R. S. and Mair, P. (1995). 'Changing Models of Party Organization and Democracy: The Emergence of the Cartel Party', *Party Politics*, 1: 5-28.

Katz, R. S. and Mair, P. (2002). 'The Ascendancy of the Party in Public Office', in R. Gunther, J. Ramón Montero and J. J. Linz (eds.), *Political Parties: Old Concepts and New Challenges*. Oxford: Oxford University Press.

Kavanagh, D. (1970). *Constituency Electioneering in Britain*. London: Longman.

Kavanagh, D. (1982). 'Representation in the Labour Party', in D. Kavanagh (ed.), *The Politics of the Labour Party*. London: George Allen and Unwin.

Kelly, R. N. (1989). *Conservative Party Conferences: The Hidden System*. Manchester: Manchester University Press.

Kelly, R. (2001). 'Farewell Conference, Hello Forum: The Making of Labour and Tory Policy', *Political Quarterly* 72(3): 329-34.

Kelly, R. (2003). 'Organisational Reform and the Extra Parliamentary Party', in M. Garnett and P. Lynch (eds.), *The Conservatives in Crisis*. Manchester: Manchester University Press.

Kirchheimer, O. (1966). 'The Transformation of the Western European Party Systems', in J. LaPalombara and M. Weiner (eds.), *Political Parties and Political Development*. Princeton: Princeton University Press.

Kogan, M. and Kogan, D. (1982). *The Battle for the Labour Party*. London: Fontana.

Labour Party (1918). *Conference Report*. London: Labour Party.
Labour Party (1955). 'Interim Report of the Sub-Committee on Party Organisation', in *Conference Report*, pp. 63-92. London: Labour Party.
Labour Party (1968). 'Report of the Committee of Enquiry into Party Organisation', in *Conference Report*, pp. 362-380. London: Labour Party.
Labour Party (1980). *Report of the Labour Party Commission of Enquiry 1980*. London: Labour Party.
Labour Party (1981). *NEC Report to Conference*. London: Labour Party.
Labour Party (1983). *Conference Report*. London: Labour Party.
Labour Party (1984). *Conference Report*. London: Labour Party.
Labour Party (1984a). *Balance of Votes at Annual Conference between the Constituency Parties and the Trade Unions*. London: Labour Party.
Labour Party (1985). *Conference Report*. London: Labour Party.
Labour Party (1987). *Party Franchise for Selection and Reselection of Parliamentary Candidates*. Consultation paper. London: Labour Party.
Labour Party (1987a). *Conference Report*. London: Labour Party.
Labour Party (1987b). *Moving Ahead*. London: Labour Party.
Labour Party (1987c). *Party Franchise for Selection and Reselection of Parliamentary Candidates*. Final document to conference. London: Labour Party.
Labour Party (1989). *Conference Report*. London: Labour Party.
Labour Party (1989a). *Future of Labour Party Conference*. London: Labour Party.
Labour Party (1990). *Selection of Parliamentary Candidates: Report of the NEC Consultation*. London: Labour Party.
Labour Party (1990a). *Democracy and Policy Making for the 1990s*. London: Labour Party.
Labour Party (1990b). *Representation of Women in the Labour Party*. London: Labour Party.
Labour Party (1990c). *Conference Report*. London: Labour Party.
Labour Party (1990d). *Future of Party Conference, Policy-Making and Party Representational Structure*. Paper to April NEC, GS:17/4/90. London: Labour Party.
Labour Party (1992). *Conference Report*. London: Labour Party.
Labour Party (1993). *Trade Unions and the Labour Party: Final Report of the Review Group on Links between Trade Unions and the Labour Party*. London: Labour Party.
Labour Party (1993a). *Conference Report*. London: Labour Party.
Labour Party (1993b). *Trade Union Links: Interim Report of the Working Group and Questionnaire*. London: Labour Party.
Labour Party (1994). *Conference Report*. London: Labour Party.
Labour Party (1995). *Conference Report*. London: Labour Party.
Labour Party (1996). *Conference Report*. London: Labour Party.
Labour Party (1997). *Labour into Power: A Framework for Partnership*.
Labour Party (1997a). *Partnership in Power*. London: Labour Party.

Labour Party (1997b). *Conference Report*. London: Labour Party.
Labour Party (1998). *Labour in Europe 1999*. London: Labour Party.
Labour Party (1998a). *Building a Healthy Women's Organisation: A Consultation Paper*. London: Labour Party.
Labour Party (1998b). *Building a Healthy Women's Organisation: Report of a Labour Party Consultation with Affiliates and Local Parties*. NECW21/7/98. London: Labour Party.
Labour Party (1999). *21ˢᵗ Century Party: Members – The Key to Our Future*. London: Labour Party.
Labour Party (1999a). *National Policy Forum Report to Conference: Volume 1*. London: Labour Party.
Labour Party (2000). *21ˢᵗ Century Party: Report to Annual Conference 2000*. London: Labour Party.
Labour Party (2003). *A Future Fair for All*. London: Labour Party.
Labour Party (2003a). *21ˢᵗ Century Party – The Next Steps*. London: Labour Party.
Labour Party (2004). *Partnership in Power Review: Interim Report*. London: Labour Party.
Laffin, M., Shaw, E. and Taylor, G. (2004). 'Devolution and Party Organisation in Britain: How Devolution has Changed the Scottish and Welsh Labour Parties', paper presented to *Devolution in Comparative Perspective* conference, University of Strathclyde.
Laffin, M., Shaw, E. and Taylor, G. (2005). 'The Parties and Intergovernmental Relations', in A. Trench (ed.), *Devolution and Power in the United Kingdom*. Manchester: Manchester University Press (to appear).
Lawrence, J. (2000). 'Labour: The Myths it has Lived By', in D. Tanner, P. Thane and N. Tiratsoo (eds.) *Labour's First Century*. Cambridge: Cambridge University Press.
LCC (1989). *Leaders and Members: A Strategy for Party Renewal in the 1990s*. London: Labour Co-ordinating Committee.
LCC (1996). *New Labour: A Stakeholders' Party*. London: Labour Co-ordinating Committee.
Linton, M. (1985). *The Swedish Road to Socialism*. London: Fabian Society.
Lipset, S. M. and Trow, M. A. (1956). *Union Democracy*. New York: The Free Press.
Lucy, R. (1993). *The Australian Form of Government*. Melbourne: Macmillan.
Ludlam, S. (2001). 'New Labour and the Unions: The End of the Contentious Alliance?', in S. Ludlam and M. J. Smith, *New Labour in Government*. Basingstoke: Macmillan.
Ludlam, S. and Smith, M. J. (eds.) (2000). *New Labour in Government*. Basingstoke: Macmillan.
Ludlam, S. and Smith, M. J. (eds.) (2004). *Governing as New Labour*. Basingstoke: Palgrave Macmillan.
Macintyre, D. (2000). *Mandelson and the Making of New Labour*. London: HarperCollins.

Maguire, G. E. (1998). *Conservative Women: A History of Women and the Conservative Party, 1874-1997*. Basingstoke: Macmillan.

Mair, P. (1994). 'Party Organisations: From Civil Society to the State', in R. S. Katz and P. Mair (eds.), *How Parties Organize: Change and Adaptation in Party Organisations in Western Democracies*. London: Sage.

Mandelson, P. and Liddle, R. (1996). *The Blair Revolution*. London: Faber and Faber.

Martin, R. (1968). 'Union Democracy: An Exploratory Framework', *Sociology*, 2(2): 205-20.

May, J. D. (1973). 'Opinion Structure of Political Parties: The Special Law of Curvilinear Disparity', *Political Studies*, 21(2): 135-51.

McDougall, L. (1998). *Westminster Women*. London: Vintage.

McKenzie, R. (1963). *British Political Parties: The Distribution of Power in the Conservative and Labour Parties*. London: Heinemann.

McKenzie, R. (1982). 'Power in the Labour Party: The Issue of Intra-Party Democracy', in D. Kavanagh (ed.). *The Politics of the Labour Party*. London: George Allen and Unwin.

McLean, I. (1975). *Keir Hardie*. London: Allen Lane.

McSmith, A. (1994). *John Smith: A Life*. London: Mandarin.

McSmith, A. (1996). *Faces of Labour*. London: Verso.

Medding, P. Y. (1970). 'A Framework for the Analysis of Power in Political Parties', *Political Studies*, 18(1): 1-17.

Michels, R. (1962). *Political Parties: A Sociological Study of the Oligarchical Tendencies of Modern Democracy*. London: Collier-Macmillan.

Miliband, R. (1961). *Parliamentary Socialism: A Study in the Politics of Labour*. London: Allen and Unwin.

Minkin, L. (1980). *The Labour Party Conference*. Manchester: Manchester University Press.

Minkin, L. (1992). *The Contentious Alliance: Trade Unions and the Labour Party*. Edinburgh: Edinburgh University Press.

Mitchell, A. (1983). *Four Years in the Death of the Labour Party*. London: Methuen.

Mitchell, J. (2000). 'New Parliament, New Politics in Scotland', *Parliamentary Affairs*, 53(3): 605-21.

Mitchell, J. (2001). 'Scotland: Maturing Devolution', in A. Trench (ed.), *The State of the Nations 2001: The Second Year of Devolution in the United Kingdom*. Thorverton: Imprint Academic.

Norris, P. (1995). 'May's Law of Curvilinear Disparity Revisited: Leaders, Officers, Members and Voters in British Political Parties', *Party Politics*, 1: 29-47.

Norris, P. (1996). 'Legislative Recruitment', in L. LeDuc, R. G. Niemi and P. Norris (eds.), *Comparing Democracies: Elections and Voting in Comparative Perspective*. London: Sage.

Norris, P. (2002). *Democratic Phoenix: Reinventing Political Activism*. Cambridge: Cambridge University Press.

Norris, P. (2004). *Electoral Engineering: Voting Rules and Political Behaviour.* Cambridge: Cambridge University Press.

Norris, P. and Lovenduski, J. (1993). 'Gender and Party Politics in Britain', in J. Lovenduski and P. Norris (eds.), *Gender and Party Politics.* London: Sage.

Osmond, J. (2000). 'A Constitutional Convention by any other Means: The First Year of the National Assembly for Wales', in R. Hazell (ed.), *The State and the Nations.* Thorverton: Imprint Academic.

Ostrogorski, M. (1902). *Democracy and the Organization of Political Parties.* London: Macmillan.

Panebianco, A. (1988). *Political Parties: Organization and Power.* Cambridge: Cambridge University Press.

Panitch, L. and Leys, C. (1997). *The End of Parliamentary Socialism: From New Left to New Labour.* London: Verso.

Pelling, H. (1992). *A History of British Trade Unionism.* London: Penguin.

Perkins, A. (2003). *Red Queen: The Authorized Biography of Barbara Castle.* Basingstoke: Pan Books.

Perrigo, S. (1995). 'Gender Struggles in the British Labour Party from 1979 to 1995', *Party Politics*, 1(3): 407-37.

Pimlott, B. (1971). 'Are CLPs Necessary?', in I. Bing (ed.), *The Labour Party: An Organisational Study.* Fabian Tract 407. London: Fabian Society.

Pimlott, B. (1977). *Labour and the Left in the 1930s.* Cambridge: Cambridge University Press.

Pitt-Watson, D. (2000). 'The Labour Party: The Voice of the People', *Renewal*, 8(2): 34-44.

Prentis, D. (2003). 'No Hidden Surprises, No Late Extras', *Fabian Review*, 115(3): 14-15.

Punnett, R. M. (1990). 'Selecting a Leader and Deputy Leader of the Labour Party: The Future of the Electoral College', *Parliamentary Affairs*, 43(2): 179-95.

Quinn, T. (2004). *Modernising the Labour Party: Organisational Change since 1983.* Basingstoke: Palgrave Macmillan.

Radice, L. (ed.) (1985). *Winning Women's Votes*, Fabian Tract 507, London: Fabian Society.

Ranney, A. (1965). *Pathways to Parliament.* London: Macmillan.

Reid, A. J. (2000). 'Labour and the Trade Unions', in D. Tanner, P. Thane and N. Tiratsoo (eds.) *Labour's First Century.* Cambridge: Cambridge University Press.

Rentoul, J. (2001). *Tony Blair: Prime Minister.* London: Time Warner.

Routledge, P. (1998). *Gordon Brown.* London: Pocket Books.

Routledge, P. (1999). *Mandy: The Unauthorised Biography of Peter Mandelson.* London: Pocket Books.

Rush, M. (1969). *The Selection of Parliamentary Candidates.* London: Thomas Nelson and Sons.

Russell, M. (2000). *Women's Representation in Elected Office: What can be done within the Law?* London: Constitution Unit.

Russell, M. and O'Cinneide, C. (2003). 'Positive Action to Promote Women in Politics: Some European Comparisons', *International and Comparative Law Quarterly*, 52: 587-614.

Russell, M., Mackay, F. and McAllister, L. (2002). 'Women's Representation in the Scottish Parliament and National Assembly for Wales: Party Dynamics for achieving Critical Mass', *Journal of Legislative Studies*, 8(2): 49-76.

Sassoon, D. (1993). 'The Union Link: The Case for Friendly Divorce', *Renewal*, 1(1): 28-35.

Sawyer, T. (1992). 'Roots and Resources', *Fabian Review*, 104(4): 3-4.

Sawyer, T., Linton, M. and Mitchell, A. (1987). *Labour's Next Moves Forward*, Fabian Tract 521, London: Fabian Society.

Scarrow, S. E. (1996). *Parties and Their Members: Organising for Victory in Britain and Germany*. Oxford: Oxford University Press.

Scarrow, S. E. (2000). 'Parties without Members?: Party Organisation in a Changing Electoral Environment', in R. J. Dalton and M. P. Wattenburg (eds.), *Parties without Partisans: Political Change in Advanced Industrial Democracies*. Oxford: Oxford University Press.

Scarrow, S. E., Webb, P. and Farrell, D. M. (2000). 'From Social Integration to Electoral Contestation: The Changing Distribution of Power within Political Parties', in R. J. Dalton and M. P. Wattenburg (eds.), *Parties without Partisans: Political Change in Advanced Industrial Democracies*. Oxford: Oxford University Press.

SCC (1995). *Scotland's Parliament: Scotland's Right*. Edinburgh: Scottish Constitutional Convention.

Scott, A. (2000). *Running on Empty: 'Modernising' the British and Australian Labour Parties*. Sydney: Pluto Press.

Seyd, P. (1987). *The Rise and Fall of the Labour Left*. Basingstoke: Macmillan.

Seyd, P. (1999). 'New Parties/New Politics: A Case Study of the British Labour Party', *Party Politics*, 5(3): 383-405.

Seyd, P. and Whiteley, P. (1992). *Labour's Grassroots: The Politics of Party Membership*. Oxford: Oxford University Press.

Seyd, P. and Whiteley, P. (2001). 'New Labour and the Party: Members and Organisation', in S. Ludlam and M. J. Smith, *New Labour in Government*. Basingstoke: Macmillan.

Seyd, P. and Whiteley, P. (2002). *New Labour's Grassroots: The Transformation of the Labour Party Membership*. Basingstoke: Palgrave Macmillan.

Seyd, P. and Whiteley, P. (2002a). *Survey of Labour Party Members, 1997 and 1999*. Computer file, SN4466. Colchester: UK Data Arvhive.

Shaw, E. (1988). *Discipline and Discord in the Labour Party*. Manchester: Manchester University Press.

Shaw, E. (1993). 'Towards Renewal? The British Labour Party's Policy Review', *Parliamentary Affairs*, 46(1): 112-32.

Shaw, E. (1994). *The Labour Party Since 1979: Crisis and Transformation.* London: Routledge.

Shaw, E. (1996). *The Labour Party Since 1945.* Oxford: Blackwell.

Shaw, E. (2001). 'New Labour: New Pathways to Parliament', *Parliamentary Affairs,* 54: 35-53.

Shaw, E. (2002). 'New Labour in Britain: New Democratic Centralism?', *West European Politics,* 25(3): 147-70.

Short, C. (1996). 'Women and the Labour Party', in J. Lovenduski and P. Norris (eds.), *Women in Politics.* Oxford: Oxford University Press.

Smyth, G. (1996). 'The Centre of My Political Life: Tony Blair's Sedgefield', in M. Perryman (ed.), *The Blair Agenda.* London: Lawrence and Wishart.

Sopel, J. (1995). *Tony Blair: The Moderniser.* London: Bantam Books.

Stark, L. P. (1996). *Choosing a Leader: Party Leadership Contests in Britain from Macmillan to Blair.* Manchester: Manchester University Press.

Stephenson, M. (1998). *The Glass Trapdoor: Women, Politics and the Media During the 1997 General Election.* London: Fawcett Society.

Straw, J. (1992). 'Leave it to Us', *Fabian Review* 104(5), 9-10.

Stuart, M. (2005). *John Smith: All We Ask.* London: Methuen (to appear).

Swan, W. and Lloyd, C. (1987). 'National Factions and the ALP', *Politics,* 22: 100-10.

Tanner, D. (2000). 'Labour and its Membership', in D. Tanner, P. Thane and N. Tiratsoo (eds.), *Labour's First Century.* Cambridge: Cambridge University Press.

Taylor, G. R. (1997). *Labour's Renewal? The Policy Review and Beyond.* Basingstoke: Macmillan.

Taylor, M. (2001). 'Party Democracy and Civic Renewal', in B. Crick (ed.), *Citizens: Towards a Citizenship Culture.* Oxford: Blackwell.

Taylor, M. (2003). 'Saving the Party: Looking Out not Up', *Renewal,* 11(1): 54-60.

Taylor, R. (1993). *The Trade Union Question in British Politics.* Oxford: Blackwell.

Teorell, J. (1999). 'A Deliberative Defence of Intra-party Democracy', *Party Politics,* 5(3): 363-82.

Thompson, P. and Lucas, B. (1998). *The Forward March of Modernisation: A History of the LCC 1978-1998.* London: Labour Co-ordinating Committee.

Tribune Group (1987). *A Mass Party.* London: Tribune Group of MPs.

Upham, M. and Watson, T. (1989). *Natural Allies: Labour and the Unions,* Fabian Tract 534, London: Fabian Society.

Wainwright, H. (1987). *Labour: A Tale of Two Parties.* London: Hogarth Press.

Walsh, T. and Tindale, S. (1992). 'Time for Divorce', *Fabian Review,* 104(4): 9-11.

Ware, A. (1987). *Citizens, Parties and the State.* Oxford: Polity Press.

Ware, A. (1996). *Political Parties and Party Systems*. Oxford: Oxford University Press.

Webb, P. (1994). 'Party Organizational Change in Britain: The Iron Law of Centralization?', in R. S. Katz and P. Mair, *How Parties Organize: Change and Adaptation in Party Organisations in Western Democracies*. London: Sage.

Webb, P. (1994a). 'Reforming the Labour-Trade Union Link: An Assessment', *British Elections and Parties Yearbook*.

Webb, P. (2000). *The Modern British Party System*. London: Sage.

Webb, P., Farrell, D. and Holliday, I. (eds.) (2002). *Political Parties in Advanced Industrial Democracies*. Oxford: Oxford University Press.

Westlake, M. (2001). *Kinnock: The Biography*. London: Little, Brown and Company.

Whiteley, P. and Seyd, P. (1992). 'The Labour Vote and Local Activism: The Impact of Local Constituency Campaigns, *Parliamentary Affairs*, 45: 582-95.

Wickham-Jones, M. (2004). 'The New Left', in R. Plant, M. Beech and K. H. Hickson (eds.), *The Struggle for Labour's Soul: Understanding Labour's Political Thought Since 1945*. London: Routledge.

Wilson, P. (2002). 'Labour and the Community – Rebuilding the Links', *Renewal*, 10(2): 66-71.

Wrigley, C. (1997). *British Trade Unions 1945-1995*. Manchester: Manchester University Press.

Wring, D., Baker, D. and Seawright, D. (2000). 'Panelism in Action: Labour's 1999 European Parliamentary Candidate Selections', *Political Quarterly*, 71(2): 234-45.

Yates, I. (1960). 'Power in the Labour Party', *Political Quarterly*, 31(3): 300-11.

Index